Richard Strauss

Richard Strauss

New Perspectives on the Composer and His Work

Bryan Gilliam, Editor

With an Introduction by Michael Kennedy

▼

DUKE UNIVERSITY PRESS   Durham and London 1992

© 1992 Duke University Press

First printing in paperback, 1997

All rights reserved

Printed in the United States of America

on acid-free paper ∞

Library of Congress

Cataloging-in-

Publication Data

appear on the last

printed page of this book.

In memory of
Alice Strauss
(1904–1991)

Contents

The Musical Works

Preface to the Paperback Edition

As we approach the year 1999, a year that marks the fiftieth anniversary of Strauss's death, scholarly interest in the composer continues to grow. In his introduction for this paperback edition, Michael Kennedy describes a current "warmer climate for Strauss." But what are the reasons for this change in climate, a change that began in the early 1980s? Or, put another way, what caused Strauss's music to become marginalized in the musical academy despite its ongoing popularity in the concert hall and opera house? The 1964 Strauss centennial, though celebrated worldwide in performance, was all but ignored in the scholarly literature. Indeed, the most memorable written document from that year was Theodor Adorno's unflattering critical appraisal of the composer's career, an essay that appeared in English a year later in *Perspectives of New Music*. During that period the ideology of musical style as a teleological process along a tonal-atonal axis was a powerful force in the academic discourse on twentieth-century music, a historical narrative that put a premium on technical progressivity. It was a worldview that embraced strong binary oppositions: tonal/atonal, progressive/regressive, high art/low art, European/non-European, and so on.

The notion of an organic, unified, linear stylistic evolution — with its nineteenth-century Germanic roots — was in opposition to the philosophy of Strauss, who recognized, if anything, a remarkable disunity in his contemporary world and saw no reason for music to be any different. With remarkable intuition, he sensed the inability of contemporary art to maintain a unified mode of expression. Throughout his mature career, Strauss delighted in creating moments of grandeur, only to undercut them — sometimes in a most jarring fashion. Unlike Schoenberg, with his romantic view of music as a transcendent, redemptive phenomenon, Strauss dealt with art and the contemporary world in his own idiosyncratic way, foreshadowing what Fredric Jameson has called the postmodern "collapse of the ideology of style." Strauss, as Peter Franklin once observed, "had effectively salvaged nineteenth-century bourgeois music for a new bourgeoisie of the twentieth century." In *Ariadne auf Naxos* the Composer may sing that "Music is a sacred art," but, as Strauss frankly demonstrated, music is also an important cultural commodity in the world of capitalism. Strauss knew full well the shock value of this duality. His was a personality very much at one with the complex age in which he lived, and he presented himself, unfiltered, to the world. (Yet this may have been the ultimate filter: by cultivating the image of a composer who treated composition as a means merely of earning an income — the pretense of being unpretentious — Strauss the artist secured the privacy necessary for creativity.)

Strauss's stance was sharply dissonant with the ethical tone of high modernism, which recognized a distinct "aesthetic immorality" in composing contemporary music in an accessible, tonal idiom considered outworn and moribund. After World War II, this artistic moralism wove in and out of the political discourse with remarkable inconsistency, as composers such as Stravinsky or Webern, who enjoyed an aesthetic "high ground," were forgiven various political sins or their views misrepresented entirely. Indeed, one senses that Strauss's composition of unabashedly tonal music may have been viewed as a greater offense than his brief but reprehensible stint as the president of the Reichsmusikkammer in the early 1930s. And perhaps because the political issues, though important, were not as resonant in the United States as in Germany, it was inevitable for the trend of academic warming toward Strauss to begin here rather than in Germany. Michael Kennedy points out that the 1990 Strauss conference at Duke University was the first major musicological symposium on an international scale. At that symposium, Reinhold Schlötterer, Professor of Music at the University of Munich, could not resist pointing out that this pathbreaking conference was taking place in Durham, North Carolina, rather than in Munich, the city of Strauss's birth. But since that conference, the academic climate for Strauss has improved rapidly within the now reunified Germany; young German scholars have produced a host of new monographs and studies on Strauss in the 1990s. I hope that the publication of this paperback edition will catalyze further Strauss research on both sides of the Atlantic.

Bryan Gilliam
Durham, North Carolina, 1997

Introduction: The Warmer Climate for Strauss

Michael Kennedy

▼

The international conference on Richard Strauss and his music that was held at Duke University in April 1990 signaled an important shift in the academic community's attitude toward this composer. The conference marked Strauss's acceptance by musicologists as a subject fit for analysis and close-focus study. No similar gathering had ever assembled in the United States. Strauss, Puccini, and other composers whose success with the general public had never waned had been in an academic and critical limbo for decades. They were composers who succeeded despite the conviction among arbiters of taste that this success had been bought too cheaply, that their music offered few intellectual challenges and was therefore unworthy of serious study. It was a supercilious attitude, to be sure, and its recent decline leaves the musical body politic much more balanced.

In his lifetime Strauss was no stranger to this brand of aesthetic criticism. His rise to fame and fortune was too rapid not to be accompanied by a counterpoint of abuse, often arising from personal jealousy. On a critical level, he encountered the hostility of Eduard Hanslick, which is predictable enough when one remembers that the young Strauss converted from Brahms worship to Wagnerism. But the most damaging criticism treated him like some short-lived musical rocket that had lit up the sky in a burst of glory but, soon after, was merely a stick falling to earth. An early example of this attitude can be found in the writings of the influential English critic Ernest Newman. After the first London performance of *Symphonia domestica* in 1905, he described a "coarse and sprawling polyphony" and concluded that "the realistic effects in the score are so pitiably foolish that one listens to them with regret that a composer of genius should ever have fallen so low." Five years later, reviewing *Elektra*, Newman described Strauss as "the greatest living musician" but considered the music of the opera "as abominably ugly as it is noisy." He hoped that the future would hold "a purified Strauss, clothed and in his right mind" rather than "a saddening mixture of genius, ranter, child and charlatan." It was this kind of overheated writing — typical, one may add, of several of Newman's scarifying misjudgments — that led to the most withering attack on Strauss by any English writer. Cecil Gray, in *A Survey of Contemporary Music* (1924), claimed that Strauss's music after *Der Rosenkavalier* bore witness to "a gradual degradation and final extinction of his creative powers. . . . From being a man of possibly unequalled genius, he has become a man of second-rate talent. . . . One can only speculate as to which works, if any, stand a chance of surviving him. . . . [T]heir manifest imperfections must inevitably tell against them in the long run, and posterity will in all probability solve the problem by performing none of them." Gray can only have been referring to the first version of *Ariadne auf Naxos*, *Josephslegende*, and *Eine Alpensinfonie*, since the likelihood of his having heard *Die Frau ohne Schatten* at the time he was writing is remote. That such a judgment has proven to be so inaccurate is perhaps the only satisfaction one receives from putting Gray's words back into circulation.

In 1924, the same year Strauss turned sixty, we find the 21-year-old Theodor Adorno diagnosing "Strauss's tragedy" in these words: "As soon as his will extended beyond the sphere of mere life, he lost what reality he possessed. It was not that Hofmannsthal robbed him of his musical vision by deceiving him with aesthetic speculations; he went to Hofmannsthal when he could no longer believe the concreteness of his musical vision." Ten years later, at the time of the composer's seventieth birthday, the English writer Eric Blom — who was perhaps never as influential as Newman but was distinguished enough to be invited to edit the fifth edition of *Grove's Dictionary of Music and Musicians* (1954) — repeated the belief that *Der Rosenkavalier* was Strauss's last great work. Blom was not polemical; it hurt him to come to this conclusion. "For the last three decades he has been, it must be said, in a decline, but a decline borne as bravely as the heroine in that most heart-searching opera bears the bitterness of ageing in body without losing the relish of life. But with him that relish was not quite great enough to induce him to strike out in new directions or to share the fresh adventures of those younger than himself. . . . One would have liked to love those later works of his which at the best one could only respect." Well, respect made a change. But again one must wonder to which works Blom was referring. In 1934 he was music critic of the *Birmingham Post*, a provincial newspaper that is unlikely to have sent him abroad to Dresden and Vienna where he might have heard *Die Frau ohne Schatten*, *Intermezzo*, *Schlagobers*, *Die ägyptische Helena*, and *Arabella*, not to mention the two works for piano left hand and orchestra. Since he could have heard none of these in Britain, I surmise that the "received opinion," spread by word of mouth, was operative here.

Nevertheless, Blom's verdict is useful in that it crystallizes two important aspects of the "Strauss-in-decline" syndrome. First, Blom echoes the belief that Strauss "peaked" with *Der Rosenkavalier*, thereafter ineffectively repeating himself until 1942 when he suddenly turned back into a genius with the second horn concerto and other "Indian summer" works culminating in the *Vier letzte Lieder*. The belief that *Der Rosenkavalier* marked a divergence from the harmonic implications of *Elektra* overlooks the cardinal fact that there was never a steady development or logical progression to Strauss's method of composing. He always liked contrast: *Feuersnot* after *Guntram*, *Salome* after *Symphonia domestica*, *Intermezzo* after *Die Frau ohne Schatten*. His initial reluctance to compose *Elektra* immediately after *Salome* was because the subjects were insufficiently contrasted, and it is no coincidence that *Elektra* took him longer to write than most of his operas, with a "creative block" of several months during the course of its gestation. Second, with Blom's throwaway remark that Strauss failed to "share the fresh adventures of those younger than himself," we are approaching the underlying reason for powerful, opinion-forming members of the academic and critical communities to cold-shoulder Strauss: he was known to be conservative by nature and inclination concerning the revolution in tonality. While he was quite prepared, in a small section of *Elektra*, virtually to abandon tonality for the purposes of dramatic characterization, atonality held no appeal for him as a style and theory of composition.

Strauss had been generously helpful to the young Schoenberg, but as works like *Verklärte Nacht* and *Pelleas und Melisande* gave way to *Five Orchestral Pieces* and *Six Little Pieces* for pianoforte, op. 19, he found it harder to enlist sympathy and support for their creator. "Nowadays only a psychiatrist can help poor Schoenberg," he said and later injudiciously offered the opinion, in writing, that "it would be better for him to be shovelling snow than scrawling on music paper." Schoenberg never forgave Strauss, saying in 1946: "I am sure he does not like my music and in this respect I know no mercy: I consider such people as enemies." So here, for Schoenberg's adherents, was a valid reason to dislike Strauss. (In Schoenberg's case there was a clear division between his opinion of the man and of the music, about which he remained, on the whole, complimentary.) From the 1920s, the struggle on behalf of atonality grew more intense and fierce. The general public preferred *Till Eulenspiegel* and *Don Juan* to the orchestral works of Alban Berg and Anton von Webern, but in the conservatoires and universities the new school of composition mattered most. Strauss, it seemed, led nowhere; Schoenberg and his acolytes led to the future. (Here it should be said that when the City of Vienna Prize was awarded to Webern and Berg in 1924, the three judges were unanimous — one of them was Strauss.)

It is hardly surprising, therefore, that when a re-examination, and to some extent rehabilitation, of post–Wagnerian romanticism began in the later 1950s, it was Gustav Mahler, not Strauss, who was elevated to "boom" proportions. Like Strauss, Mahler had encouraged Schoenberg and others. He, too, had gone to the edge of tonality in works written at the same time as *Elektra*. But he died at the age of 50 in 1911, a remarkably prescient piece of timing, if one may be irreverent; we do not know how he would have responded to the developments in music after 1912. Perhaps more sympathetically than Strauss, but in any case the admiration of the Second Viennese School for Mahler's music was always uncompromised. At the time of his centenary in 1960, he was hailed as the bridge between the romanticism of the late nineteenth century and the new music of the twentieth. Mahler thus appealed to two publics, and an astonishing revival of interest in his music swept through the concert halls and recording studios of the world. By comparison, aside from another polemical outburst from Adorno, the Strauss centenary in 1964 caused barely a ripple. (Of course, Strauss's music had never become neglected, nor was it, for the most part, in need of rehabilitation.) The audiences of the 1960s latched on to Mahler because they recognized a composer driven by neuroses and the world of the 1960s was intensely neurotic — about the bomb, about religion, about drugs. A composer who seemed to be searching for some kind of certainty amid chaos was exactly the composer they needed.

Strauss's reputation had been clouded by other factors besides his known antipathy to atonality, the 12-note system, and other modern developments, including jazz. His apparent support of the Nazi regime alienated many of his fellow artists. As man and composer, Strauss was on the blacklist of the large numbers of musicians — many of them, as it happened, devotees of Schoenberg's methods — who left Germany and Austria and eventually held influential teaching posts in the United States, Britain, and elsewhere. Not all of them were as high-minded as Schoenberg (many had suffered more than he had), and for them there was no reason to accord consideration to a man who had held, however briefly, an official position under Hitler's government.

Yet after Strauss's death in 1949, literature about him began to proliferate. Biographical studies appeared in Germany and France, although none confronted the problems of the Nazi years head-on. During the 1950s, in collaboration with the archive at Garmisch, Strauss scholars such as Willi Schuh (his chosen biographer), Franz Trenner, and Roland Tenschert supplemented the Hofmannsthal correspondence by editing and publishing Strauss's correspondence with his parents, Hans von Bülow, Joseph Gregor, Clemens Krauss, Stefan Zweig, Romain Rolland, Anton Kippenberg, and Franz Wüllner. Catalogues, documentation of the sketchbooks, bibliographies, and memoirs proliferated around the time of the centenary. The first major biographical study to appear after Strauss's death was Ernst Krause's *Richard Strauss: Gestalt und Werk* from Leipzig in 1955 and in English translation in 1964. Although tainted in places by an East German ideological stance, this was the first in-depth survey of Strauss's whole oeuvre. In scope, however, it was dwarfed by the three volumes of *Richard Strauss: A Critical Commentary on His Life and Works*, published between 1962 and 1972 and revised in 1978. Written by Noran Del Mar, a gifted conductor and horn player with a keen musical mind and an astonishing command of detail, this work is still unsurpassed in its comprehensiveness. Yet reading it afresh today, one cannot help but be disappointed by its lack of original thought, its too-ready acceptance of the conventional wisdom on Strauss at that time. For instance, Del Mar was still shocked by *Salome*, found the program of *Symphonia domestica* "intolerable," was squeamish about *Intermezzo*, generally adhered to the line that the music went downhill after *Ariadne auf Naxos*, and concluded that Strauss's personality was not complex(!). His descriptions of the later operas are detailed and illuminating, but there is a marked lack of enthusiasm. On the other hand, Del Mar's brother-in-law, William Mann, wrote an admirable critical study of the operas, published in 1964, which cautiously leaned toward a warmer appraisal of the "problem works." Other English writers who contributed to a more balanced view of Strauss were Alan Jefferson and Kenneth Birkin, the latter in a valuable examination of *Daphne* and *Friedenstag* and in a monograph on *Arabella*.

In 1971 the International Richard Strauss Society was founded in Vienna. Its *Blätter*, published several times a year, contain important contributions to Strauss scholarship. In Munich, where Reinhold Schlötterer has led a Richard Strauss Arbeitsgruppe (loosely linked with the university) since the late 1970s, a Strauss Society already existed. In addition, the Richard-Strauss-Institut was established in 1982 under the direction of Stephan Kohler and dedicated to the collection and propagation of information about the composer and his music. It has an unrivaled archive of books, scores, photographs, and other material. In 1976 came Schuh's long-awaited first volume of the official biography, covering Strauss's life through 1898. (Schuh's death halted the project, which remains in limbo.) More recently, Kurt Wilhelm's *Richard Strauss: An Intimate Portrait*, published in German in 1984 and in English in 1989, and his documentation of the genesis of *Capriccio* brought a sympathetic approach to Straussian scholarship focus. Valuable additions to the critical bibliography were the late and much lamented Derrick Puffett's collections on *Salome* and *Elektra*, in which extremely detailed analyses by some of Puffett's contributors were complemented by witty, penetrating, and provocative essays by the composer Robin Holloway. In these books it is immediately apparent that the academic climate had improved: Strauss was now under the microscope because of his genius and originality as a composer.

Yes, suddenly the climate *had* changed. A warmer wind was blowing. Whence did it come? It is virtually impossible to track down a gradual, general trend to its source, but if forced I would select Glenn Gould's article *An Argument for Richard Strauss*, which appeared in the periodical *High Fidelity* in March 1962. Gould believed that Strauss's reputation had suffered "more unjustly" with the passing years than that of any other musician of our time. He pinpointed the Schoenberg revolution as the moment in Strauss's career where "he is presumed to have gone astray," concluding that Strauss's critics considered his most egregious error to be a failure "to share actively in the technical advances of his time." Gould would have none of this. In Strauss, he boldly stated, "we have one of those rare, intense figures in whom the whole process of historical evolution is defied." What Gould admired most about Strauss was that he promised nothing for the future and was no more "a man of his time" than J. S. Bach had been. Gould's article concludes that Strauss's music "presents to us an example of the man who makes richer his own time by not being of it; who speaks for all generations by being of none."

Here at last was an iconoclastic view of Strauss, a salient statement on Strauss from North America. It was some years ahead of its time, but its truth is, I believe, incontestable. It awoke a response. Dissertations on Strauss appeared from universities in Illinois and North Carolina in 1974 and 1975. Patrick J. Smith championed the later operas. In 1979 came Barbara Petersen's pioneering study of the *Lieder* — until then a grossly neglected area — in her superb *Ton und Wort*. This brings us to the historic international conference at Duke University in 1990, organized by Bryan Gilliam, whose own writings

on Strauss — particularly a dissertation on Daphne and a book on Elektra —
appeared in the 1980s and 1990s.

The eleven contributors to this volume provide a survey of Strauss's work
of a breadth that would have been unimaginable a few years earlier (Schoenberg, Stravinsky, and Bartók could not have wished for more). It ranges
from R. Larry Todd's investigation of the Brahmsian period of Strauss's
youth to Günter Brosche's discoveries of the unusual construction of the
Oboe Concerto revealed by sketches that surfaced in 1986. Strauss's parallels
and contrasts with Mahler occupy Stephen E. Hefling and Kofi Agawu, the
former concentrating on program music, the latter on extended tonality.
The enigmas and ambiguities of the structure of Don Juan are investigated by
James Hepokoski with his characteristic zeal and perspicacity. Lewis Lockwood throws a searching new light on the harmonic achievement of Der
Rosenkavalier and explodes the old canard that it represented a regression from
Elektra. A corollary to his paper is Reinhold Schlötterer's probe into the references to Italian opera in Strauss's comedies. Strauss's work on behalf of other
composers in the realm of copyright and royalties is set forth with facts
and figures by Barbara Petersen. Pamela M. Potter's discussion of the "hot
potato" — Strauss and the Nazis — is outstanding for its level-headedness,
its compassion, its quiet demolition of the commentary in Gerhard Splitt's
Richard Strauss 1933–35 (1987), and its plea for an approach to the subject which
looks at 1933 without hindsight knowledge of the Holocaust. Finally, Bryan
Gilliam contributes an essay on Intermezzo that acknowledges its originality
and claims a high place for it in Strauss's dramatic legacy. One important
contribution that did not originate at the Duke symposium is Timothy L.
Jackson's searching, controversial, and, in many respects, irrefutable examination of the origins of Metamorphosen.

What the Duke conference achieved by way of stimulating research into
Strauss may be deduced from Gilliam's next collection, Richard Strauss and His
World (Princeton University Press), in which Hepokoski directs his analytical
searchlight on Macbeth, Jackson proposes that Ruhe, meine Seele! belongs properly to the Vier letzte Lieder, Derrick Puffett writes on Strauss's organization of
keys, and Gilliam examines Daphne. There are also essays by Leon Botstein
and Michael P. Steinberg that take a decidedly chilly view of Strauss the man
within a more sympathetic overview of his musical achievements.

It should not be thought that the wider appreciation of Strauss has been
confined to the musicologist's and writer's study; it has had practical results
in performance (including recordings and videos). Whereas the tone-poems,

Salome, Elektra, Der Rosenkavalier, and even the 1916 *Ariadne auf Naxos* and *Arabella* have been repertory pieces for many decades, other Straussian operas have appeared with increasing frequency only in the 1980s and 1990s. *Capriccio* and *Die Frau ohne Schatten,* once rarities, are now familiar. There is renewed interest in *Ariadne I* and *Die schweigsame Frau.* Thanks to the enterprise of the Santa Fe Opera, emulated by some European and British opera managements, *Daphne* and *Die Liebe der Danae* have been rediscovered. In the summer of 1997, *Die ägyptische Helena,* for many years available only to Munich audiences, had its British premiere. Dresden has restaged *Freidenstag,* and Glyndebourne triumphed with *Intermezzo,* which is no longer merely a curiosity where European audiences are concerned. The ballet *Josephslegende* has had several stagings, one of which is preserved on video.

Through this revival, even the most devout admirers of Strauss have learned anew that each of his operas, like Wagner's, inhabits its own sound world. No two are alike. One has constantly to revise opinions as new beauties and excitements are revealed. We are at last beginning to recognize how much of Strauss's greatness remains to be discovered. More than ever it seems — to this writer at least — that Glenn Gould was right when he described Richard Strauss as the greatest musical figure to live in the twentieth century.

Preface

The impulse behind this volume was an international conference on Richard Strauss that took place at Duke University in April 1990, the first such musicological gathering in the United States. Most, but not all, of these essays originated from that conference. This book is divided into two sections. The first ("The Musical-Historical Context") examines Strauss and his world from various perspectives: musical-stylistic influences, tonal language, relationships with contemporaries, political contexts, and the like. The second section ("The Musical Works") focuses on specific pieces by the composer: first instrumental works, then operatic ones. These latter essays represent manifold approaches to Strauss's music: structural analysis, studies in musical style, music and dramaturgy, source studies, and cultural context. Yet despite their varied topics and perspectives, these contributions share a common trait: they offer a fresh look at a composer quite familiar to concert and opera audiences, but who has not been a major part of the musicological discourse, especially in the United States. Strauss, indeed, embodies the paradox of a major European composer who was an integral part of the musical and cultural mainstream of the late nineteenth and early twentieth centuries, yet one who, nevertheless, has remained outside the mainstream of traditional musical scholarship.

Strauss's eighty-five years spanned one of the most remarkable stretches of modern German history. He saw an emperor come and go, witnessed the rise and fall of the Weimar Republic, endured the period of National Socialism, survived the Second World War, and died during the time of a newly divided Germany. The essays presented here examine Strauss on various fronts and from various periods of his creative life: as a young composer steeped in a conservative instrumental tradition (Todd); as a brash, young modernist tone poet of the 1890s (Hepokoski); as an important composer of twentieth-century German opera (Schlötterer, Lockwood, Gilliam); as a pioneer for the rights of composers (Petersen); and as a cultural icon manipulated by the National Socialists during the 1930s and early '40s (Potter). Other essays compare Strauss and Mahler as contemporaries who complemented each other in remarkable ways (Agawu, Hefling), and still others examine recently discovered sources that shed important light on Strauss's late period of composition (Brosche, Jackson).

There are, furthermore, a number of interconnecting threads that run through these essays, recurring issues such as the problem of defining musical modernism, new perspectives on issues of "progressive" versus "regressive" from the standpoint of postmodernism, the tension between narrative and structure in program music, and the problem of extended tonality. And while most of these essays do not attempt to find all the answers, they suggest new areas and methods of inquiry. In short, this volume offers a new portrait of Strauss, a picture different from the one presented in older historical surveys and popular literature.

A number of individuals and institutions have provided assistance in the preparation of this volume, and I should like to acknowledge their invaluable help. I am deeply grateful to the Richard-Strauss-Archiv, Garmisch; the Bavarian State Library, Munich; the Richard-Strauss-Institut, Munich; and the Austrian National Library, Vienna for their permission to cite manuscript excerpts: either in transcription or facsimile. Many thanks as well to R. Larry Todd and Peter Williams for their advice and encouragement. I am also indebted to Franz Trenner for his advice and assistance with source-related issues. All references to Garmisch sketchbooks use Trenner's numbering system (Tr. 1–144); see his *Die Skizzenbücher von Richard Strauss aus dem Richard-Strauss-Archiv in Garmisch* (Tutzing: Hans Schneider, 1977). I am most thankful to Mary Mendell and Jean Brady at Duke University Press for their tireless efforts on behalf of this volume. Thanks also to Camille Crittenden and Chuck Youmans for their diligent proofreading, Barbara Norton for her copyediting, and J. Michael Cooper for preparing the index. One final note: As this volume went to press Alice Strauss passed away. A large part of her life went to the creation and maintenance of the Richard-Strauss-Archiv, now in the capable hands of her son Richard. A number of contributors to this volume, including myself, have benefited greatly from Alice Strauss's dedication to the legacy of her father-in-law. We dedicate this book to her memory.

The Musical-Historical Context

▼

Strauss before Liszt and Wagner:
Some Observations

R. Larry Todd

▼

The signal year in Richard Strauss's early career is usually taken to be 1885, when the impressionable twenty-one-year-old came under the influence of that enigmatic Zukunftsmusiker, Alexander Ritter, and when Strauss began his conversion to the ideals of Zukunftsmusik. Ritter introduced Strauss to Liszt's symphonic poems, a body of orchestral music in which Strauss discovered, in his words, "the leading thread for my own symphonic work" ("Leitfaden für meine eigenen sinfonischen Arbeiten"), namely, the motto-like imperative, "New ideas must search out new forms" ("Neue Gedanken müssen sich neue Formen suchen").[1] In the extended series of tone poems that followed (Macbeth, the first, was conceived in 1886), Strauss vigorously pursued the Lisztian notion that the poetic idea should shape and determine the musical form. Ritter also urged upon Strauss the serious study of Wagner's music dramas and indeed encouraged Strauss to compose his first opera, Guntram (1894), for which the thirty-year-old, now a devoted Wagnerian, himself wrote the libretto. And, finally, through the philosophy of Arthur Schopenhauer, Ritter convinced Strauss that a justification could be made for music as an expression of the Will, and that the clearest path of the "Ausdrucksmusiker" proceeded from Beethoven to Liszt and Wagner. According to this formulation, Beethoven had expanded sonata form to a new extreme; with Bruckner, the "stammering Cyclops," the form, in essence, had exploded (especially in Bruckner's massive symphonic finales); and in the "complacent" work of epigonal composers, to which category no less a figure than Brahms was consigned, the form had become a kind of empty shell in which only Hanslick's flowery defense of absolute music could flourish.

This much seems clear enough, but at least one aspect of Strauss's development during the mid 1880s—his relationship with the "complacent" Brahms or, expressed another way, the case for Brahms's influence on

Strauss's emerging compositional style—poses some crucial issues that ultimately bear on Strauss's fundamental conversion. And to understand that conversion, we must consider from what Strauss chose to convert. His relationship with Brahms affords us one way to approach this problem.

In January 1884 Strauss attended the Berlin rehearsals and performances of Brahms's Third Symphony, and in a flurry of letters to his parents and his boyhood friend, Ludwig Thuille, he set down his views about Brahms's music. The first response was distinctly negative. To his parents, on 6 January 1884, he wrote: "Today my head is still humming from all this unclarity, and I admit openly that I do not yet understand it [the symphony]; but it is so wretchedly and obtusely scored, that in the first and last movements one can grab hold of only two coherent four-bar ideas, in the middle of the movements. While the scherzo substitute is very lovely and interesting, the Adagio, on the other hand, is dreary and lacking in ideas. But one cannot say this here, for Joachim etc. are enraptured with Brahms."[2] Exactly why Strauss reacted in this way is uncertain. Perhaps the letter's uncharitable tone reflected a concession to the musical tastes of his father, who, rooted in the classical trinity of Haydn, Mozart, and Beethoven, apparently could tolerate only some Mendelssohn, Schumann, and Spohr, and little further.[3]

Nevertheless, as Willi Schuh has pointed out, within only a few weeks Strauss's opinion would change decisively.[4] By March, he determined that Brahms's Third Symphony—which he had heard four times, twice under Brahms—was "not only his most beautiful symphony, but well the most significant that has now been written."[5] Adjectives such as "kolossal," "frisch," "schneidiger," and "dämonisch" (colossal, fresh, energetic, and demonic) now replace such pejorative assessments as "miserabel" and "öde" (wretched, deserted) in the accounts from January. And other works by Brahms, including the *Gesang der Parzen*, which Strauss heard in January, and the D-Minor Piano Concerto, which he heard Brahms perform in March, prompted similarly positive responses.

By 1885 Strauss's interest in Brahms had grown into a full-fledged enthusiasm, which Strauss himself later recalled as his "Brahmsschwärmerei."[6] A primary influence on this profound shift may well have been the conductor, pianist, and former Wagnerian Hans von Bülow, whom Strauss first met during the Berlin sojourn of 1884. Established in 1880 as *Hofmusikdirektor* to the Duke of Meiningen, von Bülow had worked during this period as an ardent champion of Brahms,[7] and no doubt his views encouraged and strengthened the turn in Strauss's own approach to Brahms. On 1 October 1885, Strauss arrived in Meiningen to assume a post as von Bülow's assistant; the very same month, Brahms appeared in Meiningen to "stand as godfather" to the rehearsals for the premiere of his Fourth Symphony. This historical coincidence set the stage for the climax of Strauss's Brahmsian period. The letters of the young composer now glowed with undiminished ardor for Brahms's music, and his later memoirs recount some details of the meetings he enjoyed with the composer. Thus, the Fourth Symphony is described as "a gigantic work, new and original in its greatness of conception and invention, its genius in treatment of form, period construction, and its eminent verve and strength; and yet, from A to Z it is genuine Brahms, in a word, an enrichment of our art of composition. . . ." [8] For his part, Brahms responded favorably to at least two works of Strauss, the Suite for 13 Wind Instruments, op. 4, and the Symphony in F Minor, op. 12 ("ganz hübsch, junger Mann," he is reported to have said of the symphony); his one reservation was to advise Strauss to avoid engaging in a certain "trivial pursuit" of contrapuntal combinations of triadic figures (Brahms's term was evidently "kontrapunktische Spielereien"). [9]

These essential facts suggest that in 1884 and 1885 Brahms may have played a not insignificant role in Strauss's compositional development; even so, scholarship has largely failed to measure the extent or nature of that role. A full account of the Brahms-Strauss case remains to be written; here, we can do no more than consider briefly some of its stylistic results. We need only look at Strauss's works of the mid 1880s to discover them. One example especially reminiscent of Brahms is the Piano Quartet in C Minor, op. 13 (1884). This composition belongs to a series of chamber works Strauss produced during the 1880s, including the String Quartet, op. 2 (1880), the Cello Sonata, op. 6 (1883), and the Violin Sonata, op. 18 (1887). Strauss's interest during this period in chamber music understandably would have led him to Brahms, the major contemporary composer who was still exploring the traditional genres of chamber music. Indeed, in the first movement of the C-Minor Piano Quartet, Strauss seems to have been stimulated by Brahms's own piano quartets in G minor (no. 1, op. 25) and C minor (no. 3, op. 60).

The very opening of Strauss's quartet, with its unison subject played *piano*, pause on a chord, and subsequent *fortissimo* eruption, recalls a similar series of devices Brahms had used to begin his Piano Quintet in F Minor, op. 34. Other details, however, point to the first few measures of Brahms's Piano Quartet in C Minor—notably the low-lying strings, homophonic texture, diminuendo,

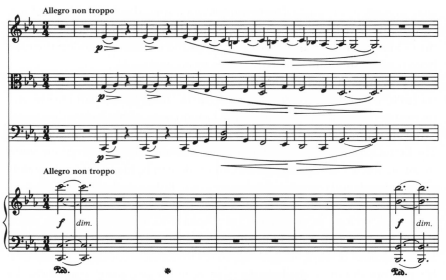

Example 1a. Brahms, Piano Quartet in C Minor, op. 60

Example 1b. Strauss, Piano Quartet in C Minor, op. 13

and the play on C-B♮ versus C-B♭ in the first violin (see example 1a and b). A few measures later, Strauss indulges in a particularly Brahmsian display: against a triplet pedal point in the bass of the piano part, we hear a turning melodic idea doubled in sixths; then the pedal is taken over by the strings, so that the melodic idea can be played by both hands of the piano in sixths and, after inversion, in thirds. The texture is one especially favored by Brahms; Strauss may have had in his ear the opening of the C-Minor Intermezzo from the G-Minor Piano Quartet (see example 2a and b; note in addition the turn from tonic to subdominant in these two examples).

Strauss himself singled out two works—the *Burleske* for piano and orchestra (1885–86) and the *Wandrers Sturmlied*, op. 14 (1884) for six-part chorus and orchestra—as works representing the culmination of his *Brahmsschwärmerei*; these, he claimed, were encouraged by von Bülow's "suggestive influence."[10] The better known *Burleske*, in D minor, is a continuous, one-movement work in sonata form. On account of its technical demands, in particular its widely spaced chords and complex passagework, von Bülow declared the work "unklaviermässig"; in fact, its premiere, given by Eugène d'Albert, was delayed until 1890. Writing to von Bülow on 7 April 1886, Strauss judged the piano part to be too detailed and found himself exhausted after an early rehearsal.[11] In any number of ways, Strauss's approach to the piano resembles Brahms at his pianistically most challenging—that is, in the two piano concertos, the first of which Strauss heard Brahms perform in 1884 (the second had appeared in 1882). Like Brahms, Strauss favored thick arrangements of chords in thirds and sixths, figuration that uses the full range of the instrument, and shifting metrical patterns, including hemiola. Occasional passages suggest points of connection with the Brahms Second Piano Concerto. In particular,

Example 2a. Brahms, Piano Quartet in G Minor, op. 25

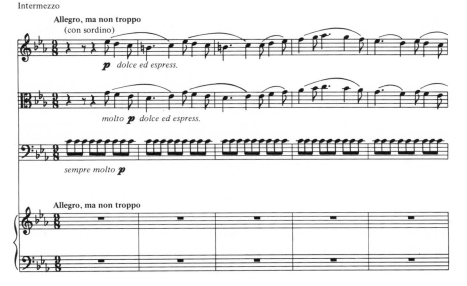

Example 2b. Strauss, Piano Quartet in C Minor, op. 13

a haunting, tranquil melody supported by a rising arpeggiated accompaniment establishes a link between the *Burleske* and the scherzo of the Brahms Second Concerto; in this scherzo, we may discover, perhaps, a primary influence for the *Burleske* (see example 3a and b). First of all, the two movements are in D minor, are similar in mood (Strauss actually referred to the *Burleske* as a scherzo[12]), and have a triple meter and similar tempo markings (Strauss, *Allegro vivace*; Brahms, *Allegro appassionato*). Moreover, both employ an essentially monothematic technique whereby a compact motive built on the first, second, and third scale degrees (D, E, and F) is first used to generate the opening theme and then redeployed in the second, "contrasting" thematic group.

In the Brahms, the opening theme is propelled by an upbeat based on the neighbor-note figure, D-E; through a redefinition of E as a passing tone, this figure is extended to F on the downbeat of the first measure (example 4). This melodic cell offers an energetic transformation of the noble horn melody that introduces the first movement, which ascends from B flat through C to D, that is, from the first to the second and third scale degrees of B-flat major. For the second theme of the scherzo proper, Brahms again begins with a neighbor-note figure, this one based on E and F, in which melodic functions are reversed: F now serves as a neighbor note and E as the fifth scale degree

Example 3a. Brahms, Piano Concerto No. 2 in B-flat Major, op. 83

Example 3b. Strauss, *Burleske*

Example 4. Brahms, Piano Concerto No. 2 in B-flat Major, op. 83

of the dominant, as we hear a plaintive melody in the dominant minor (see again example 3a).

Though the opening of the *Burleske* does not immediately bring to mind that of the Brahms scherzo, closer inspection reveals a similar melodic technique. Strauss impresses us first, of course, with the extraordinary solo for four timpani, tuned to A, D, E, and F. The use of four timpani enables him to write melodically for the instrument; furthermore, in this solo, the rising third, D-E-F, emerges as the primary melodic motive, with the E functioning as a passing tone between D and F (example 5). Truly remarkable is the manner in which this timpani figure reappears throughout the movement to articulate its principal structural divisions, and in which, indeed, its pitches are continually subsumed and reworked in the thematic material. For example, the bridge section, given *fortissimo* by the orchestra, rearranges their order to D, E, A, and F, with E functioning as a neighbor note (example 6). In the development and coda, this bridge theme is transformed into the Brahmsian piano solo cited in ex. 3b. Just before the second theme of the exposition, the timpani are assigned the three-note motive E-D-F; this cell, in which E functions as leading tone to the mediant F, is then taken up by the piano in the second theme (example 7). At the beginning of the development the timpani reappear, and we soon hear again the figure E-D-F, this time supporting a diminished-seventh harmony. Timpani solos mark the recapitulation, prepare the extended piano cadenza, and, finally, return at the very conclusion. In summary, Brahms's technique, whereby the original motive is reworked to generate the kernel of the second theme, is developed considerably further by Strauss: the thematic material for the entire movement is playfully drawn from a melodic kernel assigned to a traditionally nonmelodic instrument.

These comparisons should not encourage us to exaggerate the similarities between the *Burleske* and the scherzo. For all its passion and power, the scherzo, of course, lacks that distinct quality that sets the *Burleske* apart from nearly all other nineteenth-century piano concertos, namely, its unrelenting use of parody. The unconventional melodic application of the timpani,

Example 5. Strauss, *Burleske*

Example 6. Strauss, *Burleske*

Example 7. Strauss, *Burleske*

the shrill piccolo parts, the piano's cascading chromatic octave passage with prominent tritones (a passage which appears in the course of the movement no fewer than six times), the disproportionately swollen cadenza, and any number of other details remind us that the *Burleske*, after all, was conceived as a humorous parody. A few references are to Wagner: in at least one chromatic

Example 8. Strauss, *Burleske*

Example 9. Strauss, *Burleske*

passage from the cadenza, marked *calando*, we hear a reference to *Tristan* (example 8); and the *martellato* passage toward the end, with its insistent tremolo on D and rising octaves in the bass, sounds like a droll reenactment of the storm from *Die Walküre* (example 9).

Indeed, the opening piano solo, which Ernest Newman as early as 1908 viewed as a "reminiscence" of Brahms's *Edward* Ballade in D Minor, op. 10, no. 1,[13] projects the unmistakable quality of caricature (example 10a and b). Here Brahms's brooding folksong-like melody, with its open-spaced chords, Scotch snaps, and hint of pentatonicism, is radically transformed. Actually Strauss revamps just the first measure of the Brahms: the *piano* upbeat is now made a *mezzoforte* downbeat, which in turn displaces the Scotch snap. Even more striking, Brahms's descending third, A-F, is converted to a more dynamic, brittle ascending sixth. Strauss then repeats the fragment an octave higher before breaking off the phrase with those shrieking chromatic scales that cascade from the uppermost register of the piano. For all its Brahmsian gestures, parody thus animates this work; according to Newman, "the face of the Strauss we all know keeps peeping out of the heavy Brahmsian hood like the face of Till Eulenspiegel from under the hood of the monk."[14] Nevertheless, the *Burleske* would probably have been unthinkable if Strauss had not experienced his intense, if short-lived, *Brahmsmanie* of 1884 and 1885.

The other composition Strauss recognized as a product of his *Brahms-schwärmerei*—the *Wandrers Sturmlied*, op. 14—remains among his least-known works. It offers a rich, darkly colored setting for six-part chorus and orchestra of the first part of Goethe's celebrated imitation of a Pindaric ode. Written in 1772 during the poet's so-called *Sturm-und-Drang* period, the *Sturmlied* was conceived by Goethe as he wandered during a storm, distraught over his love affair with Frederika Brion; its mercurial, ever-shifting images and novel compound-word formations led him to describe it as "half-nonsense" (*Halbunsinn*). Filled with classical references, the poem includes an allusion to Pindar, as if to reinforce the underlying triadic structure of strophe, antistrophe, and epode. In the strophe, the portion set by Strauss, the wanderer calls upon Genius to protect the artist from the onslaught of the storm. He whom Genius does not abandon answers the storm as a singing lark and is likened to Deucalion, who in Greek mythology floated to safety during the deluge in a ship that came to rest on Mt. Parnassus. In the closing line of the strophe, the wanderer hovers above water and earth, like the gods themselves (*göttergleich*).

As was realized in 1892 by that arch-Brahmsian, Eduard Hanslick,[15] Strauss's inspiration for the *Sturmlied* was undoubtedly Brahms's *Gesang der Parzen*, op. 89,

Example 10a. Brahms, *Edward Ballade*, op. 10, no. 1

Example 10b. Strauss, *Burleske*

a setting of another Goethe poem, this one the Song of the Fates sung by Iphigenia at the close of the fourth act of *Iphigenie auf Tauris* (1779). Brahms's work, published in 1883, was dedicated to the Duke of Meiningen. Strauss heard it in Leipzig early in 1884;[16] the *Wandrers Sturmlied* was completed later that year. Both works are in D minor and specify *maestoso* characters. Both require a six-part chorus (two alto and two bass parts in the Brahms; two soprano and two bass parts in the Strauss), and they employ similar orchestras—double wood-winds expanded by a contrabassoon (in addition, Strauss adds a piccolo part, while Brahms calls for the first flute to double on piccolo), and brass with three trombones (in addition, Brahms requires a bass tuba). The shattering *fortissimo* openings are also similar (example 11a and b). In the Brahms, we hear a descending line in the strings that proceeds from D to C before leaping to an A. In the Strauss, the descending line unfolds chromatically in the same register (D-D♭-C-B♮), almost as if Strauss means to allude to the old affective convention of the descending chromatic tetrachord. Several pages into the score, toward the end of the stormy first section, Strauss reintroduces the descending figure in the violins, and here its motion (D-C-A) brings vividly to mind the opening of the Brahms (cf. examples 12 and 11a).

The end of example 12 shows how Strauss revised the descending figure so as to reinforce the descending chromatic tetrachord, D-C♯-C♮-B♭-A. Such a tetrachord, of course, was historically charged with associations of the lament. At first glance, this tetrachord may seem somewhat incongruous in a setting of a poem that celebrates, rather than bewails, the *poeticus furor*. In fact, the tetrachord may have little to do with the text; it may instead represent fur-ther stylistic evidence of Strauss's indebtedness to Brahms. But in this case, Strauss may have had in mind not the *Parzenlied* but another Brahms work for chorus and orchestra, *Nänie*, op. 82, which was published in 1881. Writ-ten in memory of the painter Anselm Feuerbach, *Nänie* is, in fact, a lament,

Example 11a. Brahms, *Gesang der Parzen*, op. 89

Example 11b. Strauss, *Wandrers Sturmlied*, op. 14

Example 12. Strauss, *Wandrers Sturmlied*, op. 14

a *Klagegesang* on a text by Friedrich Schiller. Like the *Parzenlied* and the *Wandrers Sturmlied*, Schiller's poem is filled with classical allusions. Brahms's use of the descending tetrachord in *Nänie* as an emblem of lament may have been adopted by Strauss in the *Wandrers Sturmlied* not for its topical significance but as a purely stylistic imitation.

Indeed, the introductory measures of *Nänie* may have been revived by Strauss in the *Sturmlied*. In this opening, the descent from D, subtly scored by Brahms in the first flute below the oboe, extends only as far as B, where a deceptive cadence on the subdominant is prolonged for several measures; here Brahms introduces a *piano* horn-call motive in the clarinets (example 13a). In the *Sturmlied*, that deceptive cadence appears to be brought back forcefully by the chorus (example 13b), and similar horn calls figure in the closing pages of the score, though now much more prominently (triple *forte* and scored for brass; see example 13c). The end of the *Sturmlied* is especially close to that of *Nänie*: both Brahms and Strauss write a short D-major *a cappella* passage before allowing the orchestra to join the chorus; furthermore, in the final bars of each composition, the descending tetrachord is reaffirmed (examples 14a and b). Brahms chooses the version D-C♯-B-A, no doubt in response to Schiller's text, "Auch ein Klaglied zu sein im Mund der Geliebten ist herrlich." (Perhaps his decision not to introduce the chromatic B♭ was an attempt to reinforce "herrlich.") Strauss, on the other hand, chooses the more fully chromatic version, D-C♯-B-B♭-A; also, he divides the tetrachord registrally, so that the B♭ and A are set off in a higher register. The use of the tetrachord here for "göttergleich" is curious indeed; its presence suggests more a response to the consoling conclusion of *Nänie* than a close reading of Goethe's poetry.

In 1892 Eduard Hanslick published a review of *Wandrers Sturmlied*, which the critic no doubt would have recognized as Strauss's most avowedly Brahmsian composition. Fully one half of the review is devoted to a consideration of Goethe's poem; Hanslick interprets it as a "glorification of Genius, which is manifested most clearly in a storm."[17] Strauss, he says, has done well enough

Example 13a. Brahms, *Nänie*, op. 82

Example 13b. Strauss, *Wandrers Sturmlied*, op. 14

Example 13c. Strauss, *Wandrers Sturmlied*, op. 14

Example 14a. Brahms, *Nänie*, op. 82

Example 14b. Strauss, *Wandrers Sturmlied*, op. 14

immer ruhiger werdend
pp
immer ruhiger werdend
p
dim.
pizz.
arco
gleich, göt - ter - gleich.
gleich, göt - ter - gleich.
gleich, göt - ter - gleich.
gleich, göt - ter - gleich.
gleich, göt - ter - gleich.
gleich, göt - ter - gleich.
pizz.
arco

Example 14c. Wagner, *Parsifal*, act 3

in his decision to set only the strophe; but, Hanslick continues, Strauss has nevertheless essentially misread the poem, and, further, has misapplied his reliance on Brahms:

> More exhausted and bewildered than uplifted by Richard Strauss's "Sturmlied," I nevertheless would like to prefer this work to the composer's symphonic poems. The salutary effect of the restraint, that the vocal composer must accommodate himself to the content and form of a definite poem, is made clear in Strauss's "Sturmlied." . . . The absolute freedom of purely instrumental composition appears with Strauss . . . as a fantastic rambling without any sense of mastery, which, defying any organic coherence, gladly looses itself into the unmeasurable. At least in a vocal composition there are reins. In the "Sturmlied" Strauss treats the musical substance in a more plastic, lucid manner than is usually the case; nevertheless, the feverish striving for the extraordinary sometimes

misleads him to do damage to the poetry. Goethe's poem (in its portion set by Strauss) breathes throughout a confident, godlike awareness of the one guided by genius. But in the Strauss we believe we heard in long stretches the painful lament [Klage] of one in despair. For instance, the beginning in a melancholy D minor with its cutting chords above the rumbling bass and timpani rolls! Just in this way did Brahms introduce—but with the proper expression—the gruesome Gesang der Parzen. There is little doubt that this chorus of Brahms clearly hovered before Herr Strauss's grasp. Unfortunately he did not also imitate the concise length of his model; with its incomparably lesser subject the Sturmlied lasts twice as long. It received from the public a very cool reception.[18]

Evidently Hanslick was unwilling to accept Strauss's borrowing from Brahms; if the opening of Wandrers Sturmlied strikingly invoked Brahms's Parzenlied, that borrowing was nevertheless inappropriate: Strauss in effect had failed to match the poetic content of Goethe's ode with suitable musical imagery.

By 1892, the year of Hanslick's review, Strauss had secured his reputation as a composer of tone poems; surely Hanslick's negative response was colored by his disapproval of Strauss's foray into programmatic music. But Hanslick could have discovered another reason to disparage Strauss in the closing bars of the Sturmlied. Arguably the descending tetrachord—as we have suggested, a probable reference to the close of Brahms's Nänie—suggests a second compelling reference, this one not to Brahms but to Hanslick's implacable opponent, Richard Wagner, and specifically to the Good Friday Zaubermusik from the third act of Parsifal (example 14c). In the climactic D-major section, in which Gurnemanz marvels at the renewal of nature, Wagner contraposes a descending chromatic line against a pedal point; in the treble, we hear an expressive melody formed by an ascending sixth (A-F♯) which then descends through E as an accented passing tone to D. The passage is indeed close to the Strauss (see example 14b), but the exact meaning of this allusion—if it was a deliberate allusion—is unclear. Perhaps the reference was prompted at a subconscious level. As is well known, as a favor to Hermann Levi, who conducted the premiere of Parsifal on 26 July 1882, Strauss's father played the first horn part, and young Richard journeyed with him to Bayreuth to attend the performance. Clearly the sound of Parsifal was in his ear, and thus in the closing bars of the Sturmlied we have to consider perhaps as much a Wagnerian reminiscence as the image of Strauss adjusting the "heavy hood of Brahms."

Nevertheless, the Brahms experience was a strong one for Strauss, especially in the two crucial years of 1884 and 1885. From his study of Brahms,

Strauss found reinforcement for certain conservative features of his own music written before the 1885 conversion: its reliance on traditional forms and genres (the sonata, chamber music, symphony, and concerto, for example), its use of thick, contrapuntal textures, its general preference for double-wind orchestration—in short, its awareness of and close relation to the mainstream tradition of nineteenth-century German "absolute" instrumental music. That Strauss ultimately rejected the Brahmsian mantle reflected, to be sure, his endorsement of a radically different musical aesthetic, but, paradoxically, it did not necessarily signify for Strauss the abandonment of the classical tradition, as his memoirs clarify.[19] Notwithstanding Alexander Ritter, then, for Strauss the path to the music of the future did indeed proceed, to some extent, through Brahms.

When we consider Strauss's development as a composer *before* his encounter with the music of Brahms, that is, from about 1870, the year of his first surviving composition, up to the early 1880s, we enter what is still *terra incognita* in the scholarly literature, a period, to adapt Joseph Kerman's view of Beethoven's early Bonn period, about which the twentieth century has known "little and probably cared less."[20] To carry the analogy further, just as Kerman proposed a division of Beethoven's student period into two subperiods, so too may we subdivide Strauss's early years as a composer. The first decade, roughly from 1870 to 1880, contains largely juvenile efforts—about one hundred items in all, according to Franz Trenner's recently published and updated work list,[21] with any number of references to Haydn, Mozart, Beethoven, and, occasionally, Schumann and Mendelssohn. Also, between 1877 and 1880 young Strauss undertook a systematic course in counterpoint with Friedrich Wilhelm Meyer, which included exercises in imitation, canon, and fugue; the culmination of this training came early in 1880 with a five-voice double fugue for violin and piano (Trenner 91/3). Precious little of Strauss's creative efforts during this decade was ever published; but the catalogue incipits[22] seem to confirm Strauss's assertion that, owing to his father's protective influence (*strenger Obhut*), up to his sixteenth year (1880) he was exposed only to "classical" music.[23]

In contrast, the first few years of the 1880s suggest a decided turn in Strauss's development as a composer and form a second subperiod of the student years. In short order he created several ambitious, technically accomplished works, including the two symphonies in D minor and F minor (1880 and 1883–84), the Violin Concerto (1882), the First Horn Concerto (1883), and various chamber works. Notwithstanding their traditional idioms, all of these strike one as the creations of a mature composer. Also during these years, Strauss began his first serious study of Wagner's dramas, expressly disobeying his father in 1881, when, at age seventeen, he "feverishly consumed the pages of the score of *Tristan*."[24] But full appreciation of Wagner came to Strauss only later, chiefly, of course, through his friendship with Alexander Ritter. The works of the early 1880s still show a reliance on traditional models; in particular, the music of Mendelssohn and Schumann now evidently offered Strauss specific models for study.

During this second subperiod Strauss produced some compositions evincing a curious admixture of stylistic sources, perhaps nowhere more curious than in the String Quartet in A Major, op. 2, of 1880. The initial rising triadic theme, the clearly articulated, symmetrical phrase structure, and the prevalent homophonic textures mark the first movement as a re-creation of Mozart and Haydn, as do similar features of the finale. All of this, we can well imagine, earned the young composer unstinting paternal praise. The scherzo, with its playful cross-accents that effectively interject passages in duple meter, perhaps suggests Beethoven; the rustic pedal points of the trio possibly invoke Haydn. But in the slow movement (*Andante cantabile, molto espressivo*), Strauss leaves the world of Viennese classicism to explore a romantic idiom reminiscent of Mendelssohn. He begins with a four-measure introduction; two descending chromatic lines in the cello and first violin give way to a tremolo accompaniment that supports an expressive cello melody. The passage recalls a similar opening in the slow movement of Mendelssohn's *Reformation* Symphony, op. 107, which, first published posthumously in 1868, was still a relatively "new" symphony (example 15a and b).

Example 15a. Mendelssohn, *Reformation* Symphony, op. 107

Example 15b. Strauss, String Quartet, op. 2

In a similar way, the Piano Sonata in B Minor, op. 5, of 1881 presents a juxtaposition of stylistic sources, including Beethoven and Mendelssohn. In the
last three movements, however, the reliance on Mendelssohn comes more
and more to the fore. As has been pointed out, the first movement appropriates its familiar four-note head motive from Beethoven's Fifth Symphony.
The movement is fairly saturated with the motive, which appears in the first
theme, the bridge (though not in the lyrical contrasting second theme), and
the closing section of the exposition. In addition, much of the development
is devoted to a treatment of the motive, and in the closing bars of the movement we find a major-key version of the close of Beethoven's first movement.
   The beginning of the second movement (*Adagio cantabile*) impresses as a
Mendelssohnian *Lied ohne Worte*. The first eight-bar phrase, which ends on a
half cadence, offers a singable treble melody accompanied by a syncopated
chordal pattern. This is answered by a second eight-bar phrase that reaches
a full cadence on the tonic, E major. The second phrase introduces a lyrical
tenor melodic part set against the soprano, effectively converting the solo
Lied ohne Worte to a *Duett ohne Worte*, a device encountered in Mendelssohn's

piano lieder (as in the *Lied*, op. 38, no. 6, said to have been conceived as a love duet on the occasion of Mendelssohn's engagement to Cécile Jeanrenaud in 1836). But stylistically incongruous in the Strauss is the conclusion of the second phrase, which, with its ascending triplet and $\frac{3}{8}$ meter, suspiciously resembles a cadential figure from the slow movement of Beethoven's Fifth Symphony (example 16).

Strauss sustains the duet texture in the following ten-bar section that introduces the submediant, C-sharp minor. Then the opening material returns in the tonic, suggesting the conclusion of a ternary song form. But the final cadence is interrupted, and after a bar of rest Strauss transports us to a contrasting section in the parallel minor, now expanded to form the middle

Example 16. Strauss, Piano Sonata, op. 5

section of the movement. Its staccato, scherzo-like opening unmistakably marks it as a second allusion to Mendelssohn. If the key, E minor, conjures up such works as Mendelssohn's Overture to *A Midsummer Night's Dream* and the *Rondo capriccioso*, op. 14, other details point to the *Scherzo a capriccio* in F-sharp minor (1836).[25] These include the sculpting of the tonic triad on the fifth, third, and first scale degrees, the insertion of rests to articulate the descent through the third and first scale degrees, and, finally, the application of turn-like figures to support the descent on the weak beats of the measure (example 17a and b). Strauss allows this *pianissimo* opening to reach a *fortissimo* climax before it subsides, preparing us for the resumption of the *Lied* and *Duett ohne Worte* in the tonic major. The overall shape of the movement thus describes a ternary ABA form, in which the A and B sections allude to two contrasting, but recognizably Mendelssohnian, styles.

Curiously enough, Strauss again draws on Mendelssohn's scherzo style in his third movement, a full-fledged scherzo in an expanded ABABA form.

Example 17a. Strauss, Piano Sonata, op. 5

Example 17b. Mendelssohn, *Scherzo a capriccio*

Example 18. Strauss, Piano Sonata, op. 5

The $\frac{2}{4}$ meter is possibly a debt to Mendelssohn, who wrote a number of duple-meter scherzi (see, for example, the Octet, op. 20, the Second Piano Trio, op. 66, and the *Scotch* Symphony, op. 56). Through a clever thematic manipulation, Strauss's F-sharp minor movement is related to the middle E-minor section of the Adagio; basically, Strauss reverses the two elements of the earlier scherzo theme (see example 17a), so that the theme of the third movement begins with a simple turn figure which, after several repetitions, exhausts itself through a compressed descent (example 18).

Elsewhere in the Scherzo there occur passages that closely approach individual works of Mendelssohn. The Trio, for example, has a melodic flourish reminiscent of the second theme of the finale to Mendelssohn's Violin Concerto, op. 64 (example 19a and b).[26] And at the conclusion of the scherzo

Example 19a. Mendelssohn, Violin Concerto, op. 64

Example 19b. Strauss, Piano Sonata, op. 5

Strauss creates a texture reminiscent of that at the close of the *Lied ohne Worte*, op. 19, no. 3 (the celebrated *Jagdlied*), or of the Caprice, op. 16, no. 2, in E minor. Beneath the churning turn figure in the high treble, we hear fleeting horn calls. And finally, the concluding cadence, with its modal mixture of minor subdominant and tonic major, is reminiscent, of course, of the motto with which the *Midsummer Night's Dream Overture* begins and ends.

The $\frac{6}{8}$ finale, in sonata form, presents in its opening measures a theme which may have been inspired by the finale of Mendelssohn's Second Piano Trio in C Minor, op. 66. At the repetition of the theme (example 20), Strauss redirects the melody to the middle register and adds a broken arpeggiated accompaniment above; this revision brings the passage closer to the texture of Mendelssohn's finale, which features the first theme in the cello with piano accompaniment. But Strauss approaches Mendelssohn's style most compellingly in his second theme in the mediant D major (example 21a and b). Here the melodic contour, regular phrase structure, weak half cadences, and key indicate unambiguously the beginning of Mendelssohn's D-major Cello Sonata, op. 58 as the source. And, finally, the *martellato* passage that concludes Strauss's sonata seems to belong to an earlier age of piano virtuosity and recalls devices in the piano music of Mendelssohn and his contemporaries.

The piano music of Robert Schumann also offered models that influenced Strauss during the early 1880s. In this case, we may begin by considering

Example 20. Strauss, Piano Sonata, op. 5

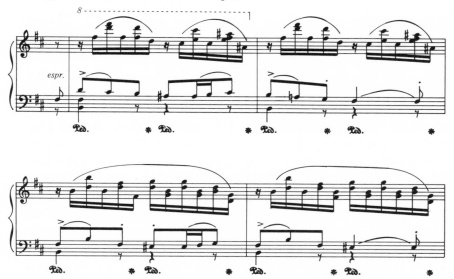

Example 21a. Strauss, Piano Sonata, op. 5

Example 21b. Mendelssohn, Cello Sonata in D Major, op. 58

the critical opinion of Franz Strauss, the composer's father: "The first piano works of Schumann up to Opus 20 were validated. The later piano works were prized somewhat less as 'Leipzig music,' for they came under Mendelssohn's influence, with their monotonous rhythms and periodic repetitions."[27] Now nowhere did the young composer reveal himself a more avid *Schumannianer* than in the first of his *Fünf Klavierstücke*, op. 3, a collection composed in 1880 and 1881. As if to confirm his father's judgment, this Andante in B-flat major is unabashedly derived from Schumann's *Humoreske* (1839), which, as Schumann's op. 20, was evidently still deemed worthy of study.

The Andante describes a three-part ABA form, as do so many individual movements of Schumann's early piano cycles. The A section, in B-flat major, draws on the opening page of the *Humoreske*, also in B flat; the B section, in the contrasting submediant G minor, on the second G-minor section of the *Humoreske*, marked *Einfach und zart*. Finally, the concluding measures of the Andante contain traces of the close of the *Humoreske*, marked *Zum Beschluss*.

Example 22a. Strauss, *Klavierstück*, op. 3, no. 1

Example 22b. Schumann, *Humoreske*, op. 20

Example 22a and b reveals just how closely Strauss adhered to his model. From the start, the texture of the Andante, with its outer voices in half and quarter notes and inner voices moving in a flowing, descending eighth-note arpeggiation, captures that special sound of the *Humoreske*. And like Schumann, Strauss begins with a nontonic opening. But whereas Schumann taunts us with an ambiguous augmented triad[28] that resolves to the subdominant before the tonic is secured in measure 4, Strauss begins less adventurously with the subdominant; this, too, gives way to a cadential phrase that establishes the tonic in m. 4. Later in the Andante, however, Strauss does insert a reference to Schumann's augmented triad, and, when it resolves not to the subdominant but to the lowered submediant, G-flat major (mm. 21ff.), we are reminded that Schumann too touches on G-flat major (mm. 8ff.), the triad of which includes two pitches from the original augmented triad.

Texturally, Strauss's B section, in the minor submediant, is also quite close to Schumann's model. Note especially in example 23a and b the soprano voice centered on D and the similar accompaniment in parallel sixths. Finally, the conclusion of the Andante, in which a descending figure in the soprano (Bb-G-Gb-F-Eb-D) appears over a tonic pedal point, sounds like a veiled allusion to Schumann's more robust conclusion (example 24a and b). Both passages incorporate references to the subdominant E flat; Strauss's ultimate cadence, in fact, is a plagal cadence, a final allusion to the nontonic opening, and an underscoring of the essential circularity of the piece—its "open-

Example 23a. Strauss, *Klavierstück*, op. 3, no. 1

Example 23b. Schumann, *Humoreske*, op. 20

endedness," which indeed captures a salient romantic feature of Schumann's early piano cycles.

Strauss's reliance, in his music of the early 1880s, on Mendelssohn and Schumann might be interpreted as a sign of the father's influence and refusal to recognize the music of Liszt and Wagner and the new views of the *Zukunfts-musiker*. As Jurgen Thym has lucidly demonstrated, a critical rethinking of Mendelssohn's and Schumann's roles in German music had already begun to emerge as early as 1845, when Franz Brendel assumed the editorship of Schumann's *Neue Zeitschrift für Musik* and gradually steered it in the direction of Zukunftsmusik.[29] For Brendel, Mendelssohn was a neoclassicist who had mastered the traditional forms with great facility, but whose "objective" and "academic" formalism was no longer congruent with the "subjective" needs of modern German music. And Schumann, who had begun his career in a highly subjective manner, was now, in his instrumental works of the early 1840s, in "danger of losing himself to the Mendelssohnian manner."[30]

In contrast, we can well imagine Franz Strauss arguing some four decades later for the very supremacy of the German tradition of absolute music. This was essentially an attempt to renew a classicist position, namely, that there existed in the instrumental music of the Viennese classicists and of nineteenth-century composers such as Mendelssohn and Schumann an exemplary instrumental tradition still worthy of emulation in the 1880s. To place Mendelssohn or Schumann in this tradition required no profound leap of thought. Mendelssohn's career at the Gewandhaus in Leipzig had established him as an upholder of traditional musical values; indeed, Schumann had referred to him as the "Mozart of the nineteenth century."[31] And Schumann, too, had continued the instrumental tradition by cultivating in systematic fashion piano, then chamber and orchestral music. In emulating Mendelssohn, young Strauss was essentially following the path of Schumann, who had turned to Mendelssohn, Schubert, Beethoven, and others for inspiration in his instrumental music.[32].

So too did Strauss's *Brahmsschwärmerei* of 1884 and 1885 enable him to cling for a while longer to the mainline German instrumental tradition. Brahms was one of the few living composers of major rank whose music resonated with any number of allusions to the German instrumental tradition[33] and who continued to cultivate the traditional genres long abandoned by the Zu-

Example 24a. Strauss, *Klavierstück*, op. 3, no. 1

Example 24b. Schumann, *Humoreske*, op. 20

kunftsmusiker. For Strauss, then, the progression that preoccupied him during the early 1880s—from Mendelssohn and Schumann to Brahms—was almost inevitable, and his personal contact with Brahms in all likelihood only reinforced it. The Brahms experience represented more or less the final stage of Strauss's student period. It enabled him to intensify his dependence on the German instrumental tradition and yet ultimately spurred him to reconsider that dependence. In the closing decades of the nineteenth century, Strauss occupied the unusual position of having thoroughly mastered the German instrumental tradition before separating from that tradition to embrace a fundamentally different musical aesthetic and to discover, at Ritter's urging, his own identity.

Notes

With great pleasure I wish to acknowledge my colleague Bryan Gilliam, whose Strauss-schwärmerei inspired the present essay and influenced its course in many ways.

1   "Aus meinen Jugend- und Lehrjahren," in Richard Strauss, Betrachtungen und Erinnerungen, ed. Willi Schuh (Zurich: Atlantis, 1957), p. 210.

2   Richard Strauss, Briefe an die Eltern, ed. Willi Schuh (Zurich: Atlantis, 1954), p. 32. "Mir brummt heute noch der Kopf von dieser Unklarheit, und ich gestehe offen, dass ich sie noch nicht verstanden habe, sie ist aber so miserabel und unklar instrumentiert, dass man während des ersten und letzten Satzes nur zwei zusammenhängende viertaktige Gedanken, [d.h.] die Mittelsätze, fassen konnte, während der scherzovertretende Satz sehr hübsch und interessant, das Adagio dagegen recht öde und gedankenarm ist. Man darf dies zwar hier nicht sagen, da von Joachim etc. sehr für Brahms geschwärmt wird. . . ."

3   "Erinnerungen an meinen Vater," in Betrachtungen und Erinnerungen, p. 194.

4   See Willi Schuh, Richard Strauss: A Chronicle of the Early Years, trans. Mary Whittall (Cambridge: Cambridge University Press, 1982), pp. 67–68.

5   Richard Strauss–Ludwig Thuille: Ein Briefwechsel, ed. Franz Trenner (Tutzing: Hans Schneider, 1980), p. 80. Letter of 8 March 1884: "Nicht nur seine schönste Sinfonie, sondern wohl mit die bedeutendste, die jetzt geschrieben worden ist."

6   "Aus meinen Jugend- und Lehrjahren," p. 207.

7   For a summary of Brahms's friendship with von Bülow, see Karl Geiringer, Brahms: His Life and Work, 2nd ed. (London: Doubleday, 1948), pp. 145ff.

8   Briefe an die Eltern, pp. 63–64. Letter of 24 October 1885: "Ein Riesenwerk, von einer Grösse der Konzeption und Erfindung, Genialität in der Formbehandlung, Periodenbau, von eminentem Schwung und Kraft, neu und originell und doch von A bis Z echter Brahms, mit einem Worte eine Bereicherung unserer Tonkunst. . . ."

9   "Aus meinen Jugend- und Lehrjahren," p. 207.

10 Ibid.

11 Willi Schuh and Franz Trenner, eds., "Hans von Bülow–Richard Strauss Briefwechsel," Richard Strauss Jahrbuch 1 (1954): 30.

12 Briefe an die Eltern, p. 68 (letter of 7 November 1885).

13 Ernest Newman, Richard Strauss (London, 1908; reprint, Westport: Greenwood, 1970), p. 35.

14 Ibid., pp. 35–36.

15 Eduard Hanslick, *Fünf Jahre Musik* (Berlin: Allgemeiner Verein für Deutsche Literatur, 1896), vol. 7, pp. 202–4.

16 *Richard Strauss–Ludwig Thuille*, p. 73. "Gesang der Parzen v. Brahms, der sehr stimmungsvoll und interessant ist . . ." (letter of 13 January 1884). Strauss also attended a rehearsal of the Brahms work in Leipzig in December 1883 and reported the work to his father as a "recht interessantes Chorwerk . . . , nur mitunter zu gesucht und bizarr" (*Briefe an die Eltern*, p. 23).

17 Hanslick, p. 203 ("eine Verherrlichung des Genius, der sich am vollkommensten im Sturme bewährt").

18 Ibid., pp. 203–4. "Von Richard Strauss' 'Sturmlied' mehr ermüdet und betäubt, als erhoben, möchte ich dasselbe den symphonischen Dichtungen dieses Komponisten doch vorziehen. Das Wohltätige dieses Zwanges, dass der Vokalkomponist sich dem Inhalt und der Form einer bestimmten Dichtung anbequemen muss, bewährt sich in Strauss' 'Sturmlied' . . . Die absolute Freiheit der Instrumental-Komposition erscheint bei Strauss . . . als ein meisterloses Schweifen der Phantasie, welche, des organischen Zusammenhanges spottend, sich gern ins Ungemessene verliert. Dem wenigstens ist in der Vokal-Komposition ein Zügel angelegt. Im 'Sturmlied' behandelt Strauss den Musikstoff plastischer, übersichtlicher als sonst, doch verleitet ihn mitunter der fieberhafte Drang nach Ausserordentlichem, der Dichtung Gewalt anzutun. Das Goethesche Poem (in seinem von Strauss komponierten Abschnitt) atmet durchaus ein siegesfrohes 'göttergleiches' Bewusstsein des vom Genius Geführten. Bei Strauss glauben wir aber ganze Strecken hindurch die schmerzliche Klage Verzweifelnder zu hören. Gleich der Anfang in düsterem D-moll mit seinen einschneidenden Akkorden über grollenden Bässen und Paukenwirbeln! So ungefähr hat Brahms mit richtiger Empfindung den schaurigen 'Gesang der Parzen' eingeleitet. Kein Zweifel, dass dieser Brahm'sche Chor Herrn Strauss deutlich, bis zum Greifen deutlich, vorschwebte. Leider ist er seinem Vorbild nicht auch in der knappen Umrahmung nachgefolgt; das 'Sturmlied' spielt bei ungleich geringerem Inhalt noch einmal so lange. Es hat im Publikum sehr kühle Aufnahme gefunden."

19 "Dieser [klassischen] Schule verdanke ich, dass mir bis heute die Liebe und Bewunderung für die klassischen Meister der Tonkunst ungetrübt verblieben ist." "Erinnerungen an meinen" *Vater*, p. 201.

20 Stanley Sadie, ed., *New Grove Dictionary of Music and Musicians* (London: Macmillan, 1979), vol. 2, "Beethoven," p. 377.

21 *Richard Strauss: Werkverzeichnis*, ed. Franz Trenner (Vienna: Doblinger, 1985).

22 See especially Max Steinitzer, *Richard Strauss* (Berlin: Schuster & Loeffler, 1914), pp. 225ff. Steinitzer was a boyhood friend of Strauss who witnessed his development as a composer firsthand.

23 "Erinnerungen an meinen" *Vater*, p. 201.

24 Ibid., p. 202.

25 Strauss's familiarity with the piano music of Mendelssohn is attested in a letter to Thuille of March 1878: "Auch Mendelsohns' [sic] Klavierwerke stehen auf einer bedeutenden Stufe und sind seine Klaviersachen sehr schön." *Richard Strauss–Ludwig Thuille*, p. 40.

26 In a letter to Thuille of June 1879, Strauss refers to opus 64 as "das herrliche Mendelsohnconzert [sic] . . . Es ist neben den Mozartschen, dem Beethovenschen zu den schönsten zu rechnen, was der Deutsche an Violinconzerten hat." *Richard Strauss–Ludwig Thuille*, p. 67.

27 "Erinnerungen an meinen" *Vater*, p. 194. ("Den ersten Klavier-Schumann bis Opus 20 liess

man gelten, der spätere wurde, als unter Mendelssohns Einfluss stehend, mit seinen rhyth-
mischen Monotonien und seinen Periodenwiederholungen als 'Leipziger Musik' etwas ge-
ringer eingeschätzt.")

28 Schumann explored the ambiguity of the augmented triad in a nontonic opening most strikingly in the Piano Concerto, op. 54. See also R. Larry Todd, "The 'Unwelcome Guest' Regaled:
Franz Liszt and the Augmented Triad," 19th-Century Music 12 (1988): 103.

29 "Schumann in Brendel's Neue Zeitschrift für Musik from 1845 to 1856," in Mendelssohn and Schumann: Essays on Their Music and Its Context, ed. Jon W. Finson and R. Larry Todd (Durham: Duke
University Press, 1984), pp. 21–36.

30 Ibid., p. 23.

31 See further my "Mozart according to Mendelssohn: A Contribution to Rezeptionsgeschichte," in
Perspectives on Mozart Performance, ed. R. Larry Todd and Peter Williams (Cambridge: Cambridge
University Press, 1991), pp. 158–62.

32 A relevant example is the finale of Schumann's Piano Trio, op. 63, which draws on the
opening of Mendelssohn's Cello Sonata, op. 58, as does the finale of Strauss's Piano Sonata,
op. 5.

33 Several of these allusions are traced in detail in Raymond Knapp, "Brahms and the Problem of the Symphony: Romantic Image, Generic Conception, and Compositional Challenge"
(Ph.D. diss., Duke University, 1987).

Miners Digging from Opposite Sides:
Mahler, Strauss, and the Problem
of Program Music

Stephen E. Hefling

▼

You have quite accurately characterized my goals in contrast to those of Strauss; you are right that my "music finally arrives at a program as the last, ideal clarification, whereas with Strauss the program stands as a given task." [1]

Thus Mahler described his relationship with Strauss to the critic Arthur Seidl in February 1897. In the same letter Mahler also acknowledges the importance of Strauss's efforts to help him get his music performed, and he declares as well that "no one may claim I regard myself as a rival (which unfortunately now happens so often)." But then Mahler presents a metaphor that he would use more than once, and which has now become well known: "Schopenhauer somewhere uses the image of two miners who dig a tunnel from opposite sides and then meet on their subterranean ways. That seems fittingly to characterize my relationship with Strauss." [2]

Three and one-half years later, Seidl published this letter, without Mahler's permission, just prior to the first performance in Munich of Mahler's Second Symphony. Mahler was furious and spoke rather heatedly of the matter to his confidante Natalie Bauer-Lechner, who recorded the discussion as follows:

"There you see the price one pays when one's not completely sincere and makes even the smallest concession out of friendship! Now they take me at my word and I appear to be an ardent advocate of Strauss and that program music which I've had to fight fiercely and openly."

. . . he held it as the greatest musical and artistic error to begin writing music according to a program. "One who can do that is no artist! It is something different if the composition of a master becomes so vivid and alive that one involuntarily believes himself to experience in it an event, an occurrence; or if the creator himself subsequently seeks to interpret his work by means of this or that picture, as always happens to me; or finally, if the content raises itself to such heights and takes on such forms that the composer no longer manages with tones alone, but seeks that highest expression which he gains only through the union of the human voice and the articulated poetic word, which is the case in Beethoven's Ninth and also in my C-minor symphony. All of this has not the least bit to do with that insipid, erroneous way of beginning, which is to choose for oneself a limited, narrowly circumscribed incident, and to follow it programmatically step by step."[3]

There is nothing new in these remarks, save for the intensity with which they are stated. Mahler had expressed serious doubts about the value of programs and program music since at least 1893, even though he continued to toy with metaphors that might somehow sum up his artistic purpose. As regards Richard Strauss, in 1894 he had written to his sister Justine:

I was together with Strauss quite a bit. I would be lying, however, if I said that many points of contact had developed between us. . . . Our goals lead away from each other. From my standpoint I can everywhere discern only old-classical, or New German, pedantry. Scarcely is Wagner recognized and understood when yet again the (priests of the one true faith) appear and establish over the entire terrain fortresses against genuine life, but what this always amounts to is that the old, even if it is greater and more significant than the new, is perpetually transformed and newly created on account of the needs of the moment. Strauss above all is the Pope, the pontiff. But nevertheless he is a nice fellow, as far as I can make him out.[4]

And in 1901, in a letter concerning program music written to his fiancée, Alma Schindler, Mahler would note: "I had a long talk with Strauss in Berlin and tried to show him the blind alley he is in. But unfortunately he couldn't completely follow me. He's a very nice chap. . . . And yet I can mean nothing to him—because I see well beyond him, whereas he sees of me only the pedestal."[5]

But of course Strauss did not think he was in a blind alley. At age twenty, to be sure, he had been an admirer of "our great master Brahms" and the classical tradition Brahms represented.[6] But by 1889 "our great master" had become "leathery St. Johannes" and "a canting, abstemious Temperance-leaguer" in Strauss's view.[7] Deeply influenced by Alexander Ritter, Strauss had been wholly won over by the music and prose writings of Wagner and Liszt.

Thus, in his view, the sonata form had been extended to its utmost limits in Beethoven, and, as he announced in a letter to Hans von Bülow, "there will be . . . no more symphonies (Brahms excepted of course), which always remind me of an immense garment, made to fit a Hercules, which a skinny tailor has tried on in the hope that he will cut a fine figure in it."[8] For Strauss, the instrumental 'music of the future' was unquestionably the tone poem.

Yet Mahler, too, was an ardent Wagnerian, and it is in their different appropriations of this common heritage that Strauss and Mahler may first be seen fundamentally to diverge on the issue of program music. As is well known, Wagner's encounter with Schopenhauerian philosophy in 1854 was highly influential upon his subsequent "ersichtlich gewordene Taten der Musik."[9] (The phrase itself derives from Schopenhauer's notion of music as a direct manifestation of the will, without mediation of other concepts.) And the "Beethoven" essay of 1870 is largely Schopenhauer reviewed from the perspective of Wagner's musical orientation.[10] In Mahler's view, "apart from Wagner in 'Beethoven,' only Schopenhauer in *Die Welt als Wille und Vorstellung* had said anything of value about the nature of music."[11] Mahler's thorough grasp of these two texts dates from his conservatory days, when he was a member of the Pernerstorfer circle in Vienna; through lengthy discourse with the brilliant philosopher-poet Siegfried Lipiner, he came to know as well the early work of Nietzsche, whose *Geburt der Tragödie* is also rooted in Schopenhauerian thought.[12]

According to Schopenhauer, music holds a superior position among the arts because of its direct relation to the *will*, which, he argues, is the purportedly unknowable, Kantian *Ding-an-sich*.[13] Whereas all other arts objectify the will indirectly, through Ideas (as Schopenhauer understands that Platonic term), music is completely independent of the phenomenal world, and "passes over the Ideas" as well—it is "as immediate an objectification and copy of the whole will as the world itself is. . . ." Like the will itself, music "gives the innermost kernel preceding all form, or the heart of things" (1: 257, 263). Our imagination is easily stirred by music, and so we try to clothe its intangible world with external images, as in opera and lieder. But the words and images remain merely analogies: "music never expresses the phenomenon, but only the inner nature"; thus, true music is never directly mimetic (1: 261, 263).

In "Beethoven," Wagner essentially endorses this position. A programmatic description of a piece may be devised *ex post facto*, as Wagner himself had done for his own overtures and for several works of Beethoven. But such an utterance remains a "mere analogy," rather like the "allegoric dream" perceived just before waking, which 'translates' the dream of inward-looking consciousness.[14] To be sure, prior to "Beethoven," Wagner had shifted position several times on the issue of program music, as Thomas Grey has pointed out.[15] In particular, his open letter of 1857 concerning Liszt's symphonic poems argues that the representation of an Orpheus or a Prometheus can provide a worthier motive for musical form than the traditional symphonic design derived from the binary dance or march; of necessity, he says, such a new form would be dictated by the subject of portrayal and its representational development.[16] Nevertheless, Wagner insists in the "Liszt" essay (although less persuasively than he would in "Beethoven") that the musician does not mimic the ordinary incidents and details of everyday life but instead "entirely sublates its chance occurrences and details, and sublimates whatever lies within it to its concrete emotional content, which indeed allows itself to be decreed solely in music." [17] *Ergo*, no bleating sheep, and no cowbells—or so one would suppose.

It is, then, scarcely surprising that Mahler would characterize his relation to Strauss in a metaphor from Schopenhauer, whom Mahler took quite seriously. But Strauss, from the point at which he "joined the Lisztians," as he put it,[18] tended to interpret the Schopenhauer–Wagner position on program music rather freely and simply—to the extent that he actually understood it. For in Schuh's view, during the late 1880s "Strauss . . . did not possess what it would have taken to get thoroughly and comprehensively to grips with Schopenhauer." [19] For Mahler, the "scanty content and spurious craftmanship" of Liszt's music were "like the threads of a badly woven garment." [20] But by 1890 Strauss considered Liszt "the only symphonist who had to come after Beethoven and represents immense progress beyond him. Everything else is pure *Dreck*." [21] And during the late 1880s and early '90s, there seemed to be an unbridgeable chasm for Strauss between "absolute music" as Hanslick upheld it and "music as expression" in Hausegger's sense. "Program music: real music!" Strauss wrote to the composer-conductor Jan Levoslav Bella. "Absolute music: can be written with the aid of a certain routine and craftsmanship by any only moderately musical person. The first:—art! The second:—craft!" [22]

Mahler's engagement with the issue was rather more tortuous. He provided no program for the disastrous premiere of his "Symphonic Poem in Two Parts," which we now know as the First Symphony, on 20 November 1889.[23] Just nine days earlier, Strauss had stepped to the forefront of modern German music with the triumphant premiere of *Don Juan* in Weimar. For the next performance of his First (Hamburg, 1893), Mahler accepted the advice of friends and drew up the well-known program and movement titles for the work, which was now called " 'Titan,' a Tone Poem in Symphony-Form"; thanks to the influence of Strauss, it was performed again the following June at the Weimar festival of the Allgemeiner Deutscher Musikverein, using the same title and virtually the same program. It remains uncertain to what extent Mahler's adoption of a program may have been influenced by the success of Strauss's early tone poems, or by the 'New German School' orientation of the ADM; but in any case, neither of these performances gained Mahler the recognition he had hoped for, and thereafter he completely dropped the titles and programs for his First Symphony.[24] Although he subsequently drafted programs for each of the Second, Third, and Fourth Symphonies, on only two occasions—and never for a premiere performance—did he permit these to be made public.[25] All the while, Mahler claimed he did not really write program music.

And indeed he did not—or at least not in the same sense as Strauss did, as surviving sketches of the two composers clearly indicate. Strauss's sketches for the tone poems are replete with lengthy and explicit comments related to the subject of portrayal.[26] In 1899 he discussed this openly with Romain Rolland, who had just heard Strauss conduct *Ein Heldenleben* in Cologne. Rolland recorded that Strauss began his tone poems by first "mapping out for himself very precisely his literary text . . . the musical phrases never come at the same time as the poetical ideas, but afterwards."[27] And indeed, one of Strauss's sketchbooks for *Ein Heldenleben* contains portions of just such a "literary" scenario, which bears noteworthy correspondences to the finished work; in the excerpt quoted below, references to rehearsal cues in the published score have been added in square brackets.

a) Following the love scene [reh. 32ff.] the envious and the critics no longer have any effect [reh. 41–1 m. before reh. 42].

b) Call to battle B-flat major [reh. 42]: he rouses himself and sinks back again in G-flat major [reh. 43] (to which the battle cry resounds / trumpets with mutes)

c) Finally he gets up [reh. 45ff.] in order to engage the inner enemies (doubt, disgust) and the external enemies: Battle (C minor) [5 after reh. 49ff.], from this battle newly strengthened in union with the beloved [reh. 75 + 2ff.; cf. also reh. 53, 55], all inner, spiritual and artistic powers continually develop and present themselves to the world [reh. 83 + 4ff.: several quotations from Strauss's earlier works]. . . . Indolence [of the world] remains nevertheless the same / Then he is seized by disgust [reh. 94] he withdraws completely into the idyll, to live only in his thoughts, wishes, and in the still, contemplative outcome of his own personality [reh. 99ff.] . . . by the side of the beloved—music dying away warm-heartedly at her side (as in the final close of the love scene) [reh. 108].[28]

Mahler, as we have noted, considered such a procedure erroneous, and his sketches suggest that this indeed was not his *modus operandi*. Only rarely do we find in them a poetic cue word or two: the somewhat ambiguous marking "Meerestille" appears above a lyrical passage in the "Todtenfeier" movement of the Second Symphony; "Pan schläft" crops up among the early sketches for the Third; the curious annotation "Steine pumpeln ins Wasser" is found in the orchestral draft of the Seventh Symphony's first movement; and the word *Grabgeläute* appears at the entrance of the tam-tam in the second half of "Der Abschied" from *Das Lied von der Erde*.[29] Notably more frequent in Mahler's sketches are common terms related to formal procedure, such as *Durchführung*, *Rückgang*, *Schlusssatz*, and so on. Even in the composition of "Todtenfeier," which was partially inspired by the 'Gustav monologue' in Mickiewicz's *Dziady*, the stages of the work's genesis clearly reveal that following the poetic narrative was by no means Mahler's chief concern.[30]

Strauss did not invariably provide a program for the premiere of a tone poem. But the well-known guides to his orchestral works compiled by Walden were drawn up with his collaboration, or at least with his consent.[31] Following the unsuccessful early performances of his First Symphony, Mahler avoided programs, claiming that at best they could offer only "a few milestones and guideposts," and at worst "audiences have been set on the wrong track by them."[32] When we explore the complex background of the outlines and commentaries that survive for Mahler's first four symphonies, it indeed becomes clear that they are inadequate allegorical summations of the personal and philosophical concerns which served as the "occasion" or "impulse," in Mahler's own words, for each of these works. All four of them are directly linked to the notions of art and redemption with which Mahler and his friend and mentor Siegfried Lipiner struggled, from their student days through Mahler's last years. To pick just one example: this "self-contained tetralogy," as Mahler thought of it,[33] culminates in the Wunderhorn song of 1892, "Das himmlische Leben," the child's vision of heaven that broke the long period of creative stagnation Mahler experienced during the genesis of his Second Symphony.[34] (In 1892 only one movement of it—"Todtenfeier"— had been completed.) Of the song's role as the finale of the Fourth, Mahler observed that "the child, which, although in a chrysalis state nevertheless already belongs to this higher realm, clarifies what everything means."[35] The phrase "in a chrysalis state" (im Puppenstand) is an allusion to the final scene of Faust; but to grasp the rest of what influenced Mahler in the seemingly naive conclusion of his tetralogy requires a review of Schopenhauer, Wagner, Nietzsche, Goethe's published conversations, Fechner, and Lipiner, as well as a thorough grasp of what he had tried to achieve in Symphonies 1 through 3.[36] Thus it is hardly surprising that Mahler ultimately decided his audience would be better off without a program.

Also sprach Zarathustra is the only one of Strauss's tone poems to brush against the complexities of nineteenth-century German philosophy; curiously enough, it was written in the same year that Mahler finished his Third Symphony, in which Zarathustra's midnight drunken song plays such a crucial role. Both of these works, tone poem and symphony, are broadly inspired by the notion of human evolution; yet the vast differences between them are tellingly characteristic of the different sides of the mountain from which each miner began digging. Not even Strauss claimed that he had embodied the essence of Nietzsche's thought in music.[37] Indeed, the episodic musical material Strauss presents under Nietzsche's subtitles often seems at variance with the philosopher's words. This is especially apparent in Strauss's conclusion of the work, "das Nachtwanderlied" (also known as Zarathustra's drunken song): except perhaps for the final pianissimo conflict between the tonal centers of B and C, this music has nothing to do with Nietzsche's doctrine of eternal recurrence, or with Zarathustra's reaction to it.

Mahler's treatment of the idea is altogether different. The text of Zarathustra's song is presented in a musical setting that evokes the hushed, mysterious midnight atmosphere in which Nietzsche's prophet first utters and elaborates it; this is the fourth movement in an evolutionary allegory that begins with primal nature and has developed to this point through flowers and animals to "What Man Tells Me," as Mahler planned to call Zarathustra's song in his latest scheme of titles.[38] But what follows next in the symphony is not the "great noon" of Zarathustra's revelatory realization that his final sin has been pity for the "higher man."[39] Instead, Mahler launches into a chorus of children's and women's voices that imitates morning church bells ("What the Morning Bells Tell Me"). The text is a Wunderhorn poem in which angels declare that St. Peter, who denied Christ, is free of sin; naive yet sincere in tone, the poem concludes thus:

> Die himmlische Freud' ist eine selige Stadt;
> Die himmlische Freud', die kein Ende mehr hat.

Die himmlische Freude war Petro bereit't
Durch Jesum und allen zur Seligkeit.

[Heavenly joy is a Blessed City;
Heavenly joy has no end anymore.
Heavenly joy was prepared through Jesus
For Peter and everyone, for bliss.]

The numerous thematic references in this chorus to "Das himmlische Leben" reflect the fact that originally the Third Symphony was to conclude with the child's celestial vision. Thus Mahler's point could not be more obvious: Nietzsche's "unconditional and infinitely repeated circular course of all things"[40] was not, in his view, the highest level of finality.[41] Strauss, on the other hand, continued to admire the teachings of Zarathustra. It was on the occasion of Mahler's death that he noted in his diary, "The Jew Mahler could still find elevation in Christianity. . . . It is absolutely clear to me that the German nation can gain new energy only through liberation from Christianity. . . . I shall call my Alpine Symphony the Antichrist, since it embodies: moral purification through one's own strength, liberation through work, worship of eternal, glorious nature."[42] These are precisely the values of Zarathustra, herald of the overman, at the close of Nietzsche's work.[43]

Mahler's Third is in many respects the most freely organized of his symphonies—the first of them to be characterized as "a world."[44] But even here, somewhat to his own surprise, the individual movement structures remain closely allied to traditional formal procedures: sonata, rondo, scherzo, and strophic variation.[45] (Zarathustra's song is, appropriately, through-composed.) And such is the case for the remainder of Mahler's oeuvre as well. Musically, it is in this respect that he differs most obviously from Strauss, for whom traditional form had lost its validity. In Zarathustra, as elsewhere, Strauss depends on a more fluid interaction of episodic contrasts, motivic interplay, and tonal relations for the organization of the tone poem. As Strauss himself wrote, "Music . . . needs to be held within bounds which determine a form, and it is the program which fixes these bounds."[46]

In one of Mahler's most explicit commentaries on the issue of program music, written in 1896, he observed that "we now stand—and of this I am certain—at the great parting of ways where the divergent paths of symphonic and dramatic music separate forever. . . . Even now, if you compare a Beethoven symphony with Wagner's tone structures, you will easily recognize the essential difference between them."[47] This was the period when he himself was abandoning with finality any thought of writing for the theater; the remainder of his works would be symphonies or lieder.[48] Strauss, on the other hand, had just made his debut as an opera composer. While both *Guntram* and *Feuersnot* were less than successful, *Salome* received enormous critical and popular acclaim. "It is emphatically a work of genius," Mahler wrote to his wife, ". . . one of the greatest masterpieces of our time."[49] By 1907 Strauss would admit to Romain Rolland that he had always wanted to write for the theater, and that his tone poems were "in a way only a poor substitute. . . ."[50] And indeed, he would compose only one additional tone poem, the *Alpensinfonie*, after the premiere of *Salome*.

Although Mahler's successes around that time were less spectacular than *Salome* or *Elektra*, he was steadily gaining ground as a symphonist. And it is striking to note that as their eminence increased, both Strauss and Mahler became less doctrinaire in their pronouncements about the problem of program music. In May 1905, Romain Rolland wrote to Strauss suggesting that he omit his program for the projected performance of the *Symphonia Domestica* in Paris. Strauss replied, "Perhaps you are right so far as the programme of the Domestica is concerned; you agree entirely with G. Mahler, who completely condemns the very principle of programme music. . . . Those who are interested in it can use it. Those who really know how to listen to music doubtless have no need for it."[51] But the previous year G. Mahler had written the following lines to Bruno Walter:

> It is undeniable that our music involves the "purely human" in one way or another (and everything that belongs to it, including the "conceptual"). . . . If one wants to make music, one must not want to paint, poetize, describe. But *what* one makes into music is always the *whole* (thus feeling, thinking, breathing, suffering, etc.) man. So there would be nothing further to object to in a "program" (even if it is not exactly the highest rung of the ladder)—but a *musician* must express himself therein, and not a man of letters, a philosopher, a painter (all of whom are contained in the musician).
>
> In a word: whoever possesses no genius should stay away from this, and whoever does possess it need not shy away from anything.[52]

And in January 1907, when Mahler conducted his Third Symphony in Berlin, the audience was provided with his programmatic titles and a commentary especially prepared by Paul Bekker.[53]

But Mahler and Strauss had not fully resolved their differences. Rather, as Strauss's diary entry following Mahler's death indicates, the two composers had come to a more secure and mutually respectful acceptance of their fundamentally different paths. Even as Mahler praised *Salome*, he still wrote to his wife in 1907 of "the problem of Strauss."[54] Mahler had come to value Strauss's musical-dramatic work more than his tone poems.[55] Yet whereas he had avoided Strauss's orchestral works as conductor of the Vienna Philharmonic during 1898–1901, in 1909 Mahler concluded his debut as director of the New York Philharmonic with *Till Eulenspiegel*, which he would perform eleven times during the next two years; *Tod und Verklärung*, *Don Juan*, *Heldenleben*, and *Zarathustra* were also prominent in his New York programs.[56] And although in the late 1920s Strauss would exclaim to Fritz Busch, "Well, Busch, as for Mahler he's not really a composer at all—he's simply a very great conductor,"[57] Strauss still conducted Mahler's music from time to time; the First and Fourth Symphonies were his favorites.[58]

The miners had met, acknowledged each other, and continued on their separate ways. Very shortly, the problem of program music, over which they had clashed, would be eclipsed by matters far more fundamental to the nature of musical language.

Notes

1   *Gustav Mahler Briefe*, new ed. by Herta Blaukopf (Vienna: Paul Zolnay, 1982) (hereafter GMB2), no. 216. Here and below, translations are mine unless otherwise noted. The letter is also found in *Selected Letters of Gustav Mahler*, ed. Knud Martner, trans. Eithne Wilkins, Ernst Kaiser, and Bill Hopkins (New York: Farrar, Straus, Giroux, 1979) (hereafter GMBE), no. 205.

2   Cf. also Alma Mahler, *Gustav Mahler: Memories and Letters*, 3d ed., rev. and enl. Donald Mitchell and Knud Martner, trans. Basil Creighton (Seattle: University of Washington Press, 1975), p. 98. A basic source for any comparative study of Strauss and Mahler is *Gustav Mahler–Richard Strauss: Briefwechsel 1888–1911*, ed. Herta Blaukopf, Bibliothek der Internationalen Gustav Mahler Gesellschaft (Munich: R. Piper, 1980); included therein is Dr. Blaukopf's essay "Rivalität und Freundschaft: Die persönlichen Beziehungen zwischen Gustav Mahler und Richard Strauss," to which I am particularly indebted. (English edition: *Gustav Mahler–Richard Strauss: Correspondence 1888–1911*, trans. Edmund Jephcott [Chicago: University of Chicago Press, 1984].) This volume effectively counterbalances Constantin Floros's excessive insistence that Mahler and Strauss were acute rivals (*Gustav Mahler*, vol. 1, *Die geistige Welt Gustav Mahlers in systematischer Darstellung* [Wiesbaden: Breitkopf & Härtel, 1977], esp. pp. 27–32).

3   *Gustav Mahler in den Erinnerungen von Natalie Bauer-Lechner*, ed. Herbert Killian, rev. and enl. edn. with annotations by Knud Martner (Hamburg: Karl Dieter Wagner, 1984) (hereafter NBL2), pp. 170–71 (not included in earlier editions of Bauer-Lechner).

4   Letter of 1894 in the Gustav Mahler/Alfred Rosé Room, Music Library, University of Western Ontario, Music MZ 1000, no. 16; also cited in *Mahler–Strauss Briefwechsel*, p. 152 (English ed., p. 116f.).

5   Alma Mahler, p. 218 (20 December 1901).

6   Strauss, letter to Otto Lessmann of 21 November 1884, cited in Willi Schuh, *Richard Strauss: A*

Chronicle of the Early Years, trans. Mary Whittall (Cambridge: Cambridge University Press, 1982), pp. 68–69.

7 Strauss, letters to Dora Wihan (9 April 1889) and Cosima Wagner (26 November 1889), cited in Schuh, pp. 165 and 207.

8 Cited in Schuh, p. 147 (24 August 1888); cf. also p. 118.

9 See Wagner's essay "Über die Benennung 'Musikdrama,'" *Gesammelte Schriften und Dichtungen von Richard Wagner*, 3d ed. (Leipzig: E. W. Fritzsch, 1898), vol. 9, pp. 302–8 (*Prose Works*, trans. W. A. Ellis [London: Routledge & Kegan Paul, 1892–99], vol. 5, pp. 299–304).

10 *Gesammelte Schriften*, 3d ed., vol. 9, pp. 61–126 (*Prose Works*, vol. 5, pp. 57–126).

11 GMB2, no. 114 (GMBE, no. 105); this is an annotation made by Alma Mahler, original editor of the volume of letters.

12 Concerning Mahler and the Pernerstorfer circle, see William J. McGrath, *Dionysian Art and Populist Politics in Austria* (New Haven: Yale University Press, 1974), as well as Hefling, *The Making of Mahler's "Todtenfeier": Programs, Sketches, Analysis* (Lanham, Md.: University Press of America, forthcoming), chapter 1.

13 Schopenhauer, *The World as Will and Representation*, 2 vols., trans. E. F. J. Payne (New York: Dover Books, 1966), 2: 195–96; henceforth page references will be provided in parentheses in the text. Useful modern discussions of Schopenhauer include *The Encyclopedia of Philosophy*, ed. Paul Edwards (New York: Macmillan and The Free Press, 1967), s. v. "Schopenhauer" by Patrick Gardiner; Alan Walker, "Schopenhauer and Music," TLS: *The Times Literary Supplement*, no. 3800 (3 January 1975): 11; L. J. Rather, *The Dream of Self-Destruction: Wagner's Ring and the Modern World* (Baton Rouge: Louisiana State University Press, 1979), esp. chapter 3; Malcolm Budd, *Music and the Emotions: The Philosophical Theories* (London: Routledge & Kegan Paul, 1985), chapter 5; and Peter Franklin, *The Idea of Music: Schoenberg and Others* (London: Macmillan, 1985), chapter 1.

14 "Beethoven," pp. 96 and 75–76 (trans. Ellis, 96 and 75).

15 Thomas S. Grey, "Wagner, the Overture, and the Aesthetics of Musical Form," *19th-Century Music* 12 (1988): 3–22.

16 Wagner, "Über Franz Liszt's symphonische Dichtungen," *Gesammelte Schriften*, vol. 5, pp. 192 and 191 (trans. Ellis, *Prose Works*, vol. 3, pp. 247 and 246).

17 "Über Franz Liszt's symphonische Dichtungen," p. 194 (trans. Ellis, pp. 249–50).

18 Strauss, letter to Dora Wihan (9 April 1889), cited in Schuh, p. 165.

19 Schuh, p. 131.

20 NBL2, p. 33; trans. Dika Newlin as *Recollections of Gustav Mahler by Natalie Bauer-Lechner*, ed. Peter Franklin (Cambridge: Cambridge University Press, 1980), pp. 37–38.

21 *Richard Strauss–Ludwig Thuille: Briefe der Freundschaft*, ed. Alfons Ott (Munich: Walter Ricke, 1969), p. 115.

22 Cited in Schuh, p. 148 (13 March 1890).

23 See Henry-Louis de La Grange, *Mahler: Chronique d'une vie* (hereafter HLGF), vol. 1: *Les chemins de la gloire* (1860–1900) (Paris: Fayard, 1979), pp. 965–72 and plates 19–20 and 27–28.

24 According to Josef Bohuslav Foerster, Mahler abandoned his titles and programs immediately following the Weimar concert (*Der Pilger: Erinnerungen eines Musikers*, trans. Pavel Eisner [Prague: Artia, 1955], p. 410).

25 For more on this issue see Hefling, "Mahler's 'Todtenfeier' and the Problem of Program Music," *19th-Century Music* 12 (1988): 27–28 and 45, n. 4.

26 See Franz Trenner, *Die Skizzenbücher von Richard Strauss aus dem Richard-Strauss-Archiv in Garmisch*

(Tutzing: Hans Schneider, 1977), pp. 1–21 and passim, as well as Schuh, pp. 420–21, 463, and 478–83, where several noteworthy facsimiles are reproduced.

27 *Richard Strauss & Romain Rolland: Correspondence*, ed. Rollo Myers (Berkeley: University of California Press, 1968), p. 113 (from Rolland's diary, April 1899).

28 Facsimiles and commentary in Schuh, pp. 478–80; German text in Trenner, p. 10 (July 1898). A complete listing of Strauss's self-quotations at reh. 83 ff. is found in Norman Del Mar, *Richard Strauss: A Critical Commentary on His Life and Works*, 3 vols. (New York: Free Press of Glencoe, 1962), vol. 1, p. 177.

29 "Todtenfeier": *A*-Wn, S.m. 4364, vol. 2, p. 12 (6v); Third Symphony: US-ST, and *A*-Wn, S.m. 2794 (facsimile in Floros, vol. 1, p. 237); Seventh Symphony: US-NYp, Bruno Walter Collection (the passage corresponds to mm. 284 ff. in the published score); *Das Lied von der Erde*: NL-DHgm, Mengelberg Stichting (facsimile in Donald Mitchell, *Gustav Mahler: Songs and Symphonies of Life and Death* [Berkeley: University of California Press, 1985], p. 476).

30 See Hefling, "Mahler's 'Todtenfeier' and the Problem of Program Music."

31 Herwarth Walden, ed., *Richard Strauss: Symphonien und Tondichtungen* (Berlin: Schlesinger'sche Buch- und Musikhandlung, n. d.); see also Schuh, p. 421.

32 GMB2, nos. 167 and 188 (GMBE, nos. 158 and 156).

33 NBL2, p. 164 (NBLE, p. 154); Bruno Walter also reflects this view in *Gustav Mahler*, translation supervised by Lotte Walter Lindt (New York: Alfred A. Knopf, 1966), pp. 134–35 and 166.

34 See NBL2, p. 172 (not in NBLE).

35 NBL2, p. 198 (NBLE, p. 178).

36 See Hefling, *The Making of Mahler's "Todtenfeier,"* chapters 1–3.

37 See Strauss's commentary for the first Berlin performance (December 1896), cited in Del Mar, vol. 1, p. 134.

38 See HLGF, vol. 1, pp. 1038–1039.

39 *Thus Spoke Zarathustra*, trans. Walter Kaufmann in *The Portable Nietzsche* (New York: The Viking Press, 1968), pt. 4, §12, p. 439:

> " '. . . *what* was it that was saved up for me as my final sin?'
>
> "And once more Zarathustra became absorbed in himself. . . . Suddenly he jumped up. 'Pity! Pity for the higher man!' he cried out, and his face changed to bronze. 'Well then, *that* has had its time! My suffering and my pity for suffering—what does it matter? Am I concerned with *happiness*? I am concerned with my *work*.
>
> " 'Well then! The lion came, my children are near, Zarathustra has ripened, my hour has come: this is my morning, my day is breaking: *rise now, rise, thou great noon!* '
>
> "Thus spoke Zarathustra, and he left his cave, glowing and strong as a morning sun that comes out of dark mountains."

40 This is Nietzsche's characterization of the eternal recurrence in *Ecce Homo*, trans. Walter Kaufman (New York: Vintage Books, 1967), pp. 273–74.

41 The literature on Mahler has been slow to grasp this; most recently Eveline Nikkels has proposed the oversimplified thesis that "Nietzsche's belief in the eternal recurrence . . . is also the guidebook of Mahler's life and creation." ("*O Mensch! Gib Acht!" Friedrich Nietzsches Bedeutung für Gustav Mahler* [Amsterdam: Rodopi, 1989], p. 1; see also, e.g., p. 92.)

42 Cited in *Gustav Mahler–Richard Strauss: Briefwechsel 1888–1911*, p. 211 (English ed., p. 153).

43 See n. 39 above.

44   NBL2, p. 35 (NBLE, p. 40).

45   Cf. NBL2, p. 64 (NBLE, p. 66).

46   *Richard Strauss & Romain Rolland: Correspondence*, p. 29 (5 July 1905).

47   Letter to Max Marschalk, 26 March 1896, GMB2, no. 167 (GMBE, no. 158).

48   See Hefling, "The Road Not Taken: Mahler's Rübezahl," *Yale University Library Gazette* 57 (1983): 166–70.

49   Alma Mahler, pp. 282 and 284.

50   *Richard Strauss & Romain Rolland: Correspondence*, p. 84 (14 May 1907).

51   Ibid., p. 29.

52   GMB2, no. 334 (GMBE, no. 313) (summer 1904).

53   See HLGF, vol. 2: *L'âge d'or de Vienne 1900–1907* (Paris: Fayard, 1983), p. 1021 n. 77.

54   Alma Mahler, p. 284 (13 January 1907).

55   Bernard Scharlitt records the following comment from 1906 in "Gespräch mit Mahler," *Musik-blätter des Anbruch* 2/7–8 (1920): 310: "Ich schätze auch sein musikdramatisches Schaffen höher denn sein symphonisches und glaube, dass die Nachwelt es ebenso tun wird."

56   See Knud Martner, *Gustav Mahler im Konzertsaal: Eine Dokumentation seiner Konzerttätigkeit 1870–1911* (Copenhagen: K. Martner, 1985), pp. 57–72, 113, 166, and passim.

57   "Sö, Busch, der Mahler, dös is überhaupt gar ka Komponist. Dös is bloss a ganz grosser Dirigent." Busch, *Pages from a Musician's Life*, trans. Marjorie Strachey (London: Hogarth Press, 1953), p. 172.

58   *Gustav Mahler–Richard Strauss: Briefwechsel 1888–1911*, p. 214 (English ed., p. 155).

Extended Tonality in Mahler and Strauss

Kofi Agawu

▼

For Strauss as for Mahler, the poetic impulse remained a central and irreducible part of the art of musical composition. Strauss's operas, tone poems, and songs, Mahler's symphonies and song cycles: all these betray in varying degrees the generative influence of the spoken word. The poetic impulse served as a foil for confronting what was perhaps the greatest technical challenge to post-Wagnerian composition: how to reconcile the conflicting demands of an inevitable resultant hierarchy in the organization of pitch with the nonhierarchic, perhaps even antihierarchic tendencies of a potent chromatic resource.[1] The history of Strauss's solutions to this challenge reveals no obvious unifying thread other than a stubborn, some might say regressive, adherence to the premises of functional tonality (the famously "anomalous" cases of *Elektra* and *Salome* notwithstanding).[2] Mahler's solutions likewise differ from genre to genre, from work to work, and even within the boundaries of a single work.[3]

The resistance to generalization is suggestive. For if a huge gap separates the musical language of *Elektra* (1906–8) from that of *Capriccio* (1940–41), or the language of *Das klagende Lied* (1878–80, revised 1892–93 and 1898–99) from that of *Das Lied von der Erde* (1908–9), then a more promising path toward understanding Strauss's and Mahler's music is to forsake the broad brush of stylistic characterization for detailed analyses of individual passages or works, the thought being that an authoritative generalization will need to be propped up by such preliminary spade work. It is with this larger project in mind, and not in an attempt to elucidate the process by which an "external" poetic impulse generates passages of music, that this essay explores the nature of musical logic in a handful of excerpts from the works of Strauss and Mahler.

The enabling procedure for analysis is a phenomenon characterized by Arnold Schoenberg as *extended tonality*.[4] Before we seek answers to what extended tonality is, where it occurs, and what technical form it takes, we need to establish a working definition of tonality itself. In an influential statement from his book *Structural Hearing*, Felix Salzer defines tonality as "prolonged motion within the framework of a single key-determining progression, constituting the ultimate structural framework of the whole piece."[5] The linear impulse in Salzer's phrase "prolonged motion" enshrines a crucial distinction between his view of tonality and Schoenberg's principle of monotonality, according to which "there is only *one tonality* in a piece, and every segment . . . is only a region, a harmonic contrast within that tonality."[6] Salzer's relentless pursuit of diatonic, chromatic, or mixed linear spans contrasts with Schoenberg's commitment to vertical sonorities that constitute his all-inclusive map of harmonic regions. Both Salzer (following Schenker) and Schoenberg agree that tonal pieces are in single keys, and that key definition is a paradoxical affair, allowing a prolongation of certain scale degrees while ultimately subverting the "egotistic tendency" (Schenker's locution) of those very *Stufen*. Extended tonality exploits a normal property of tonality by making a virtue of functionally subservient passages. In principle, all tonal writing includes a built-in tendency toward extension, so that the difference between "regular" tonality and extended tonality is largely one of degree.

Where do we find extended tonality? "In descriptive music," answers Schoenberg, where "the background, the action, the mood and the other features of the drama, poem, or story become incorporated as constituent and formative factors in musical structure. Their union thereafter is inseparable."[7] I shall forgo comment on the contradiction between this claim, made in 1948, and the thesis of an earlier (1912) essay that words function precompositionally to release a composer's creative energies, and that once this task has been accomplished, the words disappear, leaving the music to stand on its own.[8] The ready sources of extended tonality, then, are opera, tone poem, and song.

While these may be "ready sources," however, they are not the only ones. Schoenberg's claim is not only restrictive, it is contradicted by some of the examples he adduces to illustrate the functioning of extended tonality. For if we accept the presence of functionally subservient passages as the main sign of extended tonality, then it is clear that we are likely to find instances of it in music from the late seventeenth century onward. Indeed, Schoenberg himself cites passages from untexted works of J. S. Bach to illustrate the phenomenon. In a context in which the elucidation of advanced tonal harmony constitutes the main goal, it is understandable that Schoenberg should focus on nineteenth-century compositions; but this ought not lead to a denial that there are earlier manifestations of extended tonality in genres other than texted ones.

Finally, what technical form does extended tonality take? Schoenberg writes: "Remote transformations and successions of harmonies were understood as remaining within the tonality. Such progressions might or might not bring about modulations or the establishment of various regions. They function chiefly as *enrichments of the harmony* and, accordingly, often appear in a very small space, even in a single measure. Though referring them to regions may sometimes facilitate analysis, their functional effect is, in many cases, only passing, and temporary."[9] Normatively, then, extended tonality is a way of enriching a primary, diatonic tonality. Functionally, and by implication durationally, the area of extended tonality is subservient to, and at the same time inextricably linked with, the main tonality.

Example 1a shows Schoenberg's analysis of a five-measure excerpt from *Salome.*[10] A close reading of the analysis will serve to highlight some of the main features of Straussian extended tonality.

Three features of the example are worthy of note. The first is an internal conflict in the representation of closure. Although the excerpt is tonally closed, the larger context encourages a hearing of E-flat minor as a stable, recurring point of departure to a number of increasingly remote harmonic

Example 1a. Schoenberg's analysis of excerpt from *Salome*, 3 mm. after reh. 257

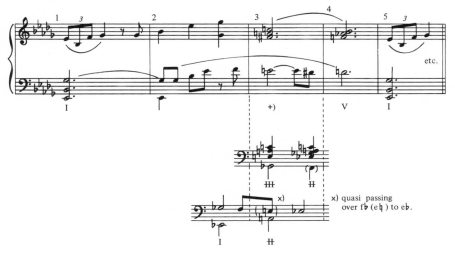

Example 1b. Generating example 1

areas. The first-inversion dominant-seventh chord in m. 4 both closes off the first four-measure phrase and points irresistibly ahead to m. 5. This dual function reinforces the monotonal structure of the passage, showing how the "purple patch" in m. 3 is neither a modulation to nor tonicization of another scale degree but an enrichment of the basic I-V-I diatonic structure.

A second feature of example 1a may be observed in the second of the two interpretations written underneath the music, where the representation of E♮ as one of two successive passing tones from a relatively stable G♭ to a relatively stable E♭ suggests an awareness of diminutional structure in this music. Schoenberg, however, is less interested in pursuing the notion of diminutions as they are manifest in linear spans than in showing what structural harmonies emerge from examining the roots of various chords. The tritonal bass progression in mm. 2–3 is interpreted as a I-II progression, the II chord modified almost beyond aural recognition.

Of particular interest is the analytic notation used to convey hierarchy, in which stemmed white notes are structurally prior to stemmed black notes. What emerges is a line descending from G♭ on the third beat of m. 2 through F, E, and D♯ to D. This type of chromatic line is a regular feature of passages of extended tonality and serves as a unifying force. Its pitches are not always conjunct registrally, but they are nevertheless present. According to this explanation, then, the most "efficient" way of hearing a passage of extended tonality is to find a stepwise progression or line that will serve as a guide. Sonorities would then be heard as "mere" resultants; it is better to understand how they came about (process) than what they are intrinsically (product).

A third feature of Schoenberg's analysis, one which in some ways runs in opposition to the second and which is already implicit in the labeling of chords in the second of the two interpretations, is the III-II progression of the first interpretation of m. 3. By a process of enharmonic substitution, and allowing for chromatic alteration of individual chord members, the two resultant chords in m. 3 are rewritten in reference to an E-flat-minor tonic. If the second of Schoenberg's interpretations stresses the linear aspect of the passage, the first stresses the horizontal aspect. There is plenty of evidence here for Schoenberg's incorrigible attachment to roots, and this may encourage the suspicion that such conceptual explanations of harmonic structure have little to do with the realm of perception. But it would be a premature judgment that failed to note the tension between concept and practice, especially the unstable limits of the latter.

In sum, the "remote transformation" in m. 3 of example 1a confers on the passage as a whole a sense of extended tonality. At the heart of this extension are two types of interaction between diatonic and chromatic elements. In the first, the elements are juxtaposed linearly, and in the second, diatonic elements form the background to chromatic ones. By-products of this process are conflicts in closure and the latent presence of chromatic lines spanning the passage.

As an alternative to Schoenberg's largely "vertical" explanation, and as a preliminary demonstration of the generative processes that underlie passages of extended tonality, example 1b provides a reading of the *Salome* excerpt on three structural levels. Level a, the background, consists of a I-V$_5^6$-I progression, the V$_5^6$ achieved by neighbor-note motion in the lowest voice. On level b, the neighbor chord itself (mm. 3–4) is prolonged by further neighbor-note motion in the soprano (B♭-C-B♭, creating the effect of an ornament of the ornament) and chromatic passing motion in the inner voice of mm. 2–3. Finally, level c restores the actual disposition of rhythmic values in the passage, showing that m. 3 arises from a confluence of neighbor-note action, rhythmic displacement, and enharmonic substitution of F♯ for G♭.

By way of contrast as well as complement, example 2 offers an analysis on three levels of seven measures from the last movement of *Das Lied von der Erde*. Unlike the excerpt from *Salome*, where a single purple patch resulted in a passage of extended tonality, the very fabric of this passage is made up of contrapuntal processes that threaten the tonal security of Mahler's music. The result, however, is not a negation but an enrichment of tonality.

The analytic presentation of example 2 (a and b) is meant to encourage a reading from a normative diatonic background (levels a and b) to Mahler's arhythmic foreground (level c). The early levels of structure show that an

Example 2a. *Das Lied von der Erde*, "Der Abschied," mm. 318–25 (piano reduction)

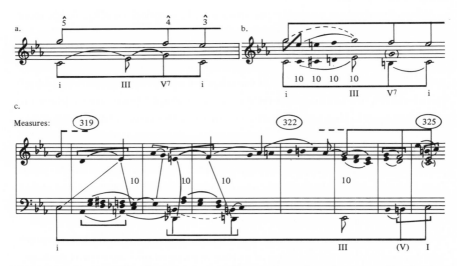

Example 2b. Voice-leading analysis of *Das Lied von der Erde*, "Der Abschied," mm. 318–25

incomplete $\hat{5}$-line, harmonized conventionally as a i-III-V^7-i progression, is enriched by chromatic prolongation of its initial dyad.

In spite of the numerous dissonances that occur in the passage, the listener is unlikely to doubt the centrality of C minor. Dissonances arise from an urgent sense of motion to consonances, a process that sometimes causes the normative simultaneity of treble and bass to be displaced. That is why an interpretation that emphasizes horizontal over vertical elements is preferable. Probably the most surprising feature of example 2 is the linear intervallic pattern, 10-10-10-10, which supports the middleground structure. There are so many dissonances obscuring this simpler progression that, as with Schoenberg's harmonic reading of m. 3 in example 1a, one is left to suspect that a normative diatonic background exists only conceptually rather than perceptually. To insist on a nonreductive chromatic element in the middleground, however, is to break with a fundamental prescription of Schenker's theory, and it is by no means clear that a chromatic middleground that is not generated either by mixture or by tonicization is not ultimately reducible to a still simpler background.[11]

What, then, makes example 2 an instance of extended tonality? Aside from the "external" factor of an illustrative (not necessarily mimetic) impetus behind this excerpt from the Great March from the finale of *Das Lied*, Mahler appropriates and in fact dramatizes the technical means of extended tonality. A simpler diatonic background is enriched by a play of diminution in which the elements of a note-against-note two-voice counterpoint are displaced in the foreground. This interpretation reinforces the continuing relevance of conventional formations like appoggiaturas, neighbor-note patterns, passing motions and arpeggiations, even where their functions seem not to coincide with their piece-specific morphology. Like the excerpt from *Salome* (example 1a), Mahler's passage is grounded in tonal counterpoint, but unlike the previous excerpt, the ground of this passage begins to shift.

It would be premature to make any claims about the differences between Mahler and Strauss on the basis of a close reading of two very short passages, but I believe that the foregoing can support some provisional generalizations. In Strauss, passages of extended tonality function in the "classical" sense in which Schoenberg defined the phenomenon—they emerge in response to specific extramusical stimuli, they have the effect of interpolations, and they are temporary enrichments of the harmony. With few exceptions, a diatonic tonality is always at hand to "rescue" the music from its dip into an extended tonal region. Furthermore, the vertical dimension of Strauss's

music is at once full and transparent, so that what we hear during such interpolations is not discordant but "concordant chromaticism," as Arnold Whittall has described it.[12] In Mahler, on the other hand, there is a contrapuntal
urgency that decisively challenges the very diatonic foundations on which
passages like the one quoted in example 2 are built. This is not to deny that
Mahler often writes long stretches of diatonic music, while Strauss's music
is not lacking in contrapuntal complexity. The difference lies in the fact that
Mahler's diatonicism vacillates between an un-Straussian refusal to act, on
the one hand, and a confident, almost carefree disposition of contrapuntal lines, on the other. Something of this distinction is conveyed in Ernst
Bloch's frequently quoted charge that "in its deepest passages, Strauss' music
wears at best the melancholy expression of a brilliant hollowness."[13] To the
extent that it is possible to strip technique of a covert aesthetic prejudice,
Bloch's claim may have valuable implications for composing middleground
reductions of Strauss's music.

Example 3, another instance of extended tonality, is an excerpt from the
quintet from Strauss's *Ariadne auf Naxos*. The analysis is Salzer's and is intended as an illustration of "the brilliant and subtle techniques of prolongation found in the music of Richard Strauss."[14] Because it encompasses
everything from the thirteenth-century motet to Stravinsky's *Symphony in Three
Movements* (1945), Salzer's definition of tonality is considerably broader than
either Schenker's or Schoenberg's. So what is sometimes discussed by Salzer
under the rubric of tonality is likely to be an instance of extended tonality in
Schoenberg's terms.

  Like examples 1a and 2, example 3 is tonally closed, although there may
be some doubt as to whether we may speak of an unproblematic F major.
Whereas in example 1a a "remote transformation" marked a clear interpolation, in example 3 the interpolations loom large, leaving F's supremacy on
the level of a beginning on F and what might be called an associative cadence
in F at the end of the passage. The force of the cadence, in other words, derives less from an immediate linear unfolding than from a cross-reference to
other F-major perfect cadences. So, although the quintet parodies a normative eighteenth-century style, Strauss's transformational procedures create a
significant gap between his style and that of a Mozart or Haydn.

  Salzer's graphs a and b show the essential progression of the passage to be
a bass arpeggiation of the tonic: I-III-V-I. The space between I and III is prolonged by motion in parallel tenths between outer voices, the same linear
intervallic pattern we saw in the Mahler extract (example 2), but articulated

Example 3. Salzer's analysis of an excerpt from *Ariadne auf Naxos*

on a level of structure closer to the surface. The pattern of tenths includes the nondiatonic bass pitches E♭ and D♭, thus showing one of the ways in which the initial I-III progression is enriched.

A crucial issue that Salzer does not address is whether, having made the initial choice of F as the tonality of the passage, this particular set of events may be made to lie in a linear Procrustean bed. What, for example, is the status of the intervening chords in example 3? If we bracket the first chord for a moment, we observe a sequential pattern: A♭-E♭; G♭-D♭; and E-A (not E-B to preserve the whole-tone descent or A-E to retain the pattern of descending fourths). It could be argued that, rhetorically at least, the successive pairs of chords work less in the service of a ruling F major than in directing the ear to their mutually resonant self-sufficiency on the most local level. It is as if the miniature I-V successions, reversed in the last instance to V-I (or I-IV), assert so much local independence that they challenge, without necessarily negating, the possibility of a larger synopsis. Framed differently, the associative dimension of the passage looms so large that it dwarfs the sense of its more immediate linear unfolding.

What is at issue in this third instance of extended tonality is partly a meta-linguistic matter: whether Salzer's graph, with its linear emphasis, adequately conveys the resistance to linearity implicit in this excerpt from *Ariadne*. To hear examples 2 and 3 as instances of a 10-10-10 prolongation is, of course, to provide a framework for comparing two passages with a similar structure but quite different methods of composing-out. While the excerpt from *Das Lied* embodies an urgent sense of forward motion, that from *Ariadne* tumbles down in an almost circular fashion, throwing into doubt the validity of a synopsis.

A less radical instance of the same I/i-III-V-I arpeggiation is shown in example 4, a harmonic summary of the opening of the fourth song from Mahler's *Kindertotenlieder* cycle. As the beamed bass notes show, the key is E-flat major, darkening to minor as the voice enters (mm. 5–7). Then, after a circle-of-fifths sequence (recall example 3), the music moves through III (G♭) to V (B♭), eventually cadencing on I. The principal source of enrichment is mixture, not only by the alternation of tonic major and tonic minor, but by means of a secondary mixture in the form of a further interpolation generated by the tonic minor (see mm. 10–14). It is these measures, therefore, that constitute a "transformation," although the transformation appears less remote than the ones we have seen so far. Here there is no doubting the possibility of a synopsis.

Example 4. Harmonic summary of *Kindertotenlieder*, song 4, mm. 1–19

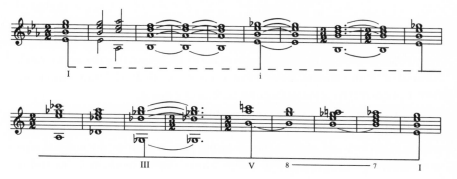

It would seem that examples 3 and 4 make a point that contradicts examples 1 and 2. Where example 1a showed itself grounded on a I-V-I progression, example 2 places the notion of a ground in question. Example 3 reduces the sense of a ground to mere presence, weakening its need for linear definition, while example 4 normatively enacts that ground. The contradictions are unavoidable if we are not to ride roughshod over certain musical realities, and it may be that the value of focusing on extended tonality is partly to problematize the gap between it and regular tonality and partly to highlight aspects of local harmonic usage that frequently disappear in the search for larger patterns of tonal coherence.

The examples discussed thus far are all tiny extracts from large works, and although there is no substantive analytical gain in moving from extracts to whole pieces, it may prove rewarding (and perhaps answer a few potential objections) to consider a slightly bigger context for extended tonality. A discussion of Strauss's remarkable 1894 song, "Ruhe, meine Seele!" op. 27, no. 1, on a text by Karl Henckell, and Mahler's equally remarkable—though for different reasons—1901 song from the collection *Des Knaben Wunderhorn*, "Der Tamboursg'sell," will serve to illustrate this larger context.

"Ruhe, meine Seele!" is in C major, although the first root-position C-major chord we hear is the very last sonority in the song. But if we keep in mind the notion that extended tonality involves enriching a primary diatonic tonality, then it is possible to analyze every single event in this song with reference to a governing C major.

A few abstract preliminaries must precede the actual analysis. Example 5a displays a standard expression of C major as a $\hat{5}$-line with a transfer of voices between the first and third dyads. In an extended tonal context, we may enrich this progression by means of mixture (example 5b), which then produces a chromaticized voice exchange.[15] Further embellishment or prolongation of the initial dyad (example 5c) produces another voice exchange between an inner and an outer voice (example 5d), and this voice exchange could in turn be chromaticized (example 5e). With these simple operations, we have assembled all the necessary resources for generating the entire pitch material of "Ruhe, meine Seele!" How, then, do we make the transition from the set of normative protostructures to Strauss's music?

The best way to understand the transition is to compare the prototypes assembled in example 5 with their specific realizations in example 6. The most straightforward and tonality-defining progression in the song occurs in measures 31–43, a realization of the $\hat{5}$-lines shown in example 5a and b.

Example 5. Prototypes for harmonic progressions in *Ruhe, meine Seele!*

Since it contains many of the song's basic relationships, the phrase, displayed in example 6a, may be described as a nexus phrase. Its concluding ii-V-I progression (mm. 35–39 of example 6a), shown in prototype in example 5f, becomes the basis for the circle-of-fifths progression in measures 4–13 (see example 5g).

Of special significance to the coherence of the song is the bass progression E-D-C♯, which opens the nexus phrase (example 6a). Measures 1–6 are an enriched harmonization of this progression (example 6b). Measures 14–19 are also based on the same progression (example 6d). Transposed up a perfect fifth and slightly abbreviated, this progression may be heard in mm. 22–26 (example 6e), and, in another transposition (this time up a semitone from the original statement but harmonized more diatonically), in mm. 27–30, which also contain the climax of the song (example 6f). The only measures that remain unaccounted for are mm. 20–21 (see example 6d), which consist

Example 6. Paradigmatic arrangement of harmonic progressions in *Ruhe, meine Seele!*

of a diminished seventh chord arrived at by stepwise motion from the $^6_5$ chord on C♯ in mm. 18 and 19. In addition to serving as a transition to m. 22 (where, as mentioned previously, a transposed version of the opening is heard), the progression between mm. 19 and 20 points ahead to that between mm. 25 and 26 and recalls that of mm. 3–4. Specifically, as example 7 shows, motion between the chords is by a combination of semitonal resolution and the retention of common tones, including enharmonic ones.

Although there are obviously numerous kinds and levels of connection to be drawn among the fragments displayed in example 6, only a few will be highlighted here to reinforce the central claim that "Ruhe, meine Seele!" is an enrichment—in the grandest possible sense—of a simpler diatonic structure. The first connection to be drawn is between the beginning and the end of the song. The last five measures of the song (example 6c), heard over a tonic pedal, are an obvious recomposition and fulfillment of a tendency set up in the first four (example 6b). Beginning and ending are thus linked organically. The recomposition emphasizes the importance of stepwise chromatic movement, and it does so by keeping two lines of the texture in the same register. Thus, beginning in measure 39, the top voice descends from G to F♯ and continues as an inner voice through F to E. Similarly, the next-to-bottom voice moves in parallel with the upper voice: B♭-A-A♭-G.

Beginning and ending constitute the song's frame, and whatever connections exist between them participate in a network of relations established during the unfolding of the song. We can best understand the rhetoric of Strauss's harmony by following this process diachronically.

The opening measure (example 6b), with its tritone-related roots, hesitates (m. 2) before moving down by step (m. 3) as if aiming for resolution on C. The C-sharp seventh chord sounded in m. 4 and held for a further two measures is therefore heard as a substitution—it signals a deferral of proper resolution.[16]

While the chord in m. 4 initiates a structural parenthesis that is not closed until m. 13, the verbal setting of mood begins here. From quiet and stillness, the voice rises to its first climax on the first syllable of "Sonnenschein" on

Example 7. Root progressions in mm. 3–4, 19–20, and 25–26 of *Ruhe, meine Seele!*

F♯ (m. 11) and returns through the important generative interval of a perfect fifth, F♯-B. (For other uses of this interval in both ascending and descending forms, see C♯-G♯ in m. 1, C♯-F♯ in m. 9, G-C in mm. 14 and 31, and, perhaps most dramatic of all, G-C again in mm. 38–39.) Note further that in mm. 11–13 the piano's upper register is opened up considerably, thus establishing a long-term connection between the opening and closing stanzas of the song. Measure 14 (see example 6d) represents a return to the opening measures as well as a poetic change from an impersonal description to directed—or rather self-directed—speech: "Ruhe, meine Seele!" says the poet, in a line that acquires a sense of refrain in the poem. The harmonic return clarifies the progression of the first four measures in one crucial respect: the C♯ in m. 18, the equivalent of that in m. 4, now supports a $^6_5$ chord, not a root-position seventh chord, thus suggesting motion toward D. D is not sounded, however, but is replaced by a diminished seventh chord in m. 20 on the highly charged word *wild*, the first explicit break in the "peaceful" mood of the song thus far. The effect of this move resembles the arrival of C♯ in m. 4. But where m. 4 marked the beginning of the vocal narrative, m. 20 sounds like an intensification of a process already begun, thus considerably reducing the feeling of return that might have come with the restatement of a transposed form of the nexus phrase beginning in m. 22. Measures 22–25 (example 6e) are equivalent to mm. 1–3 (example 6b), but m. 26, which should have consisted of an F-sharp seventh chord, departs from the precedent set earlier. Strauss responds to the troubled condition of the protagonist's soul by intensifying an earlier expression. Measure 27 initiates another transposition of the E-D-C♯ model, and this, too, reaches a different moment of harmonic crisis on the word *Not* in m. 30, which comprises the high point of the entire song. Note that m. 30 recalls both the vocal F♯ of m. 11 ("Sonnenschein") and the diminished seventh chord of measures 20–21 (on *wild*), without compromising the integrity of the bass progression F-E♭-D (example 6f), which is crucial for the ongoing reinterpretation of the nexus phrase. Finally, measure 31 (example 6a), with its quasi-refrain "Ruhe, ruhe meine Seele!" returns to the promise of mm. 14–19 and brings them to fruition in at least two ways: the $^6_5$ chord over C♯ does indeed resolve to the promised D minor or supertonic chord (mm. 34–35), and the entire progression leads inexorably to the prolonged tonic in measures 39–43.

What we hear in the song is a large-scale, goal-oriented process—organicism with a vengeance—in which the final C seems at once surprising and inevitable (as Tovey would say): surprising because of the incomplete but relatively independent sense that each fragment projects (listening from beginning to end), and inevitable because a C-major outcome seems (in retrospect) unchallenged by any other potential outcome. Within the umbrella of a normative 5̂-line, Strauss projects a predominantly semitonal logic in which now function, now stepwise resolution alternate in forceful articulation. And despite the saturation of the musical texture with chromatic elements (ten out of twelve pitch classes appear in the first four measures, the eleventh is added with the change of chord in m. 7, and the twelfth in m. 11), there is no doubting either the "hollow fullness" or the "concordant chromaticism" of the song. In this dramatically end-oriented context, extended tonality has less the character of an interpolation or digression than of a larger-than-life enrichment of a 5̂-line.

Mahler's song, "Der Tamboursg'sell," does not make a natural comparison with Strauss's "Ruhe, meine Seele!" It is an orchestral song that exploits the rich palette of the orchestra. (The fact that Strauss later orchestrated "Ruhe, meine Seele" in 1948 does not undermine this lack of obvious comparability.) "Der Tamboursg'sell" is conceived on a much grander scale, and its message and military atmosphere are more outwardly directed than Karl Henckell's deeply felt exhortation to rest one's troubled soul. Yet there are ways in which a comparison might be profitable, especially since Mahler brings together several extended-tonal techniques in "Der Tamboursg'sell."

It is hard to postulate a simple diatonic background for the song as a whole, mainly because its two main sections, in D minor and C minor respectively, do not straightforwardly define a single prolonged motion within the framework of a key-defining progression.[17] Moreover, a marked change of compositional strategy reinforces the twofold division: the first section (mm. 1–90) is predominantly harmonic, while the second (mm. 91–end) is mainly contrapuntal. The following remarks focus on the first section.

The drummer boy's relentless march to the gallows and the poem's inner repetitions encourage a relatively static portrayal of mood which contrasts with an emergent intensity in the pathetic narrative of a prisoner who is contemplating his last moments. One line of progressive tonal enrichment may be traced in the recurring phrase or motto of the song (example 8), which embodies an open I-V progression. Mahler not only plays with the metric implications of these two chords but reharmonizes them in unpredictable ways. Occurring first in (or on) the tonic (example 8a, b, and d) and then in (or on) the subdominant (example 8c and e), the pattern of successive occurrences of the motto reinforces the broad shift from D minor to G minor, the latter becoming V of C minor.

A second technique of enrichment may be observed in the opening stro-

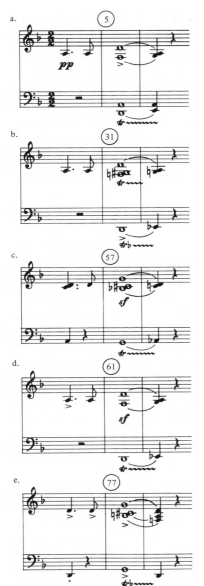

Example 8. Five different harmonizations of the motto of *Der Tamboursg'sell*

phe (mm. 8–30) which, like examples 3 and 4, constitutes a i-III-V-i progression. Mahler's rhetoric derives from a quirky, hit-or-miss approach to harmonic writing, so that while retaining a familiar ground (in the form of an overarching tonic arpeggiation) he is able to transcend some of its prescriptions by producing something different, perhaps even radical in its unpredictability. It is in the climactic third phrase of each strophe that this new harmonic writing is most evident. Example 9 assembles for ease of comparison three occurrences of the passage. It is not in the cadential measures that the listener is likely to be surprised, although the various harmonizations of the opening motto draw attention to those moments of closure. It is rather in such things as the unconventional resolution of the augmented sixth chord in mm. 22–23 (example 9a), or the progression from one dominant-functioning diminished seventh chord to another whose root is fifth-related (mm. 24–25 in example 9a), or the consonant augmented triad on the downbeat of m. 49 (example 9b) produced not by a functional progression but by pure voice leading, or the extraordinary enlargement in the bass of example 9c of the melodic figure D-C-B-C-D-G (see beamed notes). The radical nature of example 9c may further be gauged by comparing it with a conventional harmonization of the same melody in example 9d. It is in these local, hit-or-miss, sleepwalking types of harmonic gestures that the song's individuality lies. Here as elsewhere, Mahler mixes the urgency of a functional tonality with the less teleological manner of a sleepwalking harmonist. Extended tonality takes the form of a veil that hides a radically dissociated syntactic norm. Mahler composes against a sort of double tradition: that of the analyst's synchronic tonal tradition (his ordinary language), and that of a particular perspective on an extended tonal tradition (his poetic language).

I began this essay by noting that Strauss and Mahler employ a wide diversity of solutions to the central compositional challenge of achieving a convincing balance between chromatic and diatonic forces. The handful of examples discussed in this essay, chosen partly to guarantee a coherent argument, serve to underscore what was described as a resistance to generalization in the composers' oeuvre. Still, a few enabling structures cannot be denied. Understood as the process by which a primary diatonic tonality is enriched by chromatic elements, extended tonality is operative in the works of Strauss and Mahler. In most examples, it was possible to postulate or derive a diatonic background and its enriched foreground. The gap between foreground and background differs from example to example. In general, the gaps are smaller for Strauss than they are for Mahler. Put another way, Strauss's chromaticism is concordant, while Mahler's is discordant. This insight allows us to claim a greater linear energy for Mahler and to highlight Strauss's tendency to stress the vertical over the horizontal dimension. But these are no more than tentative generalizations that can only be corroborated by the results of extensive analytical research. What is beyond doubt, however, is the

Example 9. Recurring phrase in *Der Tamboursg'sell*

plurality of meanings embodied in the work of two remarkably resourceful composers.

Notes

1   For a concise introduction to methods of tonal expansion in the nineteenth and early twentieth centuries, see Jim Samson, *Music in Transition: A Study of Tonal Expansion and Atonality 1900–1920*
(London: Dent, 1977). A summary and critique of Schenkerian approaches may be found in
James M. Baker, "Schenkerian Analysis and Post-Tonal Music," in *Aspects of Schenkerian Theory*,
ed. David Beach (New Haven: Yale University Press, 1983), pp. 153–86.

2   For some recent discussions of tonality and related issues in Strauss, see Derrick Puffett, ed.,
Richard Strauss: "Salome" (Cambridge: Cambridge University Press, 1989); Derrick Puffett, ed.,
Richard Strauss: "Elektra" (Cambridge: Cambridge University Press); Graham H. Phipps, "The
Logic of Tonality in Strauss's *Don Quixote*: A Schoenbergian Evaluation," *19th-Century Music* 9
(1986): 189–305; and Bryan Gilliam, *Richard Strauss's Elektra*. (Oxford: Oxford University Press,
1991). Among specialized studies whose methods resonate with the approach taken in this
essay, see John Williamson, "Strauss and 'Macbeth': The Realisation of the Poetic Idea,"
Soundings 13 (1985): 3–21; Richard A. Kaplan, "The Musical Language of *Elektra*: A Study in
Chromatic Harmony," Ph.D. diss., University of Michigan, 1985, and Tim Jackson, "Richard
Strauss 'Winterweihe': An Analysis and Study of the Sketches," *Richard Strauss-Blätter* 17 (1987):
28–64.

3   There is no single comprehensive account of tonality and/or voice leading in the works of
Mahler. Although now superseded by more specialized work informed mainly by Schen-
kerian principles, Hans Tischler's *Die Harmonik in den Werken Gustav Mahlers* (Ph.D. diss., University of Vienna, 1937) remains a valuable point of departure (portions of the dissertation
are excerpted in "Mahler's Impact on the Crisis of Tonality," *Music Review* 12 [1951]: 113–21).
Among recent specialized studies, see Christopher Orlo Lewis, *Tonal Coherence in Mahler's Ninth
Symphony* (Ann Arbor: UMI Research Press), p. 194; Richard Kaplan, "Interpreting Surface
Harmonic Connections in the Adagio of Mahler's Tenth Symphony," *In Theory Only* 4 (1978):
32–44; Stephen Hefling, "Mahler's *Todtenfeier*: A Documentary and Analytical Study" (Ph.D.
diss., Yale University, 1985); and John Williamson, "The Structural Premises of Mahler's Intro-
ductions: Prolegomena to an Analysis of the First Movement of the Seventh Symphony,"
Music Analysis 5 (1986): 29–58.

4   Arnold Schoenberg, *Structural Functions of Harmony* (New York: Norton, 1969): 76–113.

5   Felix Salzer, *Structural Hearing: Tonal Coherence in Music*, 2 vols. (New York: Dover, 1962), p. 227.

6   Schoenberg, *Structural Functions*, p. 19. In an earlier treatise, Schoenberg railed against the
tonal-atonal "antithesis," claiming that "everything implied by a series of tones (*Tonreihe*)
constitutes tonality, whether it be brought together by means of direct reference to a single
fundamental or by more complicated connections." *Theory of Harmony*, trans. Roy E. Carter
(Berkeley: University of California Press, 1978), p. 432.

7   Schoenberg, *Structural Functions*, p. 76.

8   Schoenberg, "The Relationship to the Text" in *Style and Idea* (London: Faber, 1975), pp. 141–45.

9   Schoenberg, *Structural Functions*, pp. 76–77.

10 The analysis may be found on p. 77 of *Structural Functions*.

11   On the place of chromaticism in Schenker's theory, see Matthew Brown, "The Diatonic and the Chromatic in Schenker's Theory of Harmonic Relations," *Journal of Music Theory* 30 (1986): 1–33.

12   Arnold Whittall, *Music Since the First World War* (London: Dent, 1975), pp. 95–96.

13   Ernst Bloch, *Essays on the Philosophy of Music*, trans. Peter Palmer (Cambridge: Cambridge University Press, 1985), p. 38.

14   Salzer, *Structural Hearing*, vol. 1, p. 189.

15   On chromaticized voice exchanges, see Edward Aldwell and Carl Schachter, *Harmony and Voice Leading* (San Diego: Harcourt Brace Jovanovich, 1978; reprint, 1989), pp. 399–400, 403–4, 483–85, 488–90, and 535–41.

16   For an alternative explanation of these opening measures, see Graham H. Phipps, "Tonality in Webern's Cantata I," *Music Analysis* 3 (1984): 126–27. Invoking the principle of tritone equivalence, Phipps follows Schoenberg's theory of harmony in suggesting that the essential progression in the first four measures is F♯ (because the roots C and F♯ are equivalent), G♯ (because, as before, G♯ or A♭ is equivalent to its tritonal relation, D), and C♯. What we hear, then, according to Phipps, is "a chromatically conceived version of IV, V, I in the region of C♯" (p. 127).

17   On the theoretical issues raised by a tonal work ending in a key other than the one in which it began, see Harald Krebs, "Alternatives to Monotonality," *Journal of Music Theory* 25 (1981): 1–16.

Ironic Allusions to Italian Opera in the Musical Comedies of Richard Strauss

Reinhold Schlötterer

▼

Those familiar with the basic operatic repertoire will no doubt easily recognize explicit allusions to Italian opera in Strauss's musical comedies.[1] And while our initial reaction to these allusions is one of gentle amusement, there lies beneath that playful surface the question of a deeper significance: Has Strauss invested these seemingly harmless allusions with deeper meaning?

The ultimate source of these connections with Italian opera is not the composer's fantasy, but something already inherent in the libretti themselves. In act 1 of Der Rosenkavalier, Hofmannsthal has the Italian tenor sing the words of a real Italian aria. Hofmannsthal's libretto to Ariadne auf Naxos is informed by the Italianate world of commedia dell' arte, opera seria, and opera buffa. In Stefan Zweig's text to Die schweigsame Frau, the role of Henry—the nephew of the central character Morosus—is a tenor in an Italian opera troupe. Finally, Capriccio, which was initially inspired by an eighteenth-century Italian libretto (Prima la musica e poi le parole) of Giovanni Battista Casti and then arranged by Strauss and Clemens Krauss as a theatrical play in the historical ambience of Gluck and Piccini in Paris, offers numerous opportunities for musical allusions to Italian opera. In all of these cases, Strauss not only responds to the suggestions inherent in the libretti, but also is able, through musical means, to color these obvious references with subtle, yet effective irony.[2]

The tenor aria of Der Rosenkavalier (act 1, reh. 233)[3] is no doubt the most famous Italian reference in all of Strauss's fifteen operas. Here Strauss achieves a sense of irony through exaggeration. The composer overplays the traditional espressivo of a typical nineteenth-century Italian tenor aria (where the voice is espressivo and the accompaniment more neutral) by giving nearly every orchestral part an espressivo role; Strauss specifically designates "espr." in most cases. Furthermore, the composer intensifies the melodic line and the espressivo sonority by adorning the melody with parallel thirds or sixths. A sketchbook for *Der Rosenkavalier* specifically links this procedure with Strauss's sense of "Italianizing."[4] The singer's part itself exemplifies all the mannerisms of the genre, which are only heightened in Strauss's interpretation: the brilliant high notes are profiled in a most obvious way and then sustained with excessive fermatae, portamenti are exaggerated, and an interpolated sighing melisma on "Ah!" articulates the end of the phrase.

Word setting seems to be of relatively minor importance (*prima la musica e poi le parole!*), and one wonders whether or not this reflects an insensitivity to Italian on the part of the composer or a further—and perhaps the most subtle—example of Strauss's irony. In sum, Strauss offers us an intensified, almost concentrated version of an Italian tenor aria. But critics, such as Norman Del Mar, perhaps go too far in describing the passage as a "cruelly clever caricature of an Italian operatic aria."[5] Strauss's irony is not as biting as, for example, Mozart's in *Ein musikalischer Spass*, but is rather the gentle debunking of a music which is, to paraphrase Wagner, effect without cause.

Ariadne auf Naxos offers a curious phenomenon: Why is it that in Zerbinetta's extended coloratura aria one senses no irony at all? The mannerisms of coloratura would seem to be an easy target for ironic treatment. Perhaps the German text, especially at the sophisticated literary level of Hofmannsthal, inspired more sincere music on the part of Strauss, for in no way is it handled ironically. The Strauss-Hofmannsthal correspondence, indeed, reveals the composer's growing preoccupation with Zerbinetta—a somewhat auxiliary character. In the tradition of Mozart's "Queen of the Night," Strauss consid-

Example 1.

ered coloratura, in this case, a serious means of characterization, a means that he also applied to the genre of the lied, such as in his song *Amor*, based on a poem of Clemens Brentano. Hofmannsthal never fully agreed with Strauss on the extensive use of coloratura used to depict Zerbinetta; indeed, on one occasion he declared her role "misrepresented."[6] It may well be that Hofmannsthal failed to comprehend fully the musical ambience of Italian operatic artistry as Strauss apparently did.

Another nuance of Strauss's "all' italiana" is expressed in *Die schweigsame Frau*. To be sure, the spirit of comedy predominates in the singing lesson (act 3, reh. 18, m. 13), yet behind the comic acting there is a detectable sense of ironic exaggeration. The scene features textual as well as musical quotations from Monteverdi and Legrenzi, but, paradoxically, they are not the subject of the composer's irony. Rather, Strauss—as in *Der Rosenkavalier*—looks to the world of nineteenth-century Italian opera as his source.

Indeed, Strauss rarely misses an opportunity to recall idiosyncratic aspects of Italian singing or, more blatantly, to cite specific fragments from well-known opera tunes. At the mere mention of an "Apoll Italiens" or "Primo Tenore," Strauss shifts to a ringing high A♭ (act 1, reh. 82, m. 10 and reh. 89, m. 9), and with the line "Cavaliere Vanuzzis Ruhm ist bis in unser Vaterland gedrungen (act 1, reh. 86)," he quotes "Bella figlia di amore" and "La donna è mobile," from *Rigoletto*, in succession. Strauss articulates the citations with the indication "espr.," and casts them in the characteristic cantilena keys of A♭ and D♭ (see example 2).

Beyond allusions in the music, Strauss openly expressed his opinions of Italian opera in his letters. The brash, opinionated composer of twenty-two years once exclaimed to his father: "I shall never become a convert to Italian music, it's such trash. Even the *Barber of Seville* could only be enjoyed in an outstanding performance."[7] Later, he preferred ironic sideswipes to sweeping generalizations. At the age of seventy-eight he offered facetious praise for the three "indestructible" operas: "Long live *Tiefland, Trovatore,* [and] *Tosca!*"[8]

After examining Strauss's comments on Italian opera—in music or words —three reservations become readily apparent: the attention paid to the singer (prima donna or tenor) at the expense of the work, the careless setting of music to words or vice versa, and the paucity of orchestral polyphony. All of these points are discussed at length in Strauss's final opera, *Capriccio*. Both the opera itself and the published correspondence surrounding its genesis serve as a vital source for Strauss's opinions of Italian opera.

Like *Die schweigsame Frau*, *Capriccio* offers allusions to Italian opera both by citing or mimicking genuine operatic works (in this case a duet using words by Metastasio) and by providing musical commentary on relevant cues in the text. Letters from the Strauss-Krauss correspondence reveal that it was the composer's original plan "to find a tune which absolutely does not fit the words." He even describes the duet as an "Addio with the wrong music."[9] What, according to Strauss, constitutes "the wrong music"?

At the end of part one of the duet, Countess Madeleine remarks that she discerns a certain discrepancy between the textual content and musical expression ("A very cheerful Addio, the words don't seem to match the music" [reh. 156, m. 1]). The opinion is clearly Strauss's as well, and he creates this

Example 2.

Example 3.

important "out-of-synch" quality not by textual layout but by composing a passage based entirely on the working out of a motive. Thus, the high notes of the tenor do not articulate any relevant words; rather they highlight arbitrary syllables (see example 3).

A look at the orchestral part reveals a more complex and sophisticated irony so rich in detail that it could very well be the subject of a paper itself.[10] Two important details, however, are especially striking. The first is Strauss's intentional obfuscation of metrical stress. A glance at the opening of the duet reveals how Strauss simultaneously articulates $\frac{6}{8}$ and $\frac{3}{4}$ in the various parts, both meters being common to *bel canto* pieces.

The second detail, although still along the lines of metrical stress, particularly concerns the orchestral treatment: the accompaniment does not follow the *bel canto* norm where the orchestra should play a subdued, supportive role (quite often in the form of the so-called "oom-pah-pah," street-organ accompaniment). This element has been consigned to the bassoon part, and nearly every time it is restricted to the second half of the $\frac{6}{8}$ measure—a clever and distorted allusion to a well-known tradition. Later on, in the second part of the duet, Strauss shifts to the "normal" procedure of this tradition in the strings, but with a subtle difference: the secondary strong beat (beat 4)

Example 4.

Example 5.

remains silent in the cello and bass. The bassoons continue their distorted "oom-pah-pahs."

Three other passages from *Capriccio* exemplify Strauss's ironic tribute to Italian opera. As the Director utters the words "for the high notes of the beloved tenor" ("auf die hohen Töne des beliebten Tenors") the solo cello (marked *Appassionato*) mimics the Italian singer, working its way up to a sustained high A, complete with affected sighing in syncopation (reh. 15, m. 7; example 5).

In the ensuing passage Strauss goes from the singer to the orchestra as a medium for the expression of his musical irony. At rehearsal 16 Strauss invents a tune with the distinct flavor of Rossini. During the passage the Director exclaims: "Nothing excels Italian opera!" Olivier: "With its bad text?" Director: "With its good music! One listens full of emotion to the magic of the aria." The tune, full of affected suspensions and intensified with parallel sixths, is accompanied in the street-organ manner without a trace of the worked-out orchestral support that Strauss normally considered imperative.

Example 6.

A key phrase of text spoken early on in the work is the poet Flamand's retort to La Roche, the down-to-earth theater director: "Höheres gilt es als Zeitvertreib!" ("Higher things are at stake than mere pastime!") The implied juxtaposition of lofty human thought and amusement reveals Strauss's ideal of music, his philosophy of art. Strauss's musical depiction of this time-honored dichotomy is achieved by juxtaposing Gluck, with the famous unison passage from the *Iphigenie* overture as a symbol of high ideals, with a lighthearted passage intended to represent Piccini—a symbol of poor entertainment. Beneath this juxtaposition an even greater dichotomy is implied: German vs. Italian opera. Behind the Gluck one detects the spirit of Richard Wagner, and behind the Piccini-like tunes one senses the nineteenth-century Italian operatic tradition in general.

As a dissonance against the unison D of the Gluck, the winds play an E-flat minor triad, representing symphonic harmony,[11] which quickly resolves to the world of Piccini: the commonplace and popular key of D major. One

- sik! Man lauscht voll Rüh - rung dem Zau - ber der A - rie, be -

wonders whether or not the A harmonic tone in the cello is another high A for the tenor. All in all, these passages demonstrate a semantically determined method of composition, not mere illustrative music, as has often been said in a pejorative sense (see example 7).

With his critical attitude toward Italian opera, whether in the guise of music or expressed in words, Strauss is in good company, for many other nineteenth- and twentieth-century composers, ranging from Arthur Sullivan to Hans Pfitzner, dissociated themselves from that tradition.[12] Even earlier, Goethe was well aware of these dual musical traditions. He wrote about them in his *Anmerkung zu Diderot*:

> All newer music is treated in either of two
> ways: It is either considered as an
> independent art which develops within
> itself, maintains itself and is to be enjoyed

with a refined sense, as the Italians do. Or
it is related to understanding, feeling,
passion and is treated in such a way that it
requires the exercise of many different
qualities to comprehend it. This is the way
the French, Germans, and all Northerners
treat it and they always will do so.[13]

If we assume that Strauss believed his ironic allusions to Italian opera dissociated him from the presumed artistic vacuum there—and the evidence

Example 7.

Example 8. (Sarti)

strongly suggests it—then it is important to consider a parallel with Mozart. To be sure, Mozart's music is largely informed by the Italian tradition, yet in his later years he became ever more conscious of the superiority of his work in comparison to contemporary Italian stage music, especially that which thrived in Vienna. In the finale of the second act of *Don Giovanni*, he quotes three popular operas of the time: one by Martin y Soler, another by Giuseppe Sarti, and his own *Marriage of Figaro*. When one hears these pieces in succession, one cannot help but notice the remarkable difference in quality between Soler and Sarti on one hand and Mozart on the other. The different concept in scoring is obvious at a glance.

Particularly in his arrangement of Sarti's "Come un agnello,"[14] Mozart heightens a certain quality of stiffness in the score: the horn part, serving as a remarkably monotonous bass line, is not Sarti's but comes from Mozart's hand. Perhaps this exaggerated voice leading is an example of Mozart's dissociating irony, which in a sense foreshadows Strauss (examples 8 and 9).

However, it would be unfair to Strauss, and to Italian opera for that matter, if we neglected to mention those moments when the composer expressed his sincere envy of the tradition so seemingly foreign to his music. In a letter to Karl Böhm, Strauss expresses grave doubts about the German operatic tradition and exclaims: "Why was I not born as a Verdi or at least a Puccini? To hell with German counterpoint!"[15] And to Clemens Krauss he once affirmed that he "would not like to run down Italian music."[16]

What should one make of Strauss's apparent about-face later in his career? The change of heart expressed in these two letters signifies Strauss's keen awareness of the problems connected with German symphonic opera and of important positive qualities of Italian opera as well. Correspondence be-

Example 9. (Mozart)

tween the composer and his librettists attests to the fact that Strauss was always willing to learn when Hofmannsthal or Zweig wanted him to enhance the melodic and vocal element of the music at the expense of the orchestral apparatus.

Strauss unquestionably went in this direction when he composed, for example, *Ariadne, Intermezzo*, and *Die schweigsame Frau*—and without abandoning his own musical voice. Joseph Gregor's prosaic libretti (*Friedenstag, Daphne,* and *Die Liebe der Danae*), which immediately followed Zweig's light and witty *Schweigsame Frau*, served as a notable obstacle for Strauss's progress in this direction. Thus, a lasting and fruitful connection between German and Italian traditions remained for Strauss an unfulfilled and, perhaps for the twentieth century, anachronistic dream. Nonetheless, Strauss maintained as his ideal "ein Schöpfen aus beiden Nationalitäten" (a dipping from both national streams), an ideal that he believed had been achieved by only one composer: his idol Wolfgang Amadeus Mozart.[17]

Notes

1   *Capriccio* is, technically speaking, not a comedy or comic opera; Strauss gives it the subtitle *Konversationsstück*. Nonetheless, comic elements abound throughout the work, and it seems justified to include within the genre of comedy in this context.

2   In this essay the term "irony" is used in the sense of the Quintillian rhetorical tradition. Thus, "irony" denotes the rhetorical "pretense" (*simulatio*), in which what is meant differs from the manner in which it is stated—more narrowly, an attack under the guise of a smile. If, as will be shown below, Strauss occasionally adopts the idiom of Italian opera, but through exaggeration or distortion also introduces his own artistic distance and deliberation with regard to the idiom, then this corresponds exactly to the "attack under the guise of a smile" in the rhetorical sense of the phrase.

3   Works by Strauss are cited by indication of act, rehearsal number, and measure (when necessary), e.g., act 1, reh. 233, m. 1.

4   In an early *Rosenkavalier* sketchbook (Tr. 20) at the Richard-Strauss-Archiv in Garmisch, Strauss labels a motive in parallel sixths "Italienisierendes Liebesduett." In the printed score this motive appears for the first time in the Prelude (act 1, reh. 1, mm. 1ff).

5   Norman Del Mar, *Richard Strauss*, vol. I (London: Faber and Faber, 1986), p. 369.

6   Cf. Willi Schuh, "Die 'verzeichnete' Zerbinetta," *Hofmannsthal-Blätter* 31/32 (1985): 52–57.

7   Richard Strauss, *Briefe an die Eltern*, ed. Willi Schuh (Zurich: Atlantis, 1954), p. 94. "Zur italienischen Musik werde ich mich wohl nie bekehren, es ist eben Schund. Auch der *Barbier von Sevilla* dürfte nur mehr in einer hervorragenden Aufführung geniessbar sein."

8   *Richard Strauss–Clemens Krauss: Briefwechsel*, ed. Götz Klaus Kende and Willi Schuh (Munich: C. H. Beck, 1964), p. 234. "Der Teufel hole das Neuland, in das mich eine böse Fee bei meiner Geburt versetzt hat. Es lebe *Tiefland, Trovatore, Tosca!*"

9   *Strauss-Krauss*, pp. 112, 95. "Wenn es mir gelingt, dazu eine Melodie zu finden, die absolut

nicht zu den Worten passt." "Wenn dann die Italiener auch ein Addio mit verkehrter Musik singen . . ."

10   With regard to harmony a comparison between the Sonett (reh. 75, mm. 9ff) and the Italian duet would be of great interest.

11   This striking E-flat minor sonority, of course, does not occur in isolation. It is introduced shortly beforehand (3 mm. before reh. no. 14) in the $^6_4$ position and highlighted in an oboe "fanfare," which announces the words: "Drame héroique"—E flat being the traditional heroic key. The minor sixth (G/E♭) in the second violin maintains E♭ even though the other parts have already reached an A[7] chord: a typical instance of Strauss simultaneously combining two different harmonic layers.

12   According to a published interview in the *San Francisco Chronicle* (21 July 1885), Arthur Sullivan once observed: "Analysing the Italian grand opera, you will find that in a great many cases the most widely divergent emotions and the most opposite sentiments were expressed in the same manner. . . ." In Arthur Jacobs, *Arthur Sullivan* (Oxford, 1984), p. 218. Hans Pfitzner: "Schlechte Verdische Jugendopern . . . so dass es wohl kaum ein deutsches Opernhaus gibt, welches nicht *Die Macht des Schicksals, Don Carlos, Simone Boccanegra* und wie das Zeug alles heisst, auf dem Spielplan hat." In *Mitteilungen der Hans Pfitzner Gesellschaft*, 49 (1988): 58–59.

13   Goethe, *Anmerkung zu Diderot:*

> Alle neuere Musik wird auf zweierlei Weise
> behandelt, entweder dass man sie als eine
> selbständige Kunst betrachtet, sie in sich selbst
> ausbildet, ausübt und durch den verfeinerten
> Sinn geniesst, wie es der Italiener zu tun pflegt,
> oder dass man sie in Bezug auf Verstand,

Empfindung, Leidenschaft setzt und sie
dergestalt bearbeitet, dass sie mehrere
menschliche Geistes- und Seelenkräfte in
Anspruch nehmen könnte, wie es die Weise der
Franzosen, der Deutschen und aller Nordländer
ist und bleiben wird.

14   The variations for piano "Come un agnello" (KV 454ᵃ) is probably not a work by Mozart. Only one autograph folio survives; it contains two variations that are not identical with KV 454ᵃ. Cf. *Neue Mozart Ausgabe, Kritische Berichte*, ed. Kurt von Fischer, IX, 26.

15   Strauss to Böhm (19 May 1935) in *Der Strom der Töne trug mich fort*, ed. Franz Grasberger (Tutzing: Hans Schneider, 1967), p. 1364: "Warum bin ich nicht als Verdi oder meinetwegen als Puccini auf die Welt gekommen! Der Teufel hol' den deutschen Contrapunkt!"

16   *Strauss–Krauss*, p. 63. "Ich möchte bei dieser Gelegenheit nicht die italienischer Musik heruntersetzen müssen."

17   Letter to Hofmannsthal (16 June 1927) in *Strauss–Hofmannsthal: Briefwechsel*, ed. Willi Schuh (Zurich: Atlantis, 1978), p. 573.

Strauss and the National Socialists:
The Debate and Its Relevance

Pamela M. Potter

▼

The Nazis' twelve-year domination of cultural life during the Third Reich has figured prominently in studies of German cultural history and will continue to invite investigations into art under dictatorship for many years to come. One would expect that music, arguably the central German cultural achievement in the modern era, would be the first area of inquiry in any study dealing with the manipulation of the arts for Nazi propaganda. But such is not the case. Substantial investigations into music in Nazi Germany have been scattered, and most of them have come to light surprisingly late, lagging far behind their research counterparts in visual arts, architecture, literature, and film.

Where scholarship has failed, more popular literary ventures have taken up issues of music in the Third Reich by concentrating on the roles of prominent individuals in the Nazi state. The blunt and usually simplistic question "was he or she a Nazi?" haunts the biographers of Karajan, Furtwängler, Schwarzkopf, Orff, and especially Strauss. The question thus phrased is simplistic, because the issue involves much more than merely demonstrating membership in the Nazi party. (Many party members were unconditionally pardoned after the war, while many nonmembers, such as Richard Strauss, remained tainted because of their high visibility in the Nazi state, even if they were officially "denazified.") With the possible exception of Karajan, whose Nazi past has only recently become the center of attention, Strauss has been singled out as the most illustrious musical figure to have served the Third Reich, and although nearly half a century has passed since the end of the Second World War, the nagging question about Strauss's relationship with the German National Socialist government remains unanswered.

Why is there so much interest in Strauss, if not merely for reasons of sheer curiosity and even voyeurism? There have been far more attempts to explain the minute details of one man's problematic connections with Nazi heads of state than there have been comprehensive studies of Nazi music policy. In the place of thorough, broad-based musicological investigations of musical life in the Third Reich, studies of Strauss and the Nazis have multiplied and intensified. In the last decade a few general studies on music have deflected some of the attention away from Strauss, but only minimally.

One reason for the exclusive focus on Strauss may be that authors—wittingly or unwittingly—have made Strauss a symbol for the entire German music community's response to the policies of the Nazi regime. Subjecting his activities in the Nazi years to close scrutiny has served to satisfy our needs in determining whether or not "music" as a whole capitulated to the Nazi dictatorship. Hence the fascination with Strauss and the Nazis never dies, and the same worn question of his political allegiance always comes up in discussions concerning music in Nazi Germany. But this fascination should also alert us to question not only our perception of music as a component in the Nazi state, but also our perception of the Nazi phenomenon as a chapter in the history of German music. We must ask why the subject of music has been so blatantly ignored as a feature of the otherwise thoroughly researched history of Nazi Germany, and why, when historians can ignore it no longer, they usually present it as nothing more than an anomalous, unfortunate episode, a great source of embarrassment that is better left alone.

A survey of the treatment of Strauss's Nazi years reveals a glaring lack of historical perspective and a pressing need to treat Strauss's story for what it is and not for what we would like it to be. The treatments that have appeared in the years since Strauss's death have evolved from cursory mention, buried away in biographies, to full-scale monographs. From 1949 to 1963, authors either skipped over the period or searched for convenient labels to characterize Strauss's behavior. As more evidence came to light, they felt compelled to hand down a verdict on his moral conduct as well. Most recently, scholars have combed through archives and subjected these twelve years of Strauss's life to unprecedented scrutiny. They may believe that they have composed a definitive account of his relationship to the Nazis, but they have failed to step back and ask why the story is worth investigating at all.

After nearly half a century, a clear picture of Strauss's activities still eludes us, largely because of the complexity of events and the questionable reliability of the accounts handed down to us. Before reviewing the Strauss literature, it will be useful to summarize the main events of his interaction with the Nazi government, bearing in mind that some of the details are still being contested. The first event to place Strauss in the spotlight after Hitler's seizure of power occurred in April 1933, when he stepped in for the Jewish conductor Bruno Walter. Walter, scheduled to conduct the Berlin Philharmonic, had been warned that police protection could not be guaranteed should violence break out. Strauss agreed to fill in, giving the conducting fee back to the orchestra.

Strauss came through once again for an important musical event when Toscanini canceled his engagement at Bayreuth in protest against the treatment of the Jews. Strauss agreed to substitute for Toscanini and return to Bayreuth after a thirty-year absence. In the same summer, he signed a letter protesting Thomas Mann's speech in Brussels on the anniversary of Wagner's death, an act that prompted his critics to place him in the camp of Nazi sympathizers. However, he also allegedly used his influence to avert a catastrophe by threatening to withdraw from Bayreuth if the Munich Nazis went through with their plans to disrupt the Salzburg festival.

The high point of Strauss's cooperation with the Nazi government came in November 1933, when he was appointed president of the newly established Reich Music Chamber under the aegis of the Propaganda Ministry. In an inaugural speech in February 1934, he thanked Hitler and Goebbels for making the organization possible and expressed his optimism for the new Chamber's potential to consolidate German musical life and to bring German music back to the people. In the year that followed, Strauss used his influential position to secure copyright protection for German composers, a goal toward which he had been working since 1898.

He soon retreated from the bureaucratic duties of his office, however, disillusioned with such policies as the banning of Mendelssohn (he refused to comply with the government's request to compose new music for A Midsummer Night's Dream). Instead he diverted most of his energies to his collaboration with the Austrian Jewish writer Stephan Zweig on Die schweigsame Frau, a project he had undertaken about five months before Hitler came to power. This collaboration would be the cause of his fall from grace with the Nazi government. The Nazi press began to attack Strauss for his collaboration with Zweig in the summer of 1934. When Strauss came to Bayreuth to conduct for a second season, Goebbels indicated that there might be trouble if the opera were to be performed. Strauss and Goebbels agreed that the matter should be taken directly to Hitler, and since Hitler had no objections to the libretto and was even willing to attend the premiere, plans for the production could proceed.

But Strauss's subsequent defiance was to cause irreversible damage to the success of the opera's premiere. He was unable to secure permission to conduct *Elektra* in Salzburg that same summer because of Germany's anti-Austrian position at the time. He went to Salzburg despite the government's restrictions, and although he did not conduct, he appeared on the stage to take curtain calls as the composer. The authorities then informed Strauss that a second Zweig opera would not be possible, but the composer pushed his influential position to the limit by urging his librettist to agree to continue their collaboration in secret. When Zweig refused, Strauss wrote an irate letter to him, denying any political allegiance to the Nazis and urging Zweig not to persist in his "Jewish obstinacy." Unknown to both of them, the letter was intercepted by the Gestapo and sent to Hitler.

The consequences of these reckless actions became known at the premiere of *Die schweigsame Frau*. Shortly before the performance, Strauss asked to see the program and noticed that Zweig's name had been omitted. He insisted that Zweig's name be printed as large as Hofmannsthal's had been for *Rosenkavalier* or else he would leave immediately. The alteration was grudgingly approved, but both Hitler and Goebbels were inexplicably indisposed for the premiere, and the Dresden Intendant who showed the program to Strauss was fired.

The premiere went on as scheduled, but the production was canceled after a few performances. The government forced Strauss to resign from his office in the Music Chamber, ordering him to give reasons of poor health and advanced age. The press carried the news but gave it little attention. The existence of the intercepted letter was never publicized, and Strauss later received a copy of it marked in red by government officials. He then wrote a long, ingratiating letter to Hitler explaining the context of his statements and the anger in which it was written, but Hitler never responded. *Die schweigsame Frau* was banned in Germany, and Strauss became a *persona non grata* in his homeland. In the following year he toured Europe, conducted and attended performances of *Die schweigsame Frau*, and began to work with librettist Joseph Gregor on *Friedenstag* (based on a sketch by Zweig).

In the spring of 1936 Strauss politically rehabilitated himself by consenting to conduct his "Olympische Hymne" at the 1936 Berlin Olympic games without taking any compensation. He had composed the piece for that occasion in 1934 as one of his duties while still a government official. Having cleared the way for the production of his new opera through his rehabilitation, Strauss secured permission for *Friedenstag* to premiere in Munich in 1938. Of Strauss's last three operas, two premiered while the Nazis were still in power.

Despite these acts of reconciliation, Strauss's relationship with the Nazi government remained shaky after the Zweig affair. He continued to comply with the government's wishes, composing the *Japanische Festmusik* for the anniversary of the Japanese Empire and consenting to appear in a film about the Berlin Philharmonic that credited the Nazis for the orchestra's success. Still, he had to contend with a number of annoyances: threats to his Jewish daughter-in-law and grandsons, an attack by Martin Bormann, who wanted to use Strauss's Garmisch residence to put up wounded soldiers, and an official order to the German press not to acknowledge his eightieth birthday. But he had made friends with some influential Nazi officials, such as Baldur von Schirach (the Reichsjugendführer and Reichsstatthalter in Vienna) and Hans Frank (the Bavarian Minister of Justice, later Reich Judicial Leader, and ultimately governor of occupied Poland), both of whom interceded on his behalf on several occasions.

It took a number of years for many of these details to come to light. In the aftermath of Strauss's protracted denazification process, some of the earlier postwar Strauss scholars chose not to comment on the sensitive issues raised by the Allied tribunal. Thus the works that came out around the time of Strauss's death in 1949—those of Pfister, Rostand, and Tenschert—make no mention of the Third Reich.[1] In the next fifteen years, authors opted to wash over the episode with little more than sweeping characterizations of Strauss's political behavior, picking and choosing the events that suited these characterizations and employing such labels as "apolitical" and "opportunistic" where appropriate. Otto Erhardt's 1953 biography chronicles the highlights of Strauss's years under the Nazis and concludes that the apolitical Strauss was simply unmoved by world events.[2] Still, Erhardt feels compelled to express his "painful disappointment" that Strauss did not at least openly protest the sham of Nazi cultural policy, as one would have expected from an individual who always spoke his mind.[3] Heinrich Kralik's biography of 1963 develops this apolitical image further, maintaining that the world cannot blame Strauss for his artistic estrangement from reality.[4]

Other biographers developed the opportunist characterization. Franz Trenner's documentary study attributes all of Strauss's activities to the desire to ensure the performance of his works.[5] Ernst Krause, offering a Marxist interpretation, sees Strauss as a typical specimen of waning bourgeois society and invokes Gustav Mahler's label for Strauss as "the great opportunist."[6] Krause regards Strauss's political behavior as indicative of his ability to conform to any system that came to power; his attitude toward the Nazis serves merely as another case in point.[7] Nevertheless, he also blames Strauss for not staging an open protest.[8]

While these early works proposed the prevailing images of Strauss under the Nazis—the apolitical artist, the advocate of his own works, and the great opportunist—later authors went one step further by using such labels to arrive at moral judgments of Strauss's behavior. Authors probably felt compelled at this time to pronounce a verdict on account of two controversies raging in the 1960s. The first was the debate in Israel on whether or not to perform the works of Strauss, Wagner, and Orff.[9] The second, more important controversy was precipitated by the appearance of Joseph Wulf's *Musik im Dritten Reich* in 1963.[10] Wulf's documentation caused an uproar by bringing documents to light that showed Strauss to be more openly conciliatory to the regime, yet at the same time far less tolerated by the regime than was previously assumed. Wulf's evidence yielded a more complex picture of Strauss's character, showing him to be neither indifferent nor apolitical. Its publication represents a definite turning point in the way authors were to look at Strauss thereafter.

Walter Panofsky was one of the first to come to Strauss's defense in light of the Wulf documents. Sustaining the apolitical image, Panofsky claims that Strauss acted solely for the good of his family and his work.[11] George Marek was not so charitable, and his *Richard Strauss: The Life of a Non-Hero* has been regarded by Strauss enthusiasts as an unmitigated character assassination. Conceding Strauss's political naiveté, which by that time had been widely accepted, Marek nevertheless condemns what he calls an acquiescence to a perverse dictatorship.[12] Strauss, according to Marek, could see what was going on with the burning of the Reichstag, the vandalism of Jewish property, and the *Reichskristallnacht*. Yet he closed his eyes to these atrocities when he stood in for Walter and Toscanini, praised Goebbels for the attacks on Hindemith, and participated in the condemnation of Thomas Mann's Wagner lecture.[13] Marek describes Strauss as an opportunist in the most negative sense: "In short, Strauss's attitude to and relationship with National Socialism were as contradictory as Strauss's whole character. He swerved from pro to con; both the pro and the con were prompted by what he thought was better for him, not what was better for the world, for his country—or for music."[14] Concerning Strauss's denazification after the war, Marek adds: "It was easy to exonerate him. Was he not an artist and a great one? It was and is not so easy to excuse the man who, to protect his creative interest, could grovel and be callously devious."[15]

Marek's biography succeeded in sparking its own small controversy. His attacks evoked more sympathy for Strauss from some subsequent biographers, and although they all attested to certain character flaws—to do otherwise after Wulf's revelations would have been dishonest—their overall tone was far more conciliatory. Peter Heyworth called Marek to task in an article in *Encounter*,[16] reprimanding him for his "two-dimensional" perception of life's dilemmas, his "crass and heartless" terms, and his "nasty flavor of racial animosity."[17] Heyworth points to inconsistencies in Marek's judgment of Strauss's political awareness and to omissions on Marek's part of some of the more creditable political stands Strauss had taken.

Norman Del Mar also responded to Marek directly. He concedes that Strauss's weakness of character was a flaw that the Nazis were shrewd enough to exploit and describes in detail Strauss's lack of concern for any events transpiring beyond his villa in Garmisch.[18] Nevertheless, he attacks what he calls Marek's scurrilous speculations on what Strauss must have known of world events at the time of his collaboration.[19] Many more sympathetic judgments followed: Michael Kennedy expressed views similar to those of Heyworth—that Strauss was often envied for his success, particularly financial; that he was solely preoccupied with his music; and that, unlike Thomas Mann, he was "not a deep thinker" and "not cut out for heroics."[20] Alan Jefferson denied any weaknesses of character whatsoever, maintaining that Strauss always took honors as they came to him, did what he thought was right for the good of the art, and acted as he did to protect his family, but unfortunately his acts were misinterpreted abroad.[21]

Other authors in the 1970s offered negative moral assessments of Strauss's behavior, but they were far less strident than Marek in their manner of presentation. André Ross takes a somewhat cynical view of Strauss's activities and suggests that Strauss may have been sympathetic to the new order at first, especially after the chaos of the Weimar Republic.[22] Dominique Jameux believes that Strauss "must plead guilty," speculating that while it would have been unreasonable to expect him to resist or emigrate, he could have retired into solitude rather than serve the regime, taking the path of "inner emigration."[23]

The 1980s witnessed another turning point in the approaches to Strauss and the Nazis with the publication of studies devoted to music under the Nazi dictatorship. Aside from two unpublished American dissertations written in 1970, the first works since Wulf's documentation to deal exclusively with musical activity under Hitler,[24] no comprehensive study appeared on the subject until 1982, when Fischer-Verlag published Fred Prieberg's *Musik im NS-Staat*. German authors interested in the subject had met with countless obstacles to their research and publication of their findings. Wulf suffered for his disclosure of information exposing individuals in the music world, and

Prieberg found a willing publisher after years of unsuccessful attempts only because 1983 was the fiftieth anniversary of Hitler's seizure of power. The reasons for these difficulties had much to do with the uninterrupted success of certain leading figures in German music after 1945 for whom Wulf's and Prieberg's disclosures were potentially damaging. The central role of music in pre- and postwar German culture probably served as the very reason for its protected "sacred cow" status in the field of Nazi cultural history.

The protracted silence on music under the Nazis ended with an angry outburst. Prieberg's frustrations with acquiring materials, gaining access to archives, and even securing a publishing contract led him to lapse into polemics throughout much of his study. He challenges the consensus that Strauss was politically naive, and his treatment emphasizes the close relationships the composer cultivated with influential party officials, concluding that Strauss experienced the "crowning of [his] career" in the years of the Third Reich.[25] Stephan Kohler took issue with Prieberg's conclusions in a special issue "Musik im Nationalsozialismus" of the *Neue Zeitschrift für Musik*.[26] Kohler believes that it is fallacious to speak of career ambition when describing a long-famous septuagenarian, and it is similarly unjust to dub someone who would try to continue his illegal collaboration with Zweig after his fall from grace as an "exploiter of the Third Reich," as Prieberg does.

Despite its flaws, Prieberg's book gave young scholars the incentive to conduct thorough archival research, and it inspired such works as Gerhard Splitt's exhaustive study on Strauss's presidency in the Music Chamber.[27] Splitt's work, originally a doctoral thesis, offers a thorough presentation of available documents and demonstrates that Strauss's role as a music administrator was far more active and effective than had previously been disclosed. Unfortunately, the author's tone, reminiscent of Prieberg's, carries him to the point of exploiting and often misinterpreting material in an attempt to prove Strauss's egocentrism, anti-Semitism, and political opportunism.

As an introduction to his study, Splitt establishes a theoretical premise of isolating the political aspects of music, relying on quotes from Adorno and Dahlhaus to boost his claims. He hopes to demonstrate how Strauss's music fits these criteria by exhibiting certain "political" features. Splitt also stresses that one cannot separate the artist from the man, as so many of his predecessors have done,[28] and attempts to reexamine all of Strauss's compromising actions in light of evaluating Strauss the man. The time period of his study begins just before Strauss's appointment as Music Chamber president and ends with his resignation. Within this narrow framework, Splitt concludes that Strauss was most concerned with the reception of his music at this particular time in his musical career. Strauss therefore had no qualms about making himself useful to the Nazis as cultural "signboard" (Aushängeschild).[29]

Polemics aside, Splitt displays a remarkable ability to unearth previously unknown archival material. Given the abundant, lengthy quotations—comprising possibly fifty percent of the text—his book might have been more useful as a full-fledged documentary study rather than as a critical monograph. As it stands, however, two significant flaws compromise the value of the work: the narrow focus on two of Strauss's eighty-five years, and the liberties taken in interpreting evidence. Splitt falls into the same trap that had caught so many of his predecessors who were less interested in fact-finding than in reaching a verdict. Strauss biographers thus have continued to manipulate the evidence at hand—quoting it, interpreting it, misinterpreting it, even ignoring it—in an attempt to answer the nagging question: Was he or was he not a Nazi collaborator?

The problem of interpretation of evidence is central to the debate over Strauss and is responsible for the wide variety of judgments regarding his political culpability. Strauss scholars have had to rely heavily on their own interpretation of available documents, accounts by family and friends, memoirs, and even Strauss's musical output in an effort to determine his sympathies. They have left no stone unturned in search of the smallest hints of Strauss's political leanings, producing scraps of evidence from the most unlikely sources. The most unreliable area of investigation has been Strauss's musical style. Certain authors contend that Strauss, regarded at this point in his life as the old guard of composition, might have wanted to ally himself with the Nazis for their shared attitude toward the future of German music. Evidence indicates that Strauss was indeed nationalistic: as president of the Music Chamber, for instance, he tried to regulate music policy by stressing the importance of performing more German music and fewer foreign works.[30] His distaste for atonality was well known and seen most strikingly in his reference to the first meeting of the Permanent Council as an important, "atonal" musical event[31] and in the oft-recounted anecdotes of his exchanges with atonal composers such as Schoenberg and Hindemith.

The interpretation of such evidence, however, has been purely speculative and has often been carried too far. For example, André Ross suggests: "Strauss may justifiably have had some hope that the new regime would reject and regulate the exaggerated 'atonalism' of some artists who, in his opinion, were jeopardizing the future of German music."[32] Even more presumptuous is Splitt's interpretation of Strauss's execution of his duties as president as the realization of his aims to suppress atonality, jazz, popular music, and Italian music. Admitting that Strauss did not actually wage war on jazz and atonality, Splitt nevertheless deduces that Strauss certainly would have sympathized with the Nazis' active campaigns in the press against these types of music.[33]

If some authors can regard his musical style as evidence for his pro-Nazi leanings, others can just as easily look to Strauss's creative output as evidence for his political exoneration. Jameux proposes the unusual theory that Strauss did in fact resist the regime artistically by not producing any masterpieces, only to revive in the few years before his death in his so-called "Indian Summer" period.[34] Individual works composed under the Nazis have also been assessed for their political content: the opera *Friedenstag*, a pacifistic work produced shortly before the outbreak of the Second World War, has been subjected to various interpretations. Ross maintains that the opera, despite its pacifist theme, was "as good and subtle propaganda as could ever be devised . . . [the Commandant] is the spokesman of the tyrant himself and possesses all the qualities which the Nazis glorified in the German male . . . a fanatic."[35] Kohler defends Strauss on the question of *Friedenstag* when he attacks Prieberg for declaring it "fitting for the reality of the NS regime." Even though Prieberg never really made this declaration, Kohler nevertheless accuses him of one of the worst misinterpretations of an incontestable antiwar piece.[36] I also developed the antiwar argument in an article on *Friedenstag*, looking at the ways in which Strauss conveyed a pacifistic message by concealing it behind the façade of politically acceptable stereotypes and musical conventions.[37]

Other authors isolate some of Strauss's actions between 1933 and 1945 and use them as signposts for his political orientation, opportunism, and even anti-Semitism. Krause interprets Strauss's naive insistence that Zweig continue their collaboration after the disaster of *Die schweigsame Frau* as typical behavior for a "prisoner of his own bourgeois freedom."[38] Trenner similarly explains his assumption of the Music Chamber presidency as a manifestation of his opportunism.[39] The allegation that Strauss was an anti-Semite was more difficult to prove. Any anti-Semitic feelings he may have harbored were surely tempered by his relationships with his Jewish colleagues and family members. Nevertheless, Antoine Goléa blames Strauss for not emigrating and for writing an ingratiating plea to Hitler to spare his daughter-in-law without showing the least concern for any other Jews, thereby glorifying Hitler's anti-Semitic aims.[40] Here Goléa stands on shaky ground: his allusion to the ingratiating plea to Hitler to spare his daughter-in-law is a misreading of Panofsky's reference to the letter to Hitler published by Wulf, which contains no such plea.[41]

The Bruno Walter affair has also served as "tangible proof" of Strauss's anti-Semitism. The event is a source of embarrassment, leaving even the most well-meaning biographers at a loss for an explanation, and one author, Otto Erhardt, omits it entirely from his biography. In the inflammatory letter to Zweig (the letter intercepted by the Gestapo), Strauss does indeed describe Walter as a "mean and lousy scoundrel" ("schmierigen Lauselumpen"),[42] which indicates some personal dislike for Walter. But Splitt strives to prove that Strauss stepped in for Walter not only out of personal vengeance but also out of loyalty to the Nazi authorities and latent anti-Semitism. Splitt claims to have evidence of Strauss's long-harbored animosity toward Walter and speculates that Strauss saw this event as an opportunity to get revenge on Walter for not having performed his operas in Munich over the years.[43] After initially refusing to step in for Walter, Strauss finally conceded at the urging of the Jewish concert agent Luise Wolff and of Hugo Rasch and Julius Kopsch, both of whom were in the Nazi Party. Splitt thus concludes that Strauss's action, because it involved the influence of two Nazis who were personal friends, can only be seen as a concession to the Nazi government, hence demonstrating guilt by association.[44] He further concludes that even if Strauss were unaware of the anti-Semitic implications, he was still guilty of an anti-Semitic act.[45]

The more general questions concerning Strauss's relationship to the Nazi government have also rested entirely on the interpretation of evidence. Despite the abundance of documentation from government archives, official publications, and private correspondences, this issue has prompted a wide variety of conclusions drawn from the same materials, pointing out once again the fickleness that is characteristic of writing history. The first important revelation showing the vicissitudes of the relationship came with the publication of Wulf's collection. Wulf published Strauss's speech praising Hitler and Goebbels at the opening of the Music Chamber and the ingratiating letter sent to Hitler following his forced resignation, as well as complaints by Nazi organizations against the participation of Jews other than Zweig in the production of Die schweigsame Frau, the reactions to his refusal to cooperate during the war, and documentation of Martin Bormann's campaign to defame him in the press.[46] The letter to Hitler was perhaps the most shocking revelation for Strauss enthusiasts. Marek described it as the "nadir of Strauss's morality"[47] and used it as a springboard to give more attention than any other biographer to Strauss's activities in Nazi Germany. Even the most defensive of biographers could not ignore it: Panofsky, for example, could only regret its having been written, because it sounded respectful, and he is convinced that Strauss did not mean to be respectful.[48]

The next wave of new evidence pertaining to the relationship appeared in Prieberg's study, which is often frustrating in that it withholds specific citations for important documents.[49] Prieberg first challenges the consensus that Die schweigsame Frau was banned and, again without citing sources, demonstrates that it was instead "frozen" by the boycotts of the Nazi theater organizations.[50] He proceeds to throw much doubt upon the commonly held notion that Strauss suffered after the Schweigsame Frau affair as a persona non grata and maintains that, all in all, Strauss managed to do quite well under the Nazis by rubbing elbows with some of the highly influential Nazi elite. After being forced to step down as president of the Music Chamber, he had no difficulties living off his operas, which were performed widely throughout Germany. Furthermore, as president of the newly formed Permanent Council for International Cooperation of Composers, set up as a German challenge to the International Society for New Music, he lost none of his influence with the German government.

Prieberg supports his conclusions by describing instances that he equates with Strauss's attempts to come closer to the regime in the years following his dismissal: plans to compose a work for the "holy place" of Hindenburg's grave; settings of "national" texts by Weinheber that were concealed after 1945; an indirect commission from the Propaganda Ministry for the Japanische Festmusik in honor of twenty-six hundred years of the Japanese Empire; his election in 1942 as president of the Permanent Council for another five years; his ties with Baldur von Schirach; and his composition in 1943 of the Festmusik der Stadt Wien in commemoration of the fifth anniversary of the annexation of Austria.[51] Yet some of Prieberg's evidence is also contestable: Kohler demonstrates that the commissioned compositions mentioned by Prieberg were not commissioned by the government at all[52] and has accused Prieberg of ignoring the facts in his attempts to brand the Weinheber songs as nationalistic and to claim that the family tried to suppress them.[53]

The whole issue of the Weinheber songs and of commissioned works in general is a slippery one, raising questions about the origins of commissions and the intentions of dedications. It has given rise to debates over certain other works that might clarify Strauss's relationship to the Nazis, the best-known of which concerns the song "Das Bächlein." Norman Del Mar first drew attention to the song for its potential link to the National Socialists when he sadly remarked on its dedication to Goebbels at the opening of the Music Chamber. He quoted its closing text: "der mich gerufen aus dem Stein, der, denk ich, wird mein Führer, mein Führer, mein Führer sein!," presumably an indirect reference to Hitler.[54] Splitt carries Del Mar's speculation much farther, conscientiously carrying out a line-by-line analysis of the musical setting of the text. He concludes that the entire text, not just the last line, must be praising the Third Reich, and that the musical setting, which adds a sequential repetition on the word "mein Führer," reinforces his declaration of solidarity with Nazi aesthetics and cultural aims.[55] Once again Splitt seems to have let himself be led by his polemics; the mere repetition of the word "mein Führer" in the musical setting falls short as proof of Strauss's intended allusion to Hitler. Nevertheless, given the occasion of the opening of the Chamber, the dedication to Goebbels,[56] and especially the significance of Hitler's *Führer* designation in 1933, Strauss's choice of text was probably not coincidental.

At the center of the controversy over Strauss's relationship to the Nazis is the incontrovertible fact of his presidency in the Reich Music Chamber. Though few biographers have dared to ignore it, Strauss protagonists first confronted the issue but then argued around it by relying on the consensus of Strauss's "apolitical nature." Trenner attributes Strauss's acceptance of the post to his aim of ensuring that his works would be performed,[57] and Kralik maintains that the apolitical Strauss had no choice but to accept the appointment, because to do otherwise would have been to take a political stand.[58] Panofsky introduced the idea that Strauss was given the post without its being offered to him beforehand but, once in that position, refused to bow to the heads of the Nazi state any more than he would have to those of any other state.[59] This view was generally accepted for a number of years, until Splitt decided to investigate further. His thorough search furnished important new evidence, the most significant being a telegram in which Strauss is asked if he will accept the presidency. This vital document finally puts to rest the notion that Strauss was given the position without being asked.[60]

Splitt's monograph is by far the most detailed study of Strauss's presidency and provides us with substantial documentation indicating that Strauss was serious about his responsibilities and saw the new system as holding great potential for improving the lot of the artist in society.[61] Unfortunately, questionable interpretive methods lead Splitt to generalize that because Strauss recognized some useful aspects of Nazi cultural policy, he also must have been in favor of the entire Nazi program, including anti-Semitism.[62] The assumption that Strauss was aware of the dictatorial basis of the Culture

Chamber in 1933 furnishes proof for Splitt that Strauss must have known that the Nazis intended to take control of cultural life and to exploit German culture in the years that followed.[63] Historically speaking, however, the contrary seems more plausible: the Nazis chose Strauss, an influential composer, rather than a bureaucrat to head the Music Chamber and gave him full administrative power. This would indicate their intentions to leave the administration of musical matters in the hands of the musicians, at least at the outset.

Splitt's presumptions regarding Strauss's role in the Music Chamber create a domino effect, as one speculation engenders subsequent, more far-fetched conclusions. These lead inevitably to inconsistencies, faulty logic, and total disregard for the evidence at hand. Tracing the prehistory of the Music Chamber appointment, Splitt speculates that Strauss's act of stepping in for Toscanini at Bayreuth was calculated to bring him closer to being elected president.[64] He also speculates that by the fall of 1934, Strauss had become too powerful, that the Nazis must have wanted to get rid of him at that point, and that he must have been aware of their desire but adamantly refused to step down.[65] This scenario is based on slim evidence subjected to broad interpretation, yet Splitt allows such shaky conclusions to bear weight in determining Strauss's political aims.

Splitt also overlooks some glaring contradictions in his study of Strauss's role as president. Having demonstrated that Strauss delegated much of the administrative authority to Heinz Ihlert (business manager of the Music Chamber), he still holds Strauss responsible for all of Ihlert's directives issued "in the name of the President."[66] Yet he later cites an entire document that includes complaints that Strauss took no responsibility as president, leaving Ihlert to do all the work.[67] That same document criticizes Strauss for refusing to sign the charter of the composer's branch of the Chamber, for which he also served as president, because the charter foresaw the exclusion of Jews from the organization.[68] Having already established to his own satisfaction that Strauss was an incorrigible anti-Semite, Splitt simply ignores this detail.

Splitt's study cannot hope to tell us much about Strauss's character or his personal development by subjecting two years out of a sixty-five-year career to such close scrutiny. The very years which Splitt isolates—the first two following Hitler's seizure of power—tell us even less about society under the Nazi government and Strauss's role in it than any other two years between 1933 and 1945 the author could have chosen. Any positive impressions a German citizen may have had of the new government, any hopes and expectations held in 1933, cannot be assumed to have persisted to the end of the Second World War or even beyond 1938, when the *Reichskristallnacht*, the *Anschluss*, and ultimately the invasion of Poland brought the Nazis' political and anti-Semitic agenda into full view. Moreover, this two-year scope exemplifies larger problems in scholarship devoted to music during the Third Reich. The works of Wulf, Prieberg, and a few others offered a short-lived promise that studies on music in Nazi Germany would proliferate and mature. Instead, scholarship has lapsed back into the pitfalls of the biographical obsession. Splitt not only turns his attention away from broader issues of music under the Nazis and back to the old Strauss controversy, he also concentrates on a very brief episode in the composer's life at that, offering little insight into the reactions of Strauss and of other Germans to the entire twelve-year dictatorship.

Splitt's work may represent the culmination of investigations into Strauss's Nazi past, and it seems unlikely that further archival studies could unearth new evidence that would radically alter the composite picture we now have of those years. Yet after decades of digging, compiling, analyzing, and disputing, biographers have still not been able to determine Strauss's culpability. Scholars today have shown no more historical perspective, no more critical insight, than those who eulogized the composer in 1949, despite the advantage of chronological distance. Peter Heyworth, a notable exception, was one of the few to relate Strauss's Nazi experience to his precarious placement in history. Heyworth shows how Strauss's dizzying rise to fame at an early age, combined with financial security and a stable family life, provoked attacks from envious contemporaries against his apparent arrogance and opportunism. These petty jealousies overshadowed his earnest efforts to further the careers of less successful colleagues. Heyworth contributes a more objective look at the composer's personality and, above all, his precarious position in history, but by and large, studies have focused so exclusively on the issue of political labeling that they have ignored the question of what we as historians can learn from Strauss's saga.

Most of the authors discussed here have posed the same questions repeatedly, striving for a concrete characterization of Strauss's political behavior. Was Strauss naive and apolitical, or was he an opportunist interested only in having his works performed? Was he a musical conservative, an enemy of modern music and jazz acting to suppress anything that did not conform to his standards? Was he acting for the good of German music and musicians as president of the Music Chamber and an advocate for copyright protection? If so, was this also opportunism, since he himself was a German musician and composer? Was he not only an opportunist, but a callously devious one as well? Was he a rebellious figurehead who accepted the honors showered upon him as he would under any system with the same contempt and disrespect for authority? Was he a puppet of the Nazi political machinery, a signboard of cultural integrity, a victim of exploitation, or a powerful music dictator? Was he a resistance fighter, an advocate of pacifism on the eve of war, or a collaborator? Was he anti-Semitic, or was he worried for the safety of his Jewish family members, or was he both? Does his collaboration with Zweig disprove his anti-Semitism, or does it prove his disrespect for the Nazis, his naiveté, or his concern only for the success of his music?

Authors have also used their knowledge of Strauss's experiences to ask in retrospect how he could or should have behaved under the circumstances. Should he have openly protested? Should he have emigrated? Should he at least have gone into inner emigration? Should he have refused to be a false symbol of cultural integrity in an otherwise depraved society? Should he have known of the Nazis' extreme anti-Semitism and used his position to combat it? Should he have been aware of the Nazis' designs on culture, and if so should he have refused to cooperate, or should he have worked within the system to hinder them?

The usefulness of bestowing a convenient political label or of passing moral judgment is questionable. In the case of Strauss, some may argue that this process served to resolve one difficult practical problem of the ban in Israel that lasted until 1982. Others would argue that arriving at a verdict for Strauss aids us in understanding his works of that period: Splitt's line-by-line analysis of "Das Bächlein," for example, or Jameux's "Indian Summer" theory claims to deepen our understanding of his works by regarding their historical and psychological contexts. But in general, these exercises in armchair political analysis contribute little to music-historical scholarship and disregard the advances in historical inquiry that now guide other approaches to the study of the Third Reich.

Serious scholars must be careful not to indulge in the smugness of twenty-twenty hindsight, especially when studying the Nazi period, and Strauss scholars must be especially careful not to rely too heavily on the journalistic excesses of much of the existing literature. The aims of past authors were often simplistic: in the spirit of the highly controversial procedure of denazification, authors interested in Strauss posed the same kind of questions that one would have heard in Allied tribunals. The dearth of knowledge on musical life in Nazi Germany was one more obstacle for Strauss biographers in that the questions they asked about the choices of one individual had no learned foundation and no basis for comparison. Without an understand-ing of the operation of musical institutions, the function of the government in musical life, and the role of music performance, music scholarship, and music criticism in the broader propaganda mechanism, scholars had no op-portunity to evaluate Strauss's activities within their proper context. It was useful to treat the topic as an episode in Strauss's long and varied life, as some authors chose to do, but even this approach fell short of attaining a necessary level of objectivity in dealing with the complexity of his experience in the Nazi years.

One can place the blame for this scholarly deficiency on several heads. First, cultural historians examined all other arts in Nazi Germany but ignored music. Second, music historians wrote the history of modern German music by focusing on the 1920s, the activities of German composers in exile in the 1930s and '40s, and postwar developments, but ignored the situation within Nazi Germany. Whatever the cause, the result is the same: anyone interested in evaluating Strauss's activities in the Third Reich cannot expect to get be-yond the shortcomings of prior attempts without a broader knowledge of musical life in Nazi Germany, and such knowledge cannot be acquired with-out more critical studies of this period as an acknowledged period of music history.

Where does this leave the Strauss scholar today? Having virtually exhausted archival material and uncovered all or at least most of the significant docu-ments, having indulged our fascination with the lives of the famous com-bined with our fascination with the Nazis over the last forty years, it is now our responsibility to use the materials available in a more constructive man-ner. I would like to propose that we view Strauss in a broader social context and look at him not for what he might or should have been but for what he unquestionably was: musician, composer, international celebrity, German, late romanticist, advocate for copyright protection, and senior citizen.

Even though adequate studies of musical life are not yet available, we can draw on work done in other areas of the history of Nazi Germany to place Strauss in proper perspective. Looking at Strauss in this light presents him as an interesting case study of one response to the Nazi system as a represen-tative of his profession and his generation. Wulf's and Splitt's documenta-tion provides evidence of Strauss's earnestness especially at the beginning of his term as president of the Music Chamber. His long years of involvement in composers' organizations and in the copyright struggle are further testi-mony to his concerns for the legal protection of musicians and composers. The frustrations with earlier systems, the degradation of Germany after the

First World War, the chaos of the Weimar Republic, and perhaps even the perceived threats to tonality could have led Strauss to believe that the Nazis would not only restore order but would systematically improve the lot of cultural professionals.

Recent studies on Nazi cultural policy have revealed that many, if not most, professionals in the art world welcomed the changes proposed by the Nazis. The Weimar Republic lacked any kind of effective centralized administration of cultural matters, and the effects of general unemployment combined with budget cuts for cultural institutions left the majority of professionals in a disgruntled state. When the Nazis proposed to organize and regulate all cultural life under the auspices of the newly formed Propaganda Ministry, many undoubtedly welcomed the reforms as a new opportunity for job security. The Reich Chamber of Culture, of which the Music Chamber was a subdivision, gave cultural professionals opportunities to achieve long-standing professional goals, to expand and regulate the cultural marketplace, and to set up a social insurance system; it was not primarily concerned with censorship and the expulsion of Jews, as most histories have assumed.[69] Strauss, as an advocate for the security of German composers and of German music as a whole, was surely among the many who greeted the new policies with optimism and enthusiasm.

As for Strauss's direct relationship to Nazi officials, the recently published diaries of Joseph Goebbels may provide new insights into Strauss's role and his personality. Goebbels's direct references to Strauss are rather sparse, but many of the passages in which he mentions Strauss express his contempt for Strauss's persistence on certain pet issues regarding music policy. At the same time, Goebbels frequently hastens to add his utmost respect for Strauss the composer in spite of personal friction between them.[70] One revealing example of Strauss's importance as a cultural "signboard" is the entry of 27 August 1937, in which Goebbels reports: "Richard Strauss is ill. Unfortunately he cannot conduct in Paris. A great loss for us."

Since 1945 we have gradually become aware that most Germans were not resistance fighters, despite the overwhelming number of postwar allegations that would have us think otherwise. Placed in the difficult position of interpreting the Third Reich with the knowledge of Auschwitz, historians need to overcome this hurdle and consider the material advantages and the promise of a bright future that the Nazis offered the average German in the early years. Each German who chose not to emigrate was certainly faced at one point with the problem of rationalizing material advantages with distasteful ideological extremes. For Strauss that was especially true, since he dealt directly with so many pressing issues and experienced the Nazi government on so many different levels—as an official, as a celebrity, as a *persona non grata*, and as a friend, partner, and close relative of Jews.

To that extent, Strauss serves as an interesting case study, but little else. It is far too simplistic to expect to be able to determine whether Strauss is to be considered a Nazi or not. We cannot hope to arrive at a definitive moral verdict, nor should we expect to understand music under the Nazis on the basis of the experiences of one individual. But we can hope to use what we have learned from Strauss's story to gain insight into the concerns and attitudes of an individual in a position such as his, and we can weave this knowledge into the complex fabric of popular reaction to the Nazi dictatorship.

Notes

1 Kurt Pfister, *Richard Strauss: Weg, Gestalt, Denkmal* (Vienna: Berglandverlag, 1949); Claude Rostand, *Richard Strauss* (Paris: La Colombe, 1949); and Roland Tenschert, *Richard Strauss und Wien* (Vienna: Brüder Hollinek, 1949). Pfister mentions only that *Die schweigsame Frau* was banned.

2 Otto Erhardt, *Richard Strauss: Leben, Wirken, Schaffen* (Olten: Otto Walter, 1953), pp. 53–59.

3 Ibid., p. 71.

4 Heinrich Kralik, *Richard Strauss: Weltbürger der Musik* (Vienna: Wollzeilen, 1963), pp. 301–3.

5 Franz Trenner, *Richard Strauss: Dokumente seines Lebens und Schaffens* (Munich: C.H. Beck, 1954), p. 231.

6 Ernst Krause, *Richard Strauss: Gestalt und Werk* (Leipzig: Breitkopf & Härtel, 1955), pp. 5, 39–40. Translated by John Coombs as *Richard Strauss: The Man and His Work* (London: Collett's, 1964).

7 Ibid., pp. 52–55.

8 Ibid., p. 55.

9 An exemplary document is Eberhard Otto's discussion of Strauss's culpability in an article in the German-language periodical *Israel-Forum*. Here the author goes to extremes to explain Strauss's good intentions, even giving Strauss credit for resigning from the Music Chamber voluntarily after the fiasco of *Die schweigsame Frau*. Eberhard Otto, "Richard Strauss und das 'Dritte Reich'," *Israel-Forum* 1 (1967): 12–14.

10 Joseph Wulf, *Musik im Dritten Reich* (Gütersloh: Sigbert Mohn, 1963; repr. Frankfurt: Ullstein, 1983).

11 Walter Panofsky, *Richard Strauss: Partitur eines Lebens* (Munich: Piper, 1965), pp. 296–99.

12 George Marek, *Richard Strauss: The Life of a Non-Hero* (New York: Simon and Schuster, 1967), pp. 270–71.

13 Ibid., pp. 272–74.

14 Ibid., p. 287.

15 Ibid., p. 288.

16 "The Rise and Fall of Richard Strauss," *Encounter* 31 (1968): 49–53.

17 Ibid., p. 53.

18 Norman Del Mar, *Richard Strauss: A Critical Commentary of his Life and Works*, vol. 3 (Philadelphia: Chilton, 1972), pp. 45, 47.

19   Ibid., p. 48.

20   Michael Kennedy, *Richard Strauss* (London: J.M. Dent, 1976), p. 95.

21   Alan Jefferson, *The Life of Richard Strauss* (Newton Abbott: David & Charles, 1973), pp. 193–96; and *Richard Strauss* (London: Macmillan, 1975), pp. 89–101.

22   André Ross, *Richard Strauss: His Life and Work* (Toronto: Rococo Records, 1976).

23   Dominique Jameux, *Richard Strauss* (Paris: Editions de Seuil, 1977; new rev. ed.: Hachette, 1986), 140–41.

24   Michael Meyer, "Assumptions and Implementation of Nazi Policy toward Music" (Ph.D. diss., University of California at Los Angeles, 1970); and Donald Wesley Ellis, "Music in the Third Reich: National Socialist Aesthetic Theory as Governmental Policy" (Ph.D. diss., University of Kansas, 1970).

25   Fred K. Prieberg, *Musik im NS-Staat* (Frankfurt: Fischer, 1982), p. 203.

26   Stephan Kohler, " 'Ich als "Verfemter des Geistes" . . .'. Richard Strauss und das Dritte Reich. Zur Legendenbildung in der Musikgeschichtsschreibung," *Neue Zeitschrift für Musik* 144 (1983): 4–6.

27   Gerhard Splitt, *Richard Strauss 1933–35: Ästhetik und Musikpolitik zu Beginn der nationalsozialistischen Herrschaft* (Pfaffenweiler: Centaurus, 1987).

28   Ibid., pp. 40–41.

29   Ibid., p. 20.

30   The documents selected and compiled by Kurt Wilhelm in his illustrated biography of Strauss reveal the more reactionary and nationalistic aspects of Strauss's musical taste. See Kurt Wilhelm, *Richard Strauss persönlich: eine Bildbiographie* (Munich: Kindler, 1984), pp. 317, 318, 322.

31   Letter to Hausegger, quoted in Wilhelm, p. 322.

32   Ross, p. 32.

33   Splitt, p. 119.

34   Jameux, pp. 141–42.

35   Ross, p. 32. According to Bryan Gilliam, unpublished letters reveal that Zweig was largely responsible for the text of *Friedenstag*; thus, the allegation that it was a piece of Nazi propaganda is, at best, very weak.

36   Kohler, p. 6. See also Prieberg, p. 212.

37   Pamela M. Potter, "Strauss's *Friedenstag*: A Pacifist Attempt at Political Resistance," *The Musical Quarterly* 69 (1983): 408–24.

38   Krause, p. 57.

39   Trenner, p. 231.

40   Antoine Goléa, *Richard Strauss* (Paris: Flammarion, 1965), pp. 231–37.

41   Goléa had access to Panofsky's manuscript while preparing his book.

42   Strauss to Zweig, quoted in Splitt, p. 219. Splitt's footnote on the censorship of this term by the editors of Strauss's letters also makes interesting reading. The term is replaced by ellipses in the German edition of the Strauss-Zweig correspondence; it is completely omitted in the English translation; and it is misquoted in Kurt Wilhelm's illustrated biography (p. 328) as "schmieriger Lausejunge." Splitt confronted the editor of the letters about the omission and got the explanation that Strauss used this "ugly" term in a moment of excitement and surely would have retracted the statement a few days later. Splitt, p. 260, n. 755.

43   Splitt, p. 46. In fact, the early letters he cites include only brief references to Walter, some of which are sarcastic but hardly vindictive.

44   Ibid., p. 49.

45   Ibid., p. 58.

46   Wulf, pp. 194–202.

47   Marek, p. 283.

48   Panofsky, p. 295.

49   All too frequently the author simply states that "a copy is in the possession of the author," a citation which is of little use to the serious scholar.

50   Prieberg, p. 208.

51   Ibid., pp. 210–13.

52   Kohler, p. 5.

53   Ibid., p. 6.

54   Del Mar, pp. 395–96. The poem speaks throughout of a stream. The final stanza can be translated as follows: "Therefore I have a happy feeling of childhood, / It drives me forward, I know not whither. / The one that called me from the stone, / I believe will be my leader."

55   Splitt, pp. 87ff.

56   The dedication, as transcribed by Splitt, reads as follows: "Herrn Reichsminister Dr. Joseph Goebbels / zur Erinnerung an den 15. November 1933 / verehrungsvoll zugeeignet von / Richard Strauss." Splitt, p. 81.

57   Trenner, p. 231.

58   Kralik, p. 302.

59   Panofsky, pp. 282ff., 297.

60   Splitt, p. 81.

61   Ibid., pp. 92ff.

62   Ibid., pp. 97–98.

63   Ibid., p. 75.

64   Ibid., pp. 62–63.

65   Ibid., pp. 212ff.

66   Ibid., p. 170.

67   Ibid., pp. 209–10.

68   Ibid.

69   Alan E. Steinweis, "The Reich Chamber of Culture and the Regulation of the Culture Professions in Nazi Germany" (Ph.D. diss., University of North Carolina at Chapel Hill, 1988).

70   Elke Fröhlich, ed., *Die Tagebücher von Joseph Goebbels: Teil I: Aufzeichnungen 1924–1941* (Munich: K.G. Saur, 1987). Goebbels's comments on Strauss are found in the following entries: 23.7.33 and 24.7.33 (Goebbels first meets Strauss at Bayreuth); 21.5.34 (negative opinion of *Intermezzo*); 5.7.35, 10.7.35 and 13.7.35 (course of action on intercepted letter, cancellations, forced resignation); 20.6.36, 22.7.36, 16.12.36, 27.8.37, and 11.6.40 (opinion of *Olympische Hymne*, personal complaints against Strauss); 30.1.41, 1.3.41, and 7.3.41 (Strauss's collaboration with other composers to protect serious music and to take away financial advantages from popular music).

Die Händler und die Kunst:
Richard Strauss as Composers' Advocate

Barbara A. Petersen

▼

As both composer and conductor Richard Strauss serves as a model for present-day musicians, musical organizations, and administrators in his concern for composers' rights. A founder of the first German performing rights society, Strauss was a shrewd businessman in his negotiations with publishers, opera houses, and other professional associates. Between resident conducting engagements, tours and guest appearances, and summers largely devoted to creating new compositions, he also found time to attend to the practical business aspects of his multifaceted career. It has been estimated that Strauss wrote at least ten business letters a day throughout most of his adult life.[1] And although by the early twentieth century Strauss began to suffer from negative criticism for creating "not music but merchandise," time has in fact proven that much of his music is of lasting importance. A large number of his orchestral, operatic, and solo works are now accepted throughout the world as part of the standard repertory.

The young Strauss was fortunate in having a wealthy family to pay production costs for his first few printed works. In 1881 Breitkopf & Härtel issued his first publication, the Festmarsch, op. 1, composed in 1876. Strauss's uncle, brewery owner Georg Pschorr, to whom the nine-minute march is dedicated, subsidized the engraving costs. Yet at the same time, Breitkopf turned down two other works: the String Quartet, op. 2, and the Symphony in D Minor (AV 69).[2] By 1881 it was time for the young Strauss to find a publisher: all three of these works were receiving world premieres in March, the month after Strauss approached Breitkopf & Härtel. The symphony was not published for a century (by B. Schotts Söhne in 1980), possibly because the composer gave exclusive performing rights to the Wilde Gung'l, and thus a publisher could not have benefited from performances by other groups or expected a profit from it.

Following Breitkopf's rejection, Strauss turned to the Munich publishing house of Joseph Aibl, at the time headed by Eugen Spitzweg.[3] Thus began a long and fascinating composer-publisher relationship, which would result in a series of over thirty publications. Aibl was Strauss's principal—though not exclusive—publisher from the op. 2 quartet (composed in 1881) through a set of *Sechs Lieder*, op. 37 (completed in 1898). Over one hundred and twenty letters and postcards from Strauss to Eugen Spitzweg are part of the manuscript collection of the Munich Stadtbibliothek (housed at Monacensis);[4] some of these have been published or excerpted in writings by Alfons Ott and Willi Schuh in particular.[5] But the majority of Spitzweg's letters to Strauss most likely do not survive.[6] A second substantial collection of composer-publisher letters is less well known: it belongs to the Leipzig Staatsarchiv. Unlike the letters to Spitzweg, the Leipzig collection has rarely been cited in the standard Strauss literature.[7] These Strauss letters[8]—and many others to various correspondents—report on nearly every performance he conducted, all contractual dealings for publishing and conducting, and other detailed professional matters. Together with his unpublished diaries, they provide a full picture of his professional concerns in the years 1889 to 1904.

At the beginning of Strauss's struggle to be accepted as a published composer, his father, Franz Strauss, had to pay the engraving and printing costs for one of his son's first large works, the (Second) Symphony in F Minor, op. 12. Subsequently, the young composer sold his works to Aibl and other publishers according to the usual nineteenth-century custom: for a single one-time fee, without hope of future royalties or artistic control over new versions. By 1898, Strauss was writing to Spitzweg demanding better terms; he wanted to grant only publication, or print rights, and demanded a twenty-five percent return for himself on all the early works up to *Guntram*, op. 25. Strauss insisted on retaining performing rights, rights to arrangements, and other uses of his music. Today, lawyers speak of this as a "bundle of rights" relating to various aspects of copyright in compositions; one can imagine that Strauss would also have demanded control over mechanical and synchronization rights had these possibilities existed at the end of the nineteenth century.

At a time when Strauss's annual resident conductor's salary was only 2,000–3,000 DM, he sold his works to Joseph Aibl for such sums (in DM) as:

Orchestral works

500	*Aus Italien*, op. 16
800	*Don Juan*, op. 20
1,600	*Tod und Verklärung*, op. 24

| 1,000 | Till Eulenspiegel, op. 28 |
| 10,000 | Ein Heldenleben, op. 40 |

Lieder and choruses

200	Acht Gedichte, op. 10
200	Schlichte Weisen (5 songs), op. 21
500	Drei Lieder, op. 29
2,000	Zwei Gesänge for sixteen-voice mixed chorus, op. 34

When offering works to other publishers, his fees became considerably higher:

800	Mädchenblumen (4 songs), op. 22 (Adolph Fürstner)
35,000	Symphonia Domestica, op. 53 (Bote & Bock)
6,000	Zwei Militärmärsche, op. 57 (C. F. Peters)
50,000	Eine Alpensinfonie, op. 64 (F. E. C. Leuckart)

For Guntram, published 1894/95, Strauss asked 5,000 DM; a few years later, in 1898, he demanded twice as much for Ein Heldenleben.[9] In 1890, he proudly informed Spitzweg that he had just sold the four songs in op. 22 to Fürstner for 800 DM. He claimed to have named his high price out of sheer bravado, but when Fürstner tried to bargain, Strauss stood firm and got his fee.[10] At about the same time he offered Macbeth to the publishing house of C. F. Peters for 1,500 DM; Spitzweg advised him against placing Macbeth there and took it into his own catalog. For their part, Peters felt they should not steal him away from Spitzweg, but left the door open for future works.

While Strauss's songs of the 1880s and '90s were very likely to be successful and widely sold, Spitzweg repeatedly complained of the attendant publishing expenses. Most of Strauss's lieder were issued in high, medium and low voice editions (each requiring separate engraving), singly and in opus groups, and with various "singing" translations of the texts. Publishing instrumental works was a simpler matter: no texts to be typeset and translated, and just one version of score and parts to be engraved.[11]

By 1898–99, Strauss began to look for other publishers and sold opp. 39–44 to other firms in Berlin and Leipzig before settling on the firm of Adolph Fürstner with op. 45 (1900).[12] By then he was clearly an important enough composer and conductor to command higher fees than Spitzweg was willing to pay. The idea of a move was doubly important because Spitzweg was trying to sell the Aibl firm and could not find a buyer in Munich. Bitterly, Strauss pointed out that no music publisher in his own native city would publish works by one of its most famous composers.

This disappointment made Strauss all the more sensitive, since the public in Munich had deemed his *Guntram* to be an operatic failure upon its production there in 1895.[13] His second opera, *Feuersnot* (1901), which mocked and sniped at the citizenry of Munich, is an important outward manifestation of Strauss's frustration and rejection. Although based on a twelfth-century Netherlandish legend, Ernst von Wolgozen's libretto is a diatribe against Munich on several levels. To the librettist's topical references and double meanings, Strauss added the equivalent in music, so that the entire work would have a tone of irony, mockery, and protest against philistinism, conventional operatic texts, and even the Munich Opera Intendant, Baron von Perfall.[14]

Just at the time Strauss was looking around for a new publisher, he was also thinking about forming a society to protect the rights of composers in Germany. This was not a revolutionary idea, since the first such society actually dates from 1851, the French Société des auteurs, compositeurs et éditeurs de musique, or SACEM.[15]

In 1898 Strauss met with composers Hans Sommer (1837–1922) and Friedrich Rösch (1862–1925) to initiate plans for their proposed society. Strauss sent a circular to some one hundred sixty German composers[16] and received one hundred nineteen replies within a few weeks. After lengthy deliberations among the triumvirate and a Leipzig meeting with interested composers on 30 September 1901, Strauss and his colleagues officially called the Genossenschaft Deutscher Tonsetzer (GDT) into existence on 14 January 1903 with a membership of one hundred fifty. Another hundred composers joined within ninety days, and by July they had established a new Anstalt für musikalische Aufführungsrechte (abbreviated AFMA, AfmA, or AMA), an institute to look after the administrative aspects of performing rights.

At the outset, publishers, theater managers, and concert presenters— the bureaucracy of the music world—felt threatened by the money-hungry ("geldgieriger") Strauss and his self-protective instincts. Almost none of the nineteenth-century laws, including the Berne Convention statutes (1878) and the *droit moral* or *Persönlichkeitsrecht* (1890), extended coverage to musical works.[17] It took a new German copyright law on literary and musical works in 1901 to provide the legal basis for German performing rights royalties, and a system was clearly needed to administer them.

Performing rights societies exist to protect composers and publishers; in most countries the society is specifically named in copyright or other creative property laws. The 1901 German law did not make clear whether the performance rights being protected belonged to the composer or the publisher. Even before the 1901 law was passed, Strauss wrote to Spitzweg at Aibl that in the future he could no longer turn over performing rights to his publisher. This was the main goal of the GDT, he claimed, and as a founder he could not set a bad example:

> Publication rights to the publisher,
> Creator's rights to the creator.
> There will be no other way in the future![18]

As it turns out, he was wrong; today it is standard practice for "small" or nondramatic performing rights to be assigned to the publisher.

Through the GDT Strauss and his colleagues demanded—and ultimately obtained—protection of the melodic content in a work and control of permission in reprints, especially in collections and anthologies, which were of great value to Strauss, particularly for lieder. The length of copyright coverage also concerned GDT members: at the time their society was founded, coverage extended only thirty years beyond a creator's death (or the death of the longest-surviving collaborator, for example, either the composer or the librettist of an opera). Since French law set coverage at fifty years, several German publishers set up French branches. Only in 1935 was German copyright coverage extended to fifty years after the longest-surviving creator's death; in 1965, the period was extended to seventy years, where it remains today.

In 1915 yet another German performing rights society came into being, the Genossenschaft zur Verwertung musikalischer Aufführungsrechte, the first GEMA.[19] By 1933 the various German performing rights societies merged under yet another acronym, STAGMA (Staatlich genehmigte Gesellschaft zur Verwertung musikalischer Urheberrechte). After World War II the initials GEMA were again adopted, this time standing for a new name: Gesellschaft für musikalische Aufführungs- und mechanische Vervielfältigungsrechte. GEMA, which also licenses mechanical and synchronization rights from its Berlin and Munich headquarters, is probably the most influential performing rights organization in the world today. Recently it has collected more than 600 million DM annually. GEMA's president through 1989, Erich Schulze, has long been a friend of the Strauss family and has contributed to Strauss scholarship.[20] In 1983, Schulze received the Richard Strauss Medal for "extraordinary service to copyright." This medal is aptly named, since the results of Strauss's campaigning for copyright protection for composers endure today not only in Germany, but throughout most of the world.

The history of the German performing rights societies is complex, and Strauss monitored the new developments carefully. It is no coincidence that his early efforts to establish protection for composers date from the time of his turn-of-the-century search for the most suitable publisher. After two decades of assigning most works to Aibl, Strauss entered into his first contract with Adolph Fürstner in 1900; its terms practically guaranteed him an annual income. When Strauss wrote Spitzweg about the change, he casually announced, "My new publisher—I forgot to tell you recently—is Fürstner." [21] When the option for renewal of an exclusive contract with Fürstner came in 1903, Strauss turned it down because he did not want to feel compelled to produce for his publishers.

Meanwhile, Strauss's old friend Spitzweg was trying to interest the Berlin firm Bote & Bock in taking over the Joseph Aibl catalog, in which Strauss was by far the most important composer. After Hugo Bock turned down the offer, Strauss expressed displeasure: because no German publisher wanted his works, he lamented, he would have to accept an Austrian firm as his new publisher.[22] This turned out not to be so lamentable; Universal Edition, founded in 1901, is of course one of the preeminent publishers today, and Strauss himself later developed strong ties to the musical life of Vienna.

But Bote & Bock was not completely out of the picture; in fact, they had already issued Strauss's first set of orchestral songs, op. 33, in 1897, and in 1903 agreed to publish the *Symphonia Domestica*, op. 53.[23] Since the *Symphonia Domestica* was a large work, it was an expensive investment for Hugo Bock. Strauss reported to C. F. Peters that he sold the work to Bock for 35,000 DM. Peters would have offered "only" 30,000. In return, Bock required Strauss to sign a contract allowing them to publish his next set of lieder, from which they hoped to make a considerable income. This collection was to be in addition to the set of six songs in op. 56, which had been accepted by the publisher along with the *Symphonia*. When Strauss created no more new songs, the publisher eventually threatened to sue him for breach of contract.

Certainly the fact that Bote & Bock put more emphasis on contractual obligations than on Strauss's creative inspiration affected his desire to write more lieder. Indeed, from November 1906 through February 1918 he completed no new works in the genre. According to evidence in the Richard-Strauss-Archiv sketchbooks, he began, but then abandoned, at least eighteen lieder sketches in those years.[24] The existence of so many incomplete songs is significant: besides a few youthful efforts prior to op. 10, there are very few incomplete songs from any other period of his life.

Other significant factors further explain Strauss's lack of interest in lieder just after the turn of the century. Artistically important were his growing interest in opera and the time devoted to writing *Salome*, *Elektra*, and subsequent operas. In addition, the frequent song recitals, which Richard and Pauline had given ever since their marriage in 1894, came to an end shortly after their 1904 American tour.

The fact remains that each time Strauss became too entangled with commitments to publishers he instinctively drew back. One wonders if he knew that Ernest Newman had proclaimed that "a number of his songs may be frankly written off as not music but merchandise." [25] If Strauss did not write music to sell as merchandise, he certainly bargained when he had a successful score to offer. And he objected to publishers' insisting on deadlines or demanding works of him; even within the small-scale genre of the lied, he preferred to work on what interested him at the moment. He was proud of almost never having written on commission—something to which few composers of today would admit.

At the end of the "songless" years, Strauss returned wholeheartedly to the lied in early 1918, beginning with the orchestral *Sechs Lieder nach Gedichten von Clemens Brentano*, op. 68. He immediately found himself in a dilemma with Bote & Bock because of his earlier promises. Since he was firmly committed to Fürstner, he wanted to save op. 68 (and a further set, *Fünf kleine Lieder*, op. 69, for voice and piano) for that publisher. His only option was to set op. 68 aside and write another six songs to halt Bote & Bock's threatened lawsuit. Thus the composer embarked upon a set of songs based on satirical verses that he commissioned from the Berlin poet and critic Alfred Kerr. On 8 March 1918 Kerr mailed Strauss the completed texts, into which were woven the names of several music publishers; noticeably absent was Fürstner. Kerr required no fee for his work and encouraged Strauss to indicate any desired alterations that might suit his purposes, which Kerr would happily permit. Strauss created a cycle of twelve songs that feature the piano more prominently than the voice, which mainly serves as a vehicle for the text and its quoted names. [26] He took advantage of opportunities for self-quotation, and to accompany the publishers' names he incorporated musical quotations from *Der Rosenkavalier*, *Guntram*, *Tod und Verklärung*, and *Till Eulenspiegel*, among others. [27]

Strauss first named the cycle *Die Händler und die Kunst*; *Krämerspiegel* was added as the main title only later, upon publication. Appropriately, the work was dedicated to Friedrich Rösch, cofounder with Strauss of the GDT. A gossip column in *Signale für die musikalische Welt* reported that with these songs Strauss had indirectly declared war on the publishing industry. Naturally Bote &

Bock was not the least bit interested in publishing them,[28] nor were other music publishers. The collection ultimately appeared in 1921 as an elegant limited edition under the imprint of Paul Cassirer, a Berlin art publisher. To wait three years for the publication of a set of lieder was not Strauss's usual lot.

Later in 1918 Strauss created two sets of three songs each as op. 67: the Ophelia songs from *Hamlet* and three "bad-tempered" Goethe poems from the *West-östlicher Divan*. In choosing the Goethe texts he was still commenting on his muse's subservience to the publisher's contract, but in a more subtle way. The Goethe texts were perfectly suited to Strauss's increasingly cynical feelings about the music publishing business.[29]

Wer wird von der Welt verlangen, op. 67, no. 4 [complete]

Wer wird von der Welt verlangen,
was sie selbst vermisst und träumet,
rückwärts oder seitwärts blickend,
stets den Tag des Tags versäumet?
Ihr Bemühn, ihr guter Wille,
hinkt nur nach dem raschen Leben,
und was du vor Jahren brauchtest,
möchte sie dir heute geben.

[Who will demand of the world,
what the world itself lacks and who dreams,
looking backwards or sideways,
and always lets the day of days slip by?
Its endeavor, its good will,
always lags behind impetuous life,
and what you needed years ago,
might be given to you today.]

Hab ich euch denn je geraten, op. 67, no. 5 [stanza 1 of 4]

Hab ich euch denn je geraten,
wie ihr Kriege führen solltet?
Schalt ich euch, nach euren Taten,
wenn ihr Frieden schliessen wolltet?

[Have I ever advised you,
how you should wage wars?
Did I ever reprove you for your deeds,
when you sought to make peace?]

Wanderers Gemütsruhe, op. 67, no. 6 [stanza 1 of 3]

Übers Niederträchtige
niemand sich beklage;
denn es ist das Mächtige,
was man dir auch sage.

[Let no one complain
about baseness;
for whatever one may say,
it is most powerful.]

In *Wer wird von der Welt verlangen* Goethe expresses the cynical paradox that man cannot get what he wants when he needs it, but later—when it is no longer needed—will probably succeed. The second poem is the philosopher's outburst at fools who think they know more than the wise men, the third his advice to a traveler not to struggle against the impossible. For Strauss, the adversaries in each of these were obviously himself and his publishers. In *Hab ich euch denn je geraten,* he quotes two themes from *Eine Alpensinfonie* and hints at others in his newest opera, *Die Frau ohne Schatten;* in *Wanderers Gemütsruhe,* he uses some wonderfully cynical word painting, floridly emphasizing such words as "dirt," "dust," and "whirlwind."

Several critics have found these songs of little importance in Strauss's oeuvre, saying they were dashed off in a hurry without concern for good text setting. But the sketchbook in the RSA (Tr. 43) is quite typical of his song sketches. Two of the poems are copied into the inside covers, and drafts of the music show that he had the overall outline of each song in mind from the start, then gradually filled in the details. The final manuscripts (in the same collection) are undated—a rare omission in Strauss's final copies—and the set lacks the usual dedication. Such details prove nothing about the creative musical process, but they may indicate his desire to get the manuscript off to the publisher and rid his mind of the whole affair.

In all, Strauss completed twenty-nine lieder during 1918, signaling his enthusiastic return to the composition of songs. Bote & Bock secured the copyright for op. 67 by 1 January 1919, and Fürstner promptly printed opp. 68 and 69. Many years later, when Boosey & Hawkes took over the Fürstner catalog for English-speaking countries (with B. Schotts Söhne for most others), the new publishers issued a regular edition of *Krämerspiegel.*[30]

The dichotomy of composer vs. publisher or artist vs. businessman is a theme that recurs throughout Strauss's career. Another significant clash between Strauss and the publishing world, which predates the *Krämerspiegel* episode, involves his work not as a composer but as an editor and a scholar. Henri Hinrichsen, director of Musikverlag C.F. Peters of Leipzig, approached Strauss in 1902 (through Otto Singer) about a new, enlarged edition of Hector Berlioz's *Instrumentationslehre*.[31] An exchange of letters between composer and publisher reveals that Hinrichsen initially hoped to list the new version in his catalog on 1 October 1902. Strauss agreed but asked for time; he could not be forced to work, he said, but must always wait for the right mood and a desire to apply himself.

Indeed, more than two years elapsed from the time Hinrichsen originally intended to issue the volume until Strauss finally finished his revisions, and almost three years passed before the edition was published. Although Strauss did not complete his preface until 10 November 1904, Peters was able to issue the treatise with a copyright date of 1905. Documentation of the negotiations for this project and work on the revisions is contained in the Leipzig Staatsarchiv collection: "Korrespondenz Richard Strauss mit C. F. Peters."[32] A summary appears in the appendix to this study.

Strauss's ever-lengthening delays are not so surprising when one realizes all that he composed during that period: op. 51 (two large orchestral songs), op. 56 (six lieder, one of them also orchestrated), *Symphonia Domestica, Taillefer, Salome,* and a handful of other works not assigned opus numbers.[33] And in addition to composing and regular conducting engagements, his schedule included such extensive tours as the one to America. Having departed for the United States on 10 February 1904, the Strausses gave thirty-five concerts and lieder recitals between 1 March and 26 April.

Another significant aspect of Strauss's work on the Berlioz treatise involves finances: he was paid the large sum of 16,500 DM (not just the 5,000 DM advance agreed upon in April 1902) for his contributions to the new edition, but Hinrichsen intended to hold the price down to that of the annual reprints of the old version, only three marks. And Peters was still hoping to publish a major symphonic work, if not at Strauss's ever-mounting fees.[34] Strauss did assign them the *Zwei Militärmärsche,* op. 57 (1906), for the sum of 6,000 DM. (Fürstner had angered Strauss by offering him a mere 4,000.) In the same year, he contributed to a large collection of folksong arrangements Peters was publishing.[35] A decade later, Strauss approached Peters about publishing *Eine Alpensinfonie* for 100,000 DM, or twice what he would eventually receive from the publishing firm of F. E. C. Leuckart. But the Sander family, owners of Leuckart, had been especially helpful in the GTD and that loyalty was not forgotten.

Much of Strauss's business correspondence concerned composers' rights and his suggestions to publishers about their dealings with composers. The latter were probably as unrealistic in his day as some composers' demands are today. In his voluminous correspondence with Spitzweg during 1898–1904, Strauss offered his works for increasingly higher prices, complained of errors in scores and parts, and reported placing lieder with other publishers "and to be sure only under the most favorable terms." In 1898–1900 Strauss clashed repeatedly with Spitzweg over providing performance materials for Guntram to Angelo Neumann, director of the New German Theater in Prague. At first Strauss wanted the music sent at half price (500 DM, rather than the usual 1,000); when Spitzweg refused, Strauss countered with a request that the materials be provided without any charge whatsoever. He was clearly more interested in getting the performance than in receiving any royalty income from it. The Prague performance ultimately took place in October 1901, with Strauss conducting.

At about the same time Strauss made several requests that vocal scores of Guntram be sent to other possible producers. The lack of Spitzweg's replies makes it impossible to know his reaction to Strauss's demands and the extent of the publisher's cooperation. In all of these dealings, Strauss paradoxically wanted to secure performances and yet desired a good income from them; he was entirely unrealistic about who would pay the costs. Shortly after his requests for free performance materials for Prague, for example, he inquired how much he would receive from the sale of performing materials for Guntram to the Berlin Court Opera.

Around the turn of the century, Strauss wrote several lengthy letters about his publisher's unacceptable business practices; in one letter to Spitzweg, dated 11 November 1899, he outlined a detailed plan for clearer, more enlightened ways (i.e., more advantageous for the composer) of conducting business. In a later letter (30 June 1902), Strauss demanded the sum of 500 DM, which he claimed he was owed from the engraving and printing of his early Symphony in F Minor; his father had paid those expenses, which normally would have been borne by the publishing house.

But amid this apparent greed and concern for only his own share of income, Strauss frequently requested complimentary scores to be sent to friends and colleagues, always addressed Spitzweg "Lieber Freund," recommended other composers for the Aibl catalog (most notably Max Reger, for whom Aibl printed twenty-five compositions), and informed Spitzweg of his efforts to begin the authors' and composers' rights society as well as other projects he envisioned that would promote not only his own music but also the works of other composers.[36] Strauss was well known for encouraging his colleagues, arranging for concerts and conducting music by such contemporaries as Mahler, Pfitzner, D'Indy, Schillings, the young Schoenberg, and many lesser-known names. In spite of his first love being for the music of past masters, he believed in the works of his colleagues—and even more strongly in their right to earn respectable incomes from their compositions.

In some letters to Spitzweg, Strauss appears overly generous toward his fellow artists, too harsh on the publishing world, too naive about the economics of publishers, and too unrealistic in his expectations. For example, he asked Spitzweg to lend orchestral scores and parts free of charge to Franz Kaim for two complete concerts of his music.[37] This idea was simply bad business: the publisher was expected to provide the performance materials without rental or sales income. When Spitzweg refused, Strauss wrote back angrily. A few months later, he was even more upset about the difficulties in providing music for op. 34 to the Berlin Philharmonic Chorus: "Don't you know that a performance by this group is of greatest importance [allergrösster Wichtigkeit] for us both? What sort of business conduct is that? If you only knew how many complaints there are on all sides, how difficult you are making dissemination and acquisition of my music for concert presenters and the public. You forget that as a businessman and publisher along with your rights you have certain obligations."[38]

A composer would have a hard time making such demands today, and a publisher would hardly react kindly to such an attitude. Spitzweg's refusal angered Strauss and furthered his resolve to fight for composers' rights, often at the expense of their publishers.

Strauss's concern over his business affairs has been continued by his heirs. For decades both his son and daughter-in-law, Franz and Alice Strauss, attended to them, and more recently his grandsons, Christian and Richard, have been involved in managing the composer's estate. The family has been known to object to certain modern stagings of the operas and to exert their influence to maintain the integrity of Strauss's work. An anecdotal instance of their control over rights negotiations arose when the Bayerische Staatsoper presented a complete cycle of Strauss operas (staged or in concert) during the summer of 1988. In Germany, it is standard practice in grand rights contracts to give the publisher tickets to performances of their works. For the new production of Die Liebe der Danae an executive of another publishing firm (Bote & Bock) was unable to obtain opening-night tickets and asked if the publisher of the opera might have tickets that would not be used by their staff. He was told that there were no publishers' tickets, because the Bayerische Staatsoper had "made the arrangements with Dr. [Christian] Strauss himself." Once again, the publisher was left out of the negotiations.[39]

As a shrewd composer-businessman, Strauss is probably rivalled only by Igor Stravinsky. Both composers placed numerous publications with Boosey & Hawkes, and they are discussed together in a chapter of Ernst Roth's The Business of Music.[40] In 1942 Roth was able to acquire the rights to many of Strauss's late works even before Strauss knew about it. When the two met in 1945, Strauss was living in exile in Switzerland. Roth acknowledged that Strauss was indeed an "expensive" composer with high demands—but not excessively so, given the quality of his work.

Roth's observation points to the principal reason that Strauss was so successful in his business dealings: his music was of high quality and frequently performed. Publishers and performing organizations knew that it was worth acceding to his demands, paying him the fees he demanded, and waiting for him to meet deadlines. Strauss's concern for a decent living for composers is also understandable when we remember that he did not always live in luxury, especially during both world wars. It is fitting that Strauss's descendants receive substantial royalties from performances of his works around the world, a circumstance he himself created.

While most of Strauss's tone poems, best-known lieder, and operas through Der Rosenkavalier are already in the public domain in the United States —and thus bring in less income—their full copyright protection endures elsewhere. All of his works remain protected in United Kingdom countries to the end of 1999 and in most of Europe through 2019. Thus his heirs—as well as his publishers—receive considerable income from sales and rentals, small and grand performing rights, mechanical and synchronization licenses, and other uses of his considerable catalog of works. But Strauss's importance extends well beyond his musical legacy into the business world of music. Through his founding of the Genossenschaft Deutscher Tonsetzer, his continual efforts to improve the financial situation of composers, and his watchfulness over publishers, Strauss proved himself to be a staunch defender of composers' rights.

Appendix

From two Staatsarchiv Leipzig collections:

C. F. Peters Nr. 5032: Letters to Richard Strauss (from Peters' copybooks 1902–3)
C. F. Peters Nr. 2154: Letters to C. F. Peters from Richard Strauss (or copies thereof)

1902

18 March	CFP to RS noting he will do the Berlioz edition and requesting him to contact the publisher about his contract
12 April	CFP to RS requesting meeting 20 April
14 April	RS to CFP confirming that meeting
22 April	CFP to RS summarizing talks at the meeting; inquiring when the manuscript will be sent (it is needed at the latest during September); asking what it is to contain; agreeing on RS's fee
25 April	RS to CFP agreeing to advance of 5,000 DM to prepare a new edition; expressing uncertainty about completing his work by the end of September
19 June	CFP to RS agreeing to 31 December deadline if he can't manage 30 September; giving details on wording of the title page, publication date, advertising
13 August	RS to CFP agreeing with October announcement and with request not to print until spring 1903; requesting up-to-date instrumental method books to be sent to him
2 September	CFP to RS enclosing most method books; explaining since edition won't appear before January it cannot be listed in 1902–3 season catalog

1903

8 (5?) April	CFP to RS requesting firm date for delivery—if not completed this month, then send some of it after Easter so typesetting can begin; requesting expanded music examples; offering to obtain permissions from publishers
8 May	CFP to RS expressing awkwardness at not having manuscript before the end of August, meaning work is out of print for some time; requesting him not to postpone his work further; enclosing music examples

Strauss sent Hinrichsen eight more letters about further delays from 24 September 1903 to 13 November 1904. Finally, on 7 December 1904, he wrote, "Hier ist endlich der Berlioz!"

Notes

1   Kurt Wilhelm, *Richard Strauss persönlich: Eine Bildbiographie* (Munich: Kindler, 1984), p. 96.
2   Text of Strauss's letter (8 February 1881) in E. H. Mueller von Asow, *Richard Strauss: Thematisches Verzeichnis* (Vienna and Munich: Doblinger, 1955–74), vol. 1, pp. 4–5. Today, the managing partners of Breitkopf & Härtel treasure the relevant correspondence, even though it points to a poor business decision on the part of their predecessors.
3   The firm was founded by the lithographer Joseph Aibl (1802–34); after 1837 it was managed by Eduard Spitzweg (1811–84), brother of the painter Carl Spitzweg, and then by his son Eugen (1840–1914).

4   A catalog of these letters, with very brief mention of their principal subjects, appears in
    Günter Brosche and Karl Dachs, *Richard Strauss Autographen in München und Wien: Verzeichnis*
    (Tutzing: Hans Schneider, 1979), pp. 230–41.

5   Alfons Ott, "Richard Strauss und sein Verlegerfreund Eugen Spitzweg," in *Musik und Verlag.*
    Karl Vötterle zum 65. Geburtstag am 12. April 1968, ed. R. Baum and W. Rehm (Kassel: Bären-
    reiter, 1968), 466–75; and Willi Schuh, *Richard Strauss: Jugend und frühe Meisterjahre: Lebenschronik*
    1864–1898 (Zurich: Atlantis, 1976), passim.

6   In the Strauss–Spitzweg correspondence in *"Der Strom der Töne trug mich fort": Die Welt um Richard*
    Strauss in Briefen, ed. Franz Grasberger with Franz and Alice Strauss (Tutzing: Hans Schneider,
    1967), only two of the twelve letters are from Spitzweg.

7   It was brought to my attention by Scott Warfield in 1988, and the next year I attempted to
    secure copies for this study. The copies arrived only at the end of March 1990 and some
    of them were poorly reproduced. The two printed sources that treat this correspondence
    are a small section of a dissertation and an article, both by Hans-Martin Plesske: *Das Leipziger*
    Musikverlagswesen und seine Beziehungen zu einigen namenhaften Komponisten. Ein Beitrag zur Geschichte
    des Musikalienhandels im 19. und zu Beginn des 20. Jahrhunderts (Ph.D. diss., Karl-Marx-Universität,
    Leipzig, 1974), 197–200; and "Der Bestand Musikverlag C. F. Peters im Staatsarchiv Leipzig . . . ,"
    Jahrbuch der deutschen Bücherei 6 (1970): 75–99 (pp. 86–87 on Strauss). Plesske is also the author
    of the *New Grove* article on C. F. Peters.

8   The main group of letters relevant to this study includes twenty-four letters from Strauss to
    Musikverlag C. F. Peters Leipzig in 1902–17, eight replies (entered by hand in the publishing
    firm's copybooks, covering 1902–3), and carbon copies of letters from Peters in 1904–19. A
    later large group of letters from each party will be worth investigating, especially for the
    years after 1933. At that time, the Peters firm finally obtained copyrights to some major works
    by Strauss: eight tone poems originally in the Aibl catalog were taken over from Universal
    Edition.

9   Strauss's letter of 15 November 1898 to Spitzweg.

10 Ott, p. 470, letter of 13 November 1890.

11 For most orchestral works, the publisher usually issued a two- or four-hand piano reduc-
    tion, but since that gave the work additional circulation and increased sales there were no
    complaints about added costs.

12 Richard Forberg published *Fünf Lieder*, op. 39, and *Zwei grössere Gesänge*, op. 44; F. E. C. Leuckart
    took on *Ein Heldenleben*, op. 40, *Fünf Lieder*, op. 41, and *Zwei Männerchöre*, op. 42; and C. A. Challier
    & Co. (Richard Birnbach) accepted *Drei Gesänge*, op. 43.

13 The Wagnerian *Guntram* premiered at the Weimar Court Theater in May 1894; the Munich pro-
    duction was its second. Strauss's lifelong remembrance of its failure was commemorated by
    the wooden "Marterl," a typical Bavarian commemorative plaque, that he had constructed
    about 1909 for his garden, and which stands there today:

> Hier ruht der ehr- u. tugendsame Jüngling Guntram—
> Minnesänger der vom Symphonischen Orchester seines
> eigenen Vaters grausam erschlagen wurde.
> Er ruhe in Frieden.

> [Here lies the noble and virtuous Minnesinger Guntram—
> who was gruesomely slain by the symphony orchestra
> of his own father. May he rest in peace.]

14   Strauss and von Wolzogen called the work a "Singgedicht," not an opera. Its most extended excerptable section, Kunrad's monologue, abounds in musical and textual punning and Wagnerian reminiscences. There are references to "Reichhart der Meister," double meanings in such words as "wagen" and "Wagner," quotations from *Der Ring des Nibelungen* (the Walhalla motive at the words "Herrscher der Geister," for instance), *Der fliegende Holländer*, and so forth.

15   Most societies are known by their initials or acronyms (BMI, PRS, ASCAP, JASRAC, etc.), a particularly felicitous one being the recently established society in Hong Kong: CASH.

16   The text of Strauss's letter to his fellow composers ([14] July 1898) is printed in Schuh, pp. 505–7. Spitzweg, incidentally, paid for the printing and mailing costs.

17   The only protection nineteenth-century German copyright law provided composers and publishers was against literal reprints; there was no protection against arrangements and no compensation for performances. As early as 1829, German music publishers joined together in a protective society that became the Verein der deutschen Musikalienhändler, now the Deutscher Musikverleger-Verband.

18   Strauss's letter of 22 November 1898: "Verlagsrechte dem Verleger, / Urheberrechte dem Urheber. / Andern Modus gibt's künftig nicht!"

19   Hugo Bock, of Strauss's Berlin publisher, Bote & Bock, was a principal figure in this society.

20   Schulze retired at the end of 1989 and was succeeded by Reinhold Kreile.

21   Letter of 22 March 1900, excerpted in Ott, p. 474.

22   Without Spitzweg's replies to Strauss's letters, it is difficult to ascertain whether or not Strauss was involved in the negotiations. From such secondhand reports as that of Gustav Bock (Hugo's son) in "Richard Strauss und der Verlag Ed. Bote & Bock, Berlin," *Musikhandel* 1 (1949): 35, it would appear that Strauss was not consulted.

23   The *Symphonia Domestica* was one of Strauss's few works to be performed in the United States before it was heard at home: on 21 March 1904 the composer conducted it with the Wetzler Symphony Orchestra at Carnegie Hall in New York during a Strauss festival; Europeans first heard it under his direction in Frankfurt on 1 June 1904.

24   For sketchbook locations and descriptions of these sketches, see Barbara A. Petersen, *"Ton und Wort": The Lieder of Richard Strauss* (Ann Arbor: UMI Research Press, 1980), appendix B (pp. 201–5). The RSA sketchbooks were renumbered after that listing was completed; what was listed as no. 11 is now 10, and 40 is now 16. The numbers are correct in the German edition, *"Ton und Wort": Die Lieder von Richard Strauss*, trans. Ulrike Steinhauser (Pfaffenhofen: W. Ludwig, 1986), pp. 249–54.

25   Ernest Newman, *Richard Strauss* (London: John Lane, 1908), p. 90.

26   Some of the most obvious examples:

"Es war einmal ein Bock . . ."

(opening of the cycle)

"Einst kam der Bock als Bote / zum Rosenkavalier ans Haus;"

(beginning of song no. 2)

"Es liebte einst ein Hase
Die salbungsvolle Phrase,
obschon wie ist das sonderbar,
sein Breitkopf hart und härter war."

(beginning of no. 3; referring to the director of the publishing firm, Oskar Hase)

> "Von Händlern wird die Kunst bedroht,
> da habt ihr die Bescherung:
> Sie bringen der Musik den Tod,
> sich selber die Verklärung."

(No. 8, complete; naturally ending with the appropriate musical quotation)

27 According to Reinhold Schlötterer, *Die Texte der Lieder von Richard Strauss: Kritische Ausgabe* (Pfaffen-hofen: W. Ludwig, 1988), p. 234, neither original manuscripts of Kerr's poems nor letters that might contain alterations are known.

28 Bote & Bock's attitude has obviously changed over the years: in a recent letter to me, Hans-Jürgen Radecke, a managing partner in that firm, commented after a recent Berlin perfor-mance of *Krämerspiegel* by Dietrich Fischer-Dieskau: "After all, the text against my publisher colleagues is much harsher than against Bote & Bock."

29 Richard Strauss, *Sechs Lieder für eine hohe Singstimme mit Klavierbegleitung*, op. 67 (Berlin: Bote & Bock, 1919). Nos. 4–6 use texts from Goethe's *West–östlicher Divan, Buch des Unmuts*. Text excerpts reprinted by permission of Bote & Bock. All English translations by Barbara A. Petersen and Roger Roloff, with the kind assistance of the late Frederic Ewen.

30 An incident reported in Asow, vol. 2, p. 725, and elsewhere, proves that even bad publicity is better than no publicity at all. After a 1949 broadcast of excerpts from *Krämerspiegel*, two publishers raised the objection that the songs mentioning them had been omitted!

31 Berlioz's original treatise, *Grand Traité d'instrumentation et d'orchestration modernes*, first appeared in Paris in 1843; the German version published by Peters became a standard conservatory textbook.

32 The assistance of the following in obtaining access to these unpublished letters is grate-fully acknowledged: Mrs. Walter Hinrichsen, Chairman of the Board, and Stephen Fisher, President, both of C. F. Peters Corporation, New York; Norbert Molkenbur of V.E.B. Edition Peters, Leipzig; and the staff of the Staatsarchiv Leipzig.

33 Franz Trenner, *Richard Strauss: Werkverzeichnis* (Vienna: Doblinger, 1985), lists eight compositions (AV 95–102), which Strauss completed in 1902–6.

34 As noted previously, their offer of 30,000 DM for *Symphonia Domestica* was not enough for the composer.

35 The collection of 610 four-part choral works, assembled by a committee at the request of Kaiser Wilhelm II, encompassed repertory from several centuries and was edited by promi-nent German composers. Strauss's contribution of *Sechs Volksliedbearbeitungen*, AV 101, appeared in Peters' *Volksliederbuch für Männerchor*.

36 Among these were plans for the *Münchener Musikzeitung*, editing the thirty-two-book series *Die Musik*, serving on the board of the Allgemeine Deutsche Musikverein, and organizing music festivals in Germany and abroad.

37 Letter of 4 July 1899. Franz Kaim (1856–1935), after whom the Kaim-Saal in the Odeon and the Kaim-Konzerte series were named, founded the Munich Philharmonic Orchestra in 1893. The first fully professional orchestra in Munich, it was informally referred to as the Kaim-Orchester.

38 Strauss's letter of 11 November 1899, excerpted in Ott, p. 473.

39 In defense of the Strauss family, it must be explained that the original 1944 copyright in *Die Liebe der Danae* was in the name of Richard Strauss, not the publisher (Johannes Oertel, described in the printed score as "Kommissionsverlag"). From *Arabella* onward, Strauss was

careful to have his operas issued with copyright notices in his own name, not that of the publisher. In Europe copyright notices are often in the name of the composer, whereas in America they are more likely to bear the name of the publisher.

40 Ernst Roth, *The Business of Music* (New York: Oxford University Press, 1969), pp. 176–208. Roth first became familiar with Strauss's music (and in 1922 met the composer briefly) as head of the publications department at Universal Edition.

The Musical Works

▼

Fiery-Pulsed Libertine or Domestic Hero?
Strauss's *Don Juan* Reinvestigated

James Hepokoski

▼

> *Vielleicht ein Blitz aus Höh'n, die ich verachtet,*
> *Hat tödlich meine Liebeskraft getroffen,*
> *Und plötzlich ward die Welt mir wüst, umnachtet;*
> *Vielleicht auch nicht. . . .*
> —Nikolaus Lenau, Don Juan (1844)

Confronting a late-nineteenth-century work such as Richard Strauss's 1888–89 *Don Juan: Tondichtung (nach Nicolaus Lenau)* involves, first of all, locating a methodology and level of discourse adequate to the task. Today, when the traditional categories of music analysis strike us more as problems than as self-evident concepts, we would do well to stand clear of the temptation to simplify "modern" compositions of this sort.[1] It may be that these compositions cannot be grasped in single-dimensional terms: they are not musical puzzles to be solved by the assigning of quick analytical labels. More often, these pieces present a network of processes—structural, generic, aesthetic, social—more in need of hermeneutic untangling than of solution in any usual sense of that term. Such processes often unfold in a nonclosed realm in which aesthetic suggestion and allusion can replace concrete realization. Rather than passing over such problems, analyses need to thematize them.

Under the circumstances a more productive goal of analysis would be to uncover a "modern" composition's ambiguities. Stressing the work's unresolved tensions, such an analysis would seek the piece's essential aesthetic moment in the pull of those tensions—in the work's "embodying the contradictions, pure and uncompromised, in its innermost structure," as Adorno put it.[2] In a study of the musical form of *Don Juan*, for example, this procedure would insist that the work is reducible neither to a single analytical category nor to a flat, unelaborated statement that the piece is a hybrid of two or more. (As will be seen, "sonata" and "rondo," along with free adaptations thereof, are the categories most frequently suggested.) What does matter is the way in which the work becomes perceived as a coherent "thing in motion."[3] This essay is an exercise in this type of analysis.

Before beginning the exercise, however, it will prove useful to raise a few preliminary issues, for with *Don Juan* we also face a more generalized problem: the presence of a program. Even considered apart from a program, the nontraditional structures of modern symphonic works are notoriously complex; the difficulties increase once we have been invited to draw connections between a work's musical structure and its accompanying paratextual apparatus (its title along with the additional words or implied narratives that the composer has provided along with the otherwise untexted music). As Genette has argued with regard to literature,[4] titles (and other paratextual material) are attempts by the author to set up the framing conditions of a text's reception; they condition the way in which the text proper is to be perceived. As part of the game of reading,[5] involving the calling forth of some sort of "meaning" from a text (which, when lacking an established principle of interpretation, is normally capable of multiple readings), the reader is encouraged to interpret the text on the basis of the generic or descriptive implications of an overriding title.

A symphonic poem operates under the same premises. The relevant issues here may initially seem to be more problematic, because the paratext employs a mode of discourse (verbal) other than that of the text proper (musical), but in fact the differences are slight. The abstract problem of whether music actually can evoke nonmusical images is utterly irrelevant—and perhaps meaningless—when posed in these terms. Instead, the problem should be grounded in an actual sociohistorical system of production and reception conventions. Within such a system it would suffice that both the producer and the targeted receivers of the musical text agree that forging musical and literary-pictorial interrelationships is fully within the spirit of the game, even if it might be a "controversial" game that any given individual might not care to play.

Thus the explicit invitation is to interpret the musical processes in light of the provided paratext-complex, and this is the defining feature of the symphonic poem as a genre. The essence of a *symphonische Dichtung* is situated in the listener's act (anticipated by the composer's) of connecting text and paratext, music and nonmusical image, and grappling with the implications of the connection. The genre exists, *qua* genre, solely within the receiver, who agrees to create it reciprocally by indicating his or her willingness to play the game proposed by the composer; it does not exist abstractly in the acoustical surface of the music. Consequently, by the rules of the symphonic-poem game, we are not permitted to ask whether we could deduce the proper images had we not been supplied with them in advance, or had we not at least been given some broad hints in their direction. If we wish to play, we must abide by the rules; otherwise we are playing a different game or redefining the original one to suit our own purposes. More pointedly, there are certain "absolute music" questions that may not be asked of the symphonic poem, for at the moment of their asking the conditions of the symphonic poem's possibility as a genre are liquidated.

The verbal clues that the composer furnishes are givens within the genre. They are neither extramusical (because they are part of the essential character of this musical procedure) nor dispensable, neither accretions nor casual overlays.[6] Whether a program was introduced into a symphonic poem before, during, or after its composition is historically interesting but aesthetically unimportant to the intended transaction between producer and receiver.[7] The fact remains that at the moment of a symphonic poem's "official" presentation we are confronted with a title, epigram, or set of poetic lines, and no knowledge of a paratext's dating grants us the license either to dispense with it or to banish it to an aesthetic periphery. Withheld or "secret" programs within other musical genres, of course, are a different matter: these are covert or genesis-phase "producer's programs" that future receivers occasionally learn either inadvertently or through the result of research that the composer did not anticipate. Similarly, listeners may sometimes seek, apart from explicit composer-furnished clues, to infer programmatic narratives within pieces that were given more "abstract" titles. To be sure, these ramifications complicate the problem of extramusical connotation considered as a whole, but they need not affect the argument offered here, which is restricted to the more straightforward instances provided by explicitly titled symphonic poems. And these works, by definition, seem to insist on an inferrable simultaneity—perhaps even a metaphorical identity—between their musical and "literary" narratives.

It follows that the standard questions asked of symphonic poems—which structure, musical or verbal, is mapped onto which?; or, which is truly prior? —are not the most useful ones to pose. Such questions were passionately raised around the turn of the last century, for some argued that decisions of aesthetic validity, or even artistic morality, hung in the balance.[8] Scholars have persisted in posing these questions, with equal fervor, but without profit, in our own time: discussions of symphonic poems rapidly run aground on them. But to run these discussions aground may well have been the tactical point: the priority question typically springs from an aesthetic stance that assumes the superior status of autonomous music. "The best of [Strauss's] programmatic works," writes Ernst Krause, "always understand how to leave their programmes behind and stand on their own feet as absolute music."[9] Similarly, from Michael Kennedy's monograph on Strauss: "No music will survive unless it has independent life as music; no 'programme' will keep bad music alive. Most of Strauss's programme music can be enjoyed for its purely musical quality. How many listeners, when they have once followed the detailed programme, pay much attention to it again? Very few, I suggest. The music transcends it."[10]

Krause and Kennedy, of course—along with innumerable others—are reciting *articles de foi*, not elaborating reasoned arguments. Such issues are raised not for informational but for evaluative reasons: to lobby on behalf of (or sometimes against) a work's membership within an aesthetic system that one has tacitly agreed to universalize. There are consequently more useful, less aesthetically loaded questions to ask of a symphonic poem. For example: Are the musical and verbal planes of narrativity, both accepted here as givens, to be forced into an inevitable parallelism, or may they occasionally work at cross-purposes? Can (or must) the music drop out of the narrative at certain points for such "purely musical reasons" as the traditional requirement of formal recapitulation?[11]

As Dahlhaus has repeatedly reminded us, it is easy to interpret the programmatic intention too superficially and reduce it to a one-dimensional, concrete realism. The composers of Strauss's epoch were aware of this danger, and when pressed some relied on a strategy congruent with the privileged metaphysics of absolute music to counter it, one that claimed that a program or nonmusical image was a mere, ultimately discardable initial impulse making higher things possible. In Dahlhaus's words, a program was a " 'formal motive' [or 'form motive'—the term is Wagner's], a reason for [the piece's] existence, in order to come into being and manifest its potential."[12] Somewhat paradoxically, this standard line of defense permitted composers to argue that a program was both essential and inessential, depending on the circumstances.[13]

Still, to the Richard Strauss of the later 1880s, newly converted to the doctrines of the New German School, the main point was that the concept of absolute music that he perceived as being marketed at the time was aesthetically barren. During this period Strauss argued that the structures of his works were to be understood primarily in terms of the poetic ideas with which they were inextricably bound—a postulate derived directly from Liszt.[14] Thus his famous remarks to von Bülow on 24 August 1888, written particularly about *Macbeth*, but at the point of the completion of *Don Juan*:

> From the F minor Symphony [1884] onwards I have found myself in a gradually ever increasing contradiction between the musical-poetic content that I want to convey a[nd] the ternary sonata form that has come down to us from the classical composers. . . . Now, what was for Beethoven a "form" absolutely in congruity with the highest, most glorious content, is now, after 60 years, used as a formula inseparable from our instrumental music (which I strongly dispute), simply to accommodate and enclose a "pure musical" (in the strictest and narrowest meaning of the word) content, or worse, to stuff and expand a content with which it does not correspond.
>
> If you want to create a work of art that is unified in its mood and consistent in its structure . . . [then] this is only possible through the inspiration by a poetical idea, whether or not it be introduced as a programme. I consider it a legitimate artistic method to create a correspondingly new form for every new subject. . . . Of course, purely formalistic, Hanslickian music-making will no longer be possible, and we cannot have any more random patterns, that mean nothing either to the composer or the listener.[15]

Modern musical logic[16] was now to be wedded to modern poetic logic: Strauss claims here that his unorthodox musical structures should be understood simultaneously to be tracking a complementary poetic narrative. This narrative was doubtless to be conveyed by an ordered set of representations that, depending on the circumstances, could range from the concrete ("tone pictures," or *Tonbilder*) to the abstract or even metaphysical ("soul states," or *Seelenzustände*).[17] During the *Don Juan* period Strauss embraces a poetic logic that resembles Wagner's concept of the "form motive," but with this difference: Strauss implies that a work's poetic content is more than discardable scaffolding. He seems rather to elevate its importance, hardly surprising from a composer who has just begun to undertake the most ambitious set of symphonic poems since Liszt's. Any hermeneutics that takes Strauss at his word (at least his 1888 word) cannot shy away from the invitation proffered by the symphonic poem as a genre. Our task with *Don Juan* must involve locating a reasonable, relevant poetic narrative that would render possible the parallel music-structural process, and we should do this without collapsing into naive claims for a simplistic, consistently concrete representation or brashly excluding alternative narrative possibilities.

One potential objection at this point might be that Strauss's 1888 remarks are not representative, for later in his life he downplayed the role of poetic logic to insist that in the last analysis his symphonic poems were to be justified according to their inner musical processes. Thus his 5 July 1905 remark to Romain Rolland:

> In my opinion, too, a poetic programme is nothing but a pretext for the purely musical expression and development of my emotions, and not a simple *musical description* of concrete everyday facts. . . . But so that music should not lose itself in pure abstractions and drift in limitless directions, it needs to be held within bounds which determine a certain form, and it is the programme which fixes these bounds. And an analytic programme of this kind should be nothing more than a starting-point. Those who are interested in it can use it. Those who really know how to listen to music doubtless have no need for it.[18]

This seems to accept the concept of a "form motive," as does his often-quoted statement from many years later: "A poetic programme can certainly lead to the establishment of new forms, but if the music does not develop logically out of itself the result is 'Literaturmusik.' " And: "In reality, of course [!], there is no genuine programme music. This is merely a term of abuse used by all those who are incapable of being original."[19]

These things are not easy to reconcile either with his letter to von Bülow or with several of his other earlier remarks. Consider, for example, his reported boasts: "I regard the ability to express outward events as the highest triumph of musical technique"; and "Anyone who wants to be a real musician must be able to compose a menu."[20] Or, specifically from the years of *Don Juan*, in a letter to Johann L. Bella from March 1890: "Programme music! real music! Absolute music: it can be put together with the aid of routine and rule-of-thumb techniques by everybody who is at all musical! First: true art! Second: artificiality."[21]

Ultimately, Strauss's verbal position on the essential relevance of his programs is deeply problematic and probably unresolvable. It would appear, though, that the later "antiprogrammatic" utterances are less contrite confessions of what had always been the truth than part of a strategy to parry the criticisms of the autonomous-music partisans (who, in fact, continue to quote the passages for the purpose of reassuring their own readers of the aesthetic legitimacy of Strauss's enterprise). Strauss's famous 1905 remark to Rolland, for instance, was not delivered, nor should it be read, in the abstract; rather, it was a diplomatic, pacifying response to Rolland's sharp criticism of the *Symphonia Domestica*. In his letter of eight days earlier, 29 May 1905, Rolland had claimed that he had been "shocked" by the program and that it "pre-vented me from judging the work itself. It was only in the evening, at the concert, that I really heard [the piece], forgetting the whole programme," and so on.[22] Under the circumstances, the most reasonable conclusion would be neither that the later Strauss encouraged a revisionist reading of his earlier works nor that he intended to readjust the balances of his original aesthetic aims, but rather that he wished to call attention to those aspects of his oeuvre that his "absolute-music-oriented" readers would be most likely to respect. In short, it would seem that Strauss's remarks on programs are neither objec-tive nor neutral; they were probably conditioned by the expected reactions of their intended recipients.

To write today under the automatic assumption of the aesthetic superi-ority of autonomous music (or, stated more cautiously, of music that asks to be perceived as autonomous) seems dated, as if one were unwilling to re-lease oneself from the grasp of the system that one is attempting to explain. In practice, restriction exclusively to either a privileged musical or verbal sphere of discourse proves inefficient, if not naive. For us, and probably for the late nineteenth century as well, the two commingle in ways that it would be unwise to separate: the form-creating element is synonymous with the form per se—with the form as narrative process, a thing in motion.

If for no other reason than to steer clear of elementary (and by now tedious) issues, I shall not repeat here the most basic and widely available information about *Don Juan*: Strauss's linking of the music with Lenau's 1844 (but published posthumously in 1851) *dramatisches Gedicht* of the same name; his preceding of the printed score with thirty-two expressive (not narrative) lines, subdivided into $7 + 17 + 8$, the first two subdivisions extracted from near the beginning, the last near the end, of the poem; and so on.[23] This study is concerned not with laying out these details, but with the larger question of how we can come to perceive adequately the work's structure, content, and represented meaning.

The following discussion subdivides into three sections (2–4). Section 2 is more attentive to musical structure than to that of its implied programma-tic companion. As an overview, not a complete analysis, of the most crucial elements of *Don Juan*, it attempts to sketch out the issues involved in appre-hending the work's form as interactive process. Section 3 takes up more directly the problem of verbal meaning—metaphorical or actual—within the musical representations of the symphonic poem. Section 4 provides a brief summary and final consideration of the issues raised in the preceding sections.

2

Riddled with ambiguities, the musical structure of Don Juan has elicited a variety of analyses over the past century. Most commentators have heard it as a free sonata: this position is clearly discernible in the discussions of Gustav Brecher (1899), Otto Klauwell (1910), and Max Steinitzer (1911), and it continues with such writers as Hermann W. von Waltershausen (1921), Reinhold Muschler (1924), Norman Del Mar (1962), Michael Kennedy (1976), Robert Bailey (1980), and Kenneth Levy (1983).[24] Another group, however, has considered it a rondo or a free rondo: one of the earliest writers to take this position was Ernst Otto Nodnagel (1902), and the case for the rondo was argued with particular vigor by Richard Specht (1921). We also find discussions on its behalf from such later commentators as Gerald Abraham (1938, rev. 1964), Antoine Goléa (1965), Edward Murphy (1983), and Heinz Becker (1989).[25]

A few others—most notably Reinhold Gerlach (1966) and Arno Forchert (1975)—have tried to effect a synthesis between the two formal positions by discussing Don Juan as a mixture of sonata and rondo (sometimes incorporating aspects of other structures as well).[26] In these analyses the sonata is the ultimately defining category, but it is a category loosened in the direction of others for programmatic or innovative reasons, although those reasons have gone largely unspecified. Thus Gerlach writes:

> The adventurous element in the symphonic poem Don Juan, its aversion to a stringent coherence [Zusammenhang], is expressed in that its sonata form may be perceived only as something fragmentary, [as a structure] that passes over into something else: the sonata layout, which [first] dissolves itself into a rondo, is then confused still further with a four-movement, symphony-like cycle (Allegro, Andante, Scherzo, and Allegro). . . . A new, scarcely describable form is trying to realize itself in and with the fragmentarily appearing forms. . . . Neither [a sonata nor a rondo] is actually composed out in an intact manner in Don Juan. The newness of Don Juan is the compounded aspect of its many-layered "modern" form, which arises out of fragments.[27]

For the sake of completeness one might add that Don Juan has also provoked other analytical positions. Echoing similar remarks of Erich Urban (1901) and doubtless many others, Wilhelm Mauke (1908), the main source of the programmatic details usually assigned to the work, was content to assert the freedom of its form without specifying further ("breaking every traditional form . . . a proof of the artistic justification of disdainfully potent [selbstherrlichen] expression vis-à-vis the conventionally formal appeal to schematics"), primarily to make claims for its modernism and avoidance of *idées reçues*.[28] Nearly thirty years later Alfred Lorenz, in a quirky but by no means negligible essay of 1936, proposed (in recognizably post–*Geheimnis-der-Form* fashion) that *Don Juan* is neither a sonata nor a rondo, but rather traces out a massive *Reprisenbar*.[29] And in his textbook *Form in Tonal Music* (1965, rev. 1979) Douglass Green noted the work's resemblance to a sonata form but urged us for harmonic reasons to disregard it, to hear *Don Juan* as a "unique form" governed by its patterns of tonal closure, "a continuous four-part form with coda having the over-all design AA'BA''."[30]

Such solutions as Green's (and to some extent Lorenz's), which arrive at unexpected or ad hoc forms, dismiss the expressive power of generic implications. In response, current genre theory would stress that our ability to interpret a work's gestures resides in our decision regarding to which generic family they belong.[31] The genre decision attempts to locate the "horizon of expectations"[32] or pattern of defaults against which the individual work may be understood; it identifies the rules or the "social code"[33] by which a work's sequence of signals may be processed; it involves facing a network of traditional structures, contents, tones, and social purposes.

Making this decision can be difficult for turn-of-the-century modern works, since they often confront us with generic mixtures and unusual interactions with the traditions, things that I have elsewhere called generic or structural deformations.[34] In brief, the term "deformation" (for example, "sonata deformation") is most appropriate when one encounters a strikingly nonnormative individual structure, one that contravenes some of the most central defining traditions, or default gestures, of a genre while explicitly retaining others. (I refer here especially to the normative practice, or set of reified defaults, urged by the *Formenlehre* traditions, for better or worse a fundamental frame of reference for the institution of Germanic art music at least from the time of A. B. Marx onward. Indeed, Strauss's essential complaint in his 24 August 1888 letter to von Bülow, quoted above, is that the "ternary sonata form that has come down to us from the classical masters" is in fact reified, an inflexible given, a mere formula.) The advantage of the term "deformation" is that one may refer to a generic aspect of a piece without reducing that piece into a mere exemplar of the genre.

In any event, it is the presence of such deformations that has led *Don Juan* commentators to produce markedly differing analyses. More important, this is why both a simple, reductive labeling of the structure (sonata? rondo? a mixture?) and the appeal to a nongeneric "unique form" are insufficient. What is needed is to proceed beyond the reductions into hermeneutics.

When confronted with such problems in any individual piece, we need first to determine with which generic traditions it is in dialogue. In most cases these traditions will be ones immediately at hand; one normally should be advised against seeking out exotic or unusual genres. (This follows Dahlhaus's dictum, "One may establish in analysis the rule that a movement is to be interpreted, within sensible limits, as a variant of the form characteristic of the genre, and not as exemplifying another schema unusual for the genre.")[35] And second, we need to discover the principle that shapes these traditions into a unique but still coherent process guided by both musical and poetic logic.

The formal issues at stake in Don Juan may be clarified by investigating the rondo and sonata positions in their purer forms. The programmatic argument in favor of the rondo is the more enticing, for this structure, as Alfred Lorenz pointed out even while archly rejecting the position, may be heard as a formal analogue of sexual libertinism: "Don Juan is a man who has had many adventures. The structure of the work, therefore, is very simple: a rondo! Don Juan—adventure—Don Juan—adventure—Don Juan—adventure—and so on."[36] In this scheme the "rondo theme," a representation of Don Juan, is first sounded as a complex of two related E-major ideas: the introductory figure, m. 1 (DJ^{int}, beginning on a seeming "C^6" that is actually an E chord subjected to a ♮6-♮3 shift) and the Don Juan theme proper, m. 9 (DJ). The rondo theme recurs most clearly in m. 62 (a fleeting reference to DJ^{int} only, expressing here an ephemeral $V^7/B♭$), m. 169 (DJ: as in m. 1 the initial "C^6" is an expression of the E bass), and m. 474 (DJ^{int}, shortened, and DJ, in E major). The "Hero Theme" or Heldenthema sounded in the horns (V/C major), beginning with the upbeat to m. 315, is often considered a substitute for the rondo theme,[37] and some commentators consider it a rondo-theme recurrence.[38]

The rondo reappearances alternate with four adventures, or episodes, although various Don Juan motives also invade each of the episodes. The first three are commonly (and doubtless correctly) interpreted as representing the subject's aggressive seduction of three mistresses. Strauss constructs each of these episodes to be more ardent and prolonged than its predecessor. Episode 1 (mm. 44–62) is brief and tonally unstable. Although all commentators have considered it to signify the first of Don Juan's sexual encounters, it has been a problematic passage within the proposed rondo structures because of its brevity and tonal instability and because of the incomplete appearance of DJ^{int} only (and on $V^7/B♭$, the "wrong" key) at its end, mm. 62–65. Most commentators have refused it the status of a full-fledged rondo episode and, not unreasonably, have relegated it to the status of a transition (or "transition episode") to the more stable B major of the following episode.[39] However we categorize it, it begins with what is clearly the first appearance of "the Other"—a radical change of texture, motive, and dynamic, along with a sudden shift onto what would seem to be C major (m. 44). This C major is overpowered at once, however, by a potent, *fortissimo* cadential $^{6\text{-}5}_{4\text{-}3}$ in E (that is, in the rondo key, m. 46) that deflects it first onto a deceptive-cadence C-sharp minor chord (m. 48), tonicizes that C sharp via an authentic cadence on its dominant (m. 51), moves via sequences toward B-flat major (mm. 57ff.: now an augmented fourth away from the rondo's E), and rushes toward an abrupt diminished-seventh close (m. 62, enharmonically vii^{o7}/B♭).

Episode 2 (mm. 90–160, preceded by a lengthy dominant) is conceived essentially in B major, although it moves through other keys and builds to climactic E-minor chords in triplets in mm. 149–52 and 156–59. Episode 3 (mm. 197–314) is even longer and is subdivided into two sections: an ardent G-minor one (mm. 197–232) that relaxes into a slower, G-major idyll (mm. 232–314). Following the announcement of the subsequent *Heldenthema* (mm. 315ff., V/C), Strauss brings us to a modulatory Episode 4 (mm. 351–424) that begins in D major and proceeds to developmental activity (mm. 386ff.) that ends catastrophically (mm. 421–24). This episode is usually referred to (following Mauke, who was evoking an incident in Lenau's *Don Juan*) as the "Carnival" or "Masked Ball" Scene, although Lorenz also refers to it as the "Orgy."[40] The E-major tonic reprise of the initial Don Juan themes and the *Heldenthema* leads to the suicide-duel, invariably interpreted as a coda (mm. 567–606).

The argument in favor of a free-rondo structure has its musical and pro-grammatic attractions, but there are also some strong objections to it. First, as Abraham admitted, "Some of the sections . . . are disproportionately long; themes are freely interwoven, sections skilfully fused into one another."[41] Similarly, Lorenz had opposed the notion of a rondo on the grounds that it led to a sprawling, insufficiently regulated plan, from which "not the slight-est artistic pleasure could arise"; moreover, to interpret the *Heldenthema* as a rondo-recurrence was unconvincing, since it bore "not the slightest musical resemblance to the other principal themes."[42] In addition, two of the mo-ments that we might wish to count as DJ-rondo appearances, measures 62–66 and measures 169ff. (not to mention the first statement of the *Heldenthema*), do not articulate the theme in the tonic. (In this respect the form seems ori-ented more toward a "ritornello" than a "rondo" structure.) Most important, however, the expansive E-major tonic reprise, reinitiating the vigor of the opening and then moving to an apotheosis of the *Heldenthema* introduced on the tonic (but over a dominant pedal), seems unmistakably to suggest a varied recapitulation. In short, *Don Juan* is no standard rondo, although portions of it, especially its episodic first half—at least up to the *Heldenthema*, and perhaps up to the reprise—seem clearly to be in dialogue with the rondo tradition. Hence one may consider it to be, at least in part, a "rondo deformation."

The "free-sonata" position avoids some of these problems but introduces others. Its strongest piece of evidence is the recapitulatory reprise, and it also makes appeals to the dominant-key, second-subject-like effect of Episode 2 (preceded by what is now interpreted as a transition) and to some developmental aspects of the Carnival Scene. In 1921 Waltershausen stated what has become more or less the standard sonata argument—"a sonata form with a thematically free development and a shortened reprise"—and even suggested that the structure of Wagner's *Siegfried-Idyll* provided an interesting comparison, an argument echoed by Reinhold Muschler three years later.[43] (The comparison is indeed apt. Grounded, of course, in Lisztian practice, *Siegfried-Idyll* could well have provided one of the most influential models for late-century sonata deformations. More precisely, it was one of the key representatives of a deformation family that, particularly in symphonic poems or related genres, featured a developmental space given largely over to an episode or, more commonly, to a set of episodes—in this case, to a pair of them.[44] Some other family members include Liszt's *Tasso*, in which the episodes are little more than rudimentary thematic transformations of expositional material, along with Strauss's more complex *Macbeth* and *Death and Transfiguration*.)

Discussions along this line have been furthered by current writers in English, particularly in the variant disseminated by Norman Del Mar: "The form of the work is fundamentally the same as that of [his immediately preceding symphonic poem] *Macbeth*: i.e. a sonata first movement with two major independent episodes inserted into the development."[45] The episodes in question are the G-minor/major "Episode 3" and the "Episode 4" Carnival Scene, which ends developmentally: they are separated, of course, by the appearance of the *Heldenthema*. In this view the development is considered to begin with DJ in m. 169 (Green concurs, for example, even while denying priority to the "sonata" aspects of the work), to be interrupted by the episodes, and then to resume midway through the Carnival Scene, in the vicinity of m. 386. This seems to me to be the most satisfying sonata-based arrangement of subsections within *Don Juan*.

Other solutions, however, are imaginable (although, I believe, less de-

fensible). Some commentators might wish to consider the development to
begin only after the highly stable "Episode 3," which would argue on behalf
of a lengthy, three-key, triple-theme exposition, in which the second and
third themes are separated by a brief, developmental (or transitional) appearance of the DJ theme.[46] Given the ambiguities tolerated, or even encouraged,
within deformational practice, anything is possible, one supposes, and to
some extent within that practice we ought not to insist so inflexibly upon
our *Formenlehre* subcategories. Still, it should be remarked, first, that such an
expansive exposition would be highly unusual for Strauss, who during this
period seemed to favor, as in *Macbeth*, references to bithematic expositional
spaces. Moreover, the problem that the "triple-theme exposition" argument
would be intended to solve, the presence of the "static," clearly thematic
G-major/minor episode, disappears once we become aware of the existence
of a normative sonata-deformation family with an "episodic" treatment of
the developmental space. Along these lines, though, we should acknowledge
Kenneth Levy's related—and highly unusual—suggestion that *Don Juan* provides us with a double exposition, the second beginning with DJ in m. 169
(which he mistakenly identifies as being "in the home key") and leading to
the G-minor/major section as a "new second theme," with the *Heldenthema*
serving as a link to the "Carnival" development.[47] This solution seems the
least satisfactory for at least three reasons: it is either unaware of or unconcerned with the actual *Rezeptionsgeschichte* of *Don Juan*, from which it differs
markedly; a repeated or double exposition is emphatically not part of the generic tradition of the symphonic poem (hence Levy draws his sonata-model
from what would appear to be a less appropriate genre, the classical "first-
movement" sonata form); and none of Strauss's other symphonic poems
shows the slightest interest in either a repeated or a double exposition.

As opposed to the libertine suggestions of the rondo structure, the programmatic connotations of a sonata, a form that stresses rounding, balances,
symmetries, and resolution, pose considerable problems. What does a quasi-
symmetrical resolution, for example, have to do with the cynical denouement of what is normally taken to be the program, the unraveling of Don
Juan's desire to live and his renunciation of a meaningless life by means of
the suicide-duel? Sonata-resolutions function well enough with *per aspera ad
astra* contents, but not with perverse (and rare) ones of the opposite type,
per astra ad aspera. More specifically: if Strauss leads the second development
episode (the Carnival Scene) to a catastrophe (mm. 421ff.) that ushers in Don
Juan's loss of sexual appetite and his lack of desire to continue living (which
seems unarguable), why does he follow it up with a triumphant reprise fea-

turing a *Heldenthema* apotheosis (mm. 510ff.) prior to the suicide duel in the coda? The jubilant recapitulation has proven to be difficult to assimilate into the assumed program of the work, and even the most programmatically conscientious of writers—Del Mar, for example—drop their discussions of the program at this point, only to resume them again at the point of the coda-duel.[48]

Nor are programmatic matters the only difficulties faced by the sonata interpretation. As might be inferred from what has preceded, on "purely formal grounds" the "nondevelopmental" episodes within the developmental space have been a perennial sticking point in *Don Juan*. Coming so directly after the narrative presentations in the exposition, these new episodes seem only to string out further the succession of self-contained adventures (rondo-like!), thus denying the work, at least up to the moment of the reprise, the "feel" of a standard sonata. Considered from the point of view of the expectations within a reified, *Formenlehre* sonata—and not, as seems preferable, from that of the far less restrictive ones within a characteristic "symphonic-poem" family of late-century sonata deformations—this can become a serious problem. Defenders of the sonata position's priority, such as Forchert, have consequently tended to see the looseness of the structure as a symptom of the disintegration of the late-century sonata, one in which the earlier ideals of functional musical coherence, motivic-tonal interconnections, and "[the sonata's] most important principle, thematic economy" are being undermined by the fracturing of the whole into "stylistically differing sections" that strive to become self-sufficient, sharply characterized, contrasting units.[49]

A second "sonata" problem mentioned by some commentators is what is often judged to be its lack of a sufficient symmetry in the recapitulation, in which the exposition's "transition" and "second theme" (Mistresses One and Two) fail to reappear and are replaced instead by a grand statement of the seemingly post-expositional *Heldenthema*. Lorenz, for example, refused to grant sonata status to *Don Juan* on the combined effects of the episodic development and this "blow in the face of sonata form" in the reprise.[50] Forchert, on the other hand, noted the recapitulation problem and ascribed it to programmatic considerations: "For it is surely not by chance that a Don-Juan-based piece, on the one hand, has more than one 'feminine' theme and, on the other, adheres to none of them all the way to the end."[51]

But in fact, the rationale for such a structure is not exclusively programmatic. As was the case with the episodic-development problem, the recapitulation problem is best addressed by considering it within the category of another of the characteristic fin-de-siècle deformation families: that of the "breakthrough" (Durchbruch) sonata deformation. (Late-century works, such as this one, not uncommonly mix the features of two or more deformation families.) Durchbruch, of course, is one of the central content-categories that Adorno devised in 1960 to interpret the music of Gustav Mahler,[52] and in the past two decades the concept has received some attention from German writers, particularly in Bernd Sponheuer's work on Mahler.[53] The concept of breakthrough, closely related to the category of peripeteia, or sudden reversal of fortune, involves abandoning or profoundly correcting the originally proposed sonata (the one proposed in the exposition) through the inbreaking of an emphatic, unforeseen idea at some post-expositional point, usually during the space customarily given over to development. The mid-piece inbreaking of the new from outside the proposed structure, sundering the piece's immanent logic, is sufficiently powerful to render a default recapitulation inadequate. The breakthrough thus triggers a recomposed or totally reconsidered recapitulation, in which the breakthrough idea itself usually plays a prominent role. Although there are many ways of realizing the concept, it can be seen to have arisen historically as one solution to the problem of a potentially redundant recapitulation within an aesthetic system that increasingly validated only original ideas.[54]

While tailored to explicate Mahler's First Symphony, Sponheuer's remarks on the concept of breakthrough are not without relevance to *Don Juan*:

> [In a piece that relies on a breakthrough] what is constitutive is its claim to contrast the "world" as the embodiment of the real, historical life-process [of which the given music is initially a reflection] . . . with that "other world" [that is, with the redemptive condition that invalidates the given world of the music]. . . . Such a contrast corresponds to the critical moment of breakthrough. [As Adorno put it,] "for a few seconds the symphony believes that what it has hoped for so anxiously and for so long, the earthly glimpse of heaven, has actually become real . . . the tearing of the veil. . . ." [In Mahler Durchbruch is] a breaking into the closed formal immanence through the unexpected ("as though it were dropping down from heaven"), peripeteia-like turn to chorale-like transcendence.[55]

The structural analogue in *Don Juan* is clear. Strauss proclaims this new condition with the *Heldenthema* in the horns (m. 315), which arrives emphatically as (to quote Lenau) "a thunderbolt from the heights," *ein Blitz aus Höh'n*.[56] This can be considered the announcement of the breakthrough-intention, and it eventually results in a radically altered recapitulation in which the break-through is more fully realized. There Strauss, following the guidelines of the deformation family, collapses the exposition schema to produce an apotheosis, or true breakthrough, in which the *Heldenthema* is sounded *fortissimo* on the tonic E major, mm. 510ff., as a substitute second subject. This event is clearly the sonorous high point of the work to which all else has led. Significantly, in the recapitulation the *Heldenthema* is sounded over a dominant pedal: its initial sonority is a powerful $^6_4$ chord proclaiming both arrival and expectation. The larger point, however, is that it is not yet resolved. The composer subsequently drives the climactic music to an ecstatic C-major *Jubelruf* in measures 543ff., seemingly its true goal, to a series of sequences that land on F major (heard as IV/C), and finally to a cadence back in E to begin the suicide-duel coda. These details—particularly the crucial significance of C major, which functions as a kind of "second (or redemptive) tonic" in *Don Juan*—will be taken up again in Section 3 below.

But what about the rondo argument, which was also so cogent, at least up to the moment of the *Heldenthema*'s appearance—indeed, up to the point of the reprise? That, too, can be accommodated through a shift from the concept of form-as-schema to that of form-as-process. The actual musical logic of *Don Juan* is best described as a process by which what initially appears to unfold as a rondo deformation is conceptually recast, toward the end, as a sonata deformation.[57] Notwithstanding the general sonata-deformational orientation of its genre, Strauss begins *Don Juan* by providing us with what would seem to be rondo-like signals: cyclical thematic recurrences (albeit in various keys, some of them "wrong") and episodic adventures. None of this need be problematic until the moment of the first sounding of the C-major *Heldenthema* (m. 315)—seemingly an unforeseen regeneration of some sort—which is puzzling within the rondo-deformation context. (Equally important, however, is that up to this point the evidence that the piece might be a sonata is even slimmer.) Notwithstanding the inbreaking of the Hero-Theme, the piece proceeds, rondo-like, into another episode, the Carnival Scene, in which the new *Heldenthema* plays a prominent role. But instead of suggesting another conquest for Don Juan, the Carnival music suggests instead catastrophe and collapse (mm. 421–24). What Strauss also collapses here is the rondo principle itself: the inner momentum of the rondo, ideally capable of an infinite number of self-replications, is now spent and cannot continue. This precipitates a crisis of form and formal continuation.

The musical zone that connects the Carnival Scene catastrophe to the onset of the reprise (m. 474) comprises a series of brief recollections of the

a. Oboe Idyll, mm. 236-44

b. *Heldenthema*, mm. 315-26

Example 1.

episodes, a barren review of the path that has led to the present structural crisis: images from Episode 1 (mm. 431–33), Episode 2 (mm. 438–41), Episode 3 (mm. 444–47), and, again, Episode 2 (mm. 448–57).[58] The sudden dominant-seventh "snap" in m. 457 (initiating a prolonged V^7 of E) would appear to be connected with Strauss's decision to shift genres: it is as if a solution is glimpsed, and we hear a dominant intensification into what we may now interpret as the recapitulation of a breakthrough sonata deformation. It is only at the moment of the reprise, then (m. 474ff.), and especially at the moment of the *Heldenthema* apotheosis (m. 510), that we realize that the rondo principle has been supplanted by that of the sonata (more specifically, by that of the breakthrough deformational variant). Retrospectively, we may now recall the sonata potential embedded in the dominant-key, second-subject-like Episode 2 (mm. 90–160), the transition potential in Episode 1, the piece's overall structural similarity to other "developmentally episodic" symphonic poems, and so on, and we may accordingly reshape our understanding of the piece under a new generic category.

As we rethink our way through the piece, it would at first appear that the crucial moment for the structure was the initial appearance of the *Heldenthema*. This unforeseen event seems to have disempowered the rondo and made its successful continuation impossible; the subsequent attempt to do so has ended in crisis. But as Strauss tells the tale, the proximate cause of the *Heldenthema Durchbruch* is the experience of the idyllic third episode, for the *Heldenthema* is itself a thematic transformation of (or complement to) Episode 3's oboe theme. One hears once again in the *Heldenthema*, for example, the octave leap to the held note (example 1, at [a]), the oboe's coy grace note transformed into a powerful iambic rhythm (b), the subsequent descent with reiterated subphrase (c), and so on. The breakthrough that precipitates the generic crisis (and ultimately, as the agent of peripeteia, that makes the ensuing sonata deformation possible) is itself generated by the experience of the third episode. Episode 3, then, is the crux of the matter: it is an episode with unforeseen structural consequences.[59]

Before pursuing those consequences, we might finally recall Gerlach's observation, quoted at the beginning of this section, that *Don Juan* is also mixed throughout with an overarching "four-movements-in-one" structure. As has also been noted by Lorenz and Green, the oboe idyll in Episode 3 corresponds with a closed slow movement, the Carnival Scene with a scherzo, and the recapitulation with a finale.[60] And as Dahlhaus has argued, this multi-movement principle is one of the key categories of the post-Lisztian sonata,[61] and it, too, has its own expressive consequences, which will also be considered below.

To summarize the musical-logic argument presented thus far: *Don Juan* is structurally in no single form; rather, it is a structural process in dialogue with several generic traditions. Most important, these traditions are not presented randomly: Strauss undermines the initial rondo deformation's force with the material in the third episode along with its immediate consequences, the *Heldenthema* breakthrough (the *Blitz aus Höh'n*) and the catastrophic Carnival, then liquidates it by presenting subsequent events that permit us to reinterpret the piece as a sonata deformation (a reinterpretation that, however ultimately decisive, must not ignore the earlier presence of the rondo, which had by no means been a false presence); and the whole complex is suffused with the urge to be perceived as a multimovement form in a single movement. This narrative of structural dissolution and replacement could be pursued in a purely musical language by elaborating its tonal ("double-tonic"), harmonic, melodic, rhythmic, and textural details. But this is a symphonic poem—the genre that asks us to consider these things in conjunction with a verbally based, poetic logic. And it is to that more uncertain, but generically defining, realm that we now turn.

3

The obvious base text for an inquiry into the poetic logic of *Don Juan* is the set of brief extracts from Lenau's poem that Strauss provided along with the score.[62] Establishing a clear link between the music and the extracts, however, has proven problematic over the past century. The cited lines furnish only a generalized expressive shape, that of an initial erotic energy ultimately transformed into loss and disillusionment; but with regard to specifics, as Muschler put it, they have "nothing to do with a chain of events."[63] For this reason, seekers of a more vivid narrative program have tended to follow the

1908 strategy of Wilhelm Mauke, who refused to be limited to the thirty-two provided lines and insisted that "the whole poem of Lenau must be considered, for we find all of its principal episodes expressed here in sounds."[64] This procedure encouraged a closer identification of what seems to be unambiguously represented in the musical work: three specific sexual encounters, the catastrophic Carnival Scene and its immediate aftermath, and the concluding suicide-duel, none of which is mentioned in the provided lines.

Still, the connection of the Strauss work to the Lenau poem has not been easy to explain, and opinions have ranged from Mauke's Lenau-based concreteness to Specht's 1921 assertion that a far wider program or poetic idea dominates the work: "the symphonic expression of the strongest, most primitive human feeling, the erotic, a series of sensuality masks in their most potent forms. . . . Lenau's *Don Juan* gives [Strauss's work] only its name."[65] Specht's expansion of the poetic content into the general concept of Don-Juanism as the key image of masculine sexual desire was echoed by Lorenz in 1936. "The work's material is not that of Lenau's *Don Juan*. This shape is only a symbol for something far more general . . . the representation of the Will to Life in its most undisguised shape, in Eros."[66]

Particularly because the music's most significant structural events reside outside the confines of both any simple reading of Lenau and any unproblematized celebration of sheer libido, what is needed is a closer study of the work's imagery. Much of this centers around the erotics of the music. On the most basic level it could scarcely be more evident that the work's prevailing images are clearly musical representations of male sexuality—both of its physical mechanics and of nineteenth-century masculine conceptions of the feminine. These allusions are as explicit as the degree to which they have been euphemized by past commentators. One may be certain, however, that on certain basic levels of poetic content this piece concerns itself neither with innocent hand-holding nor with mere serenades to an idealized object of beauty: as Leporello reminds us about another Don Juan, "Voi sapete quel che fa."

In a 1934 study of the typology of Strauss's melodies Roland Tenschert identified certain theme types as masculine and feminine. Masculine themes were those displaying an initial, vigorously rising anacrusis incorporating "activity and positive engagement . . . ascending impetus [*Auftrieb*], power, will"; feminine themes were lyrically rich, legato, descending lines embodying "sinking downward, conceding to another [*Gewährenlassen*], emotion, and also, not infrequently, a specific disposition [*Gemüt*]."[67] More current perspectives would probably consider it self-evident that the leading symbol of the principal Don Juan themes (mm. 1 and 9ff.) is that of the phallus, here also to be understood as a signifier of potential conquest (Lenau's *immer neuen Siegen*, mentioned in the lines quoted by Strauss), of the drive toward libertinism (the magic circle, *Den Zauberkreis*), and of blind sexual desire (*der Jugend Feuerpulse* in pursuit of the *Sturm des Genusses*). The appropriateness of its initial reappearances as a rondo theme—the unfailing regeneration of sexual potency after finishing with the feminine episodes—is obvious enough (cf. Lenau's *Sie kann nur sterben hier, dort neu entspringen*), and at least one commentator, Bryan Gilliam, has explicitly identified E major in Strauss as "typically associated with the passionate or erotic."[68]

Observations such as these can help us to interpret the significance of an important motive used near the onset of both the first and second episodes (that is, in Don Juan's seductions of Mistresses One and Two, mm. 46–48 and 90–92: see example 2a and b). To be sure, this figure need not be identified exclusively as a musical metaphor of sexual penetration (although the case that could be argued on its behalf is obvious enough, to insist too strongly upon it would be both crudely reductive and unnecessary), but whatever our graphic interpretation might be, the far more important point is that on a broader level of metaphor it would appear to represent Don Juan as possessor, the invader of episodic "other-space" that he is now claiming as his own. In this regard, it is also easy to perceive in the music's early narratives a classic unfolding of what gender theory would identify as one characteristic type of masculine discourse: the conversion of sexual desire (the principal theme) into acts of power and possession (the episodes).

In the first episode Strauss employs this figure *fortissimo* to overwhelm Mistress One's brief C-major identity. "Her" C in mm. 44–45, which in its non sequitur appearance can strike us as a potentially stable, "other" tonic approaching E major as if "from outside" (this is surely its programmatic point, as virtually all commentators have noted), is instantly appropriated and nor-

Example 2.

a. mm. 46–48

b. mm. 90–92

malized as a mere upper neighbor to "his" dominant, V/E. Thus a subject-centered tonic control is insisted upon; through the possession figure "for itself" is consumed and converted into "for him." The composer then leads the episode, now confidently centered on "Don Juan–related keys" (those more relatable to "his" E than to "her" C), into the musical interplay of the assertive masculine and the alternating *flebile* and stereotypically giggling feminine.

In the second episode the possession figure serves as the less aggressive incipit of a more prolonged, lyrical, and *tranquillo* seduction. (To those who, following the interpretive tradition, would argue that this figure represents Mistress Two here, one may respond very simply: it may in fact "be" her, but only in the limited sense that, in actuality, it is nothing more than Don Juan's perception—or Strauss's construction—of her as something beautiful to be possessed. In any event, the tradition does not account for the prominent appearance of this figure in the prior episode.) The second episode begins in B major, moves through other keys, and leads to what is probably a musical representation of masculine sexual climax (the E-minor chords in triplets, mm. 149–52 and 156–59; cf. "Don Juan's tonic," E major).

Without question, there is an aspect of the modernistically sensational in Strauss's treatment here of the erotic, and it is a simple enough task to propose interpretations of the musical details as representations of graphic concretes once the basic premise is accepted. Needless to say, however, the main risks in any interpretive multiplication of specific erotic referents are, first, the difficulty of sensing at what points our supposed concretes pass over into either the unlikely or the preposterous—tastes and temperaments will differ on this point—and, second, the danger of becoming so taken with a single line of sensational representations that we overlook other possibilities or broader interpretations.

All of this bears on Strauss's construction of the third episode, Don Juan's sexual encounter with Mistress Three. As already mentioned, this episode differs significantly from its predecessors in that it subdivides into two complementary sections, in G minor and G major, traditionally interpreted as an ardent wooing followed by a more intimate love scene.[69] But on this point the tradition seems mistaken, or perhaps squeamish. Although the first section, in G minor, (mm. 197–232) lacks the possession incipit, it is helpful, I think, to interpret it as precisely what we might expect on the basis of the preceding episodes: another musical representation of the sexual act, initiated, as before, without delay by the indefatigable seducer. Once again the composer presents us with a dominating, ascending masculine theme, now syncopatedly assertive and *molto appassionato*, in dialogue (as in Episode 1) with *flebile*, gasping feminine responses.

But Episode 3—or Mistress Three—is not immediately discarded, as her predecessors had been. On the contrary, the G-minor episode now relaxes into a second section, the prolonged G-major idyll, *sehr getragen und ausdrucksvoll*. The most obvious inference would be that Strauss, as narrator, is suggesting that Don Juan is lingering in a prolonged embrace, now released (or "redeemed"—Wagner's *erlöst*) from a roguishly coital G minor into a radiant, and doubtless postcoital, G major. For the first time—and this must be the *raison d'être* of the nonnormative "double episode"—Don Juan is portrayed as accepting satisfaction and stasis. This is a reversal of that which had defined his essence (Lenau's *Ich fliehe Ueberdruss und Lustermattung . . . Hinaus und fort nach immer neuen Siegen, / So lang der Jugend Feuerpulse fliegen!*). In the G-major episode, then, Strauss begins the process of undoing Don Juan *qua* Don Juan; the melodic, harmonic-tonal, and structural signs associated with him are now seriously threatened. (We may recall that Episode Three's idyll is the musical event through which, and after which, the ongoing rondo deformation will be dissolved. After this third episode Don Juan is permitted no more episodic successes, or conquests.) In this pivotal G-major idyll Don Juan the penetrator is himself penetrated—presumably by such things as genuine emotion, fulfillment, and so on—and the rondo principle, his structural sign, is incapable of continuing as if nothing had happened.

With the G-major idyll emerges the famous oboe theme (mm. 236ff.); Don Juan's prior "Episode 3 seduction" motive has now collapsed into a cozily satisfied prop (in the muted cellos and violas, *divisi*, above a settled tonic pedal) for the theme itself. Here too, in the new attention to the feminine, Strauss overturns the piece's basic premises, and this first peripeteia is simultaneously linked with the problem of placing a slow movement into a multimovement-form-in-a-single-movement that claims to convey the fiery pulses (*Feuerpulse*) of libidinal insatiability. Because the slow movement would inevitably be the contradictory movement of such a piece, one might have expected Strauss to have suppressed it or to have treated it in a less substantial way. The composer's solution to this structural dilemma is as simple as it is brilliant. By expanding the slow movement into a prolonged, sensual stasis, and by subsequently abandoning the rondo principle in a negative scherzo, Strauss invites us to interpret the slow movement as the irreversible wounding of the piece's initial principles. Thus Don Juan's encounter with Mistress Three becomes the cardinal event of his life, at least as traced out in this narrative.

Virtually all commentators interpret the idyll as displaying a new depth to Don Juan's emotion, although as a rule they draw no further conclusions from this apart from pointing us toward the beauty of the music. Mauke touches here on the German Romantic tradition that Don Juan did indeed fall in love with one woman, Donna Anna (in fact, such an event is mentioned, but not explicitly dramatized, in the Lenau poem);[70] Specht conjures up "das uralte Mysterium von Mann und Weib"; and Del Mar, while hesitant to accept Mauke's identification of Mistress Three with Anna, assures us that "there is not the slightest doubt that Strauss is now concerned with Juan's deepest love-experience."[71]

Moreover, the opening of the G-major passage is not without its Wagnerian resonances. In terms of affect, allusion, and even melodic contour, the oboe theme can easily recall such nineteenth-century masculine constructions of the ideal woman—almost invariably represented as a gentle, centered voice of security, the domestic complement to masculine striving—as heard, for instance, in the E-major portion of the love duet in *Siegfried*, act 3, the rescued and newly awakened Brünnhilde's "anmüthiges Bild vor die Seele" (see example 3a and b).[72] Perhaps even more to the point, this passage was also familiar as the principal theme of the *Siegfried-Idyll*, one of the principal models for late-nineteenth-century sonata deformation, and one which, as mentioned above, Waltershausen and Muschler claimed as the prototype for the structure of *Don Juan*. Related examples of this familiar "ideal-partner" *topos* (which frequently features a solo woodwind instrument, often an oboe) include Liszt's representation of Gretchen in *Eine Faust-Symphonie* (example 3c) and the theme, sung by a newly blissful Eva, that opens the quintet from *Die Meistersinger*, act 3 (example 3d; certain features of the quintet seem to be explicitly echoed in this *Don Juan* episode). Strauss would reuse the *topos* for Dulcinea del Toboso (or, as Del Mar argues for its first appearance only, for "the ideal Lady of Knighthood") in *Don Quixote* (example 3e).[73]

The idyll closes in its tonic, G major (m. 296), and a *molto tranquillo/dolcissimo* codetta is appended (mm. 296–307). At this point we hear Don Juan's "seduction" motive—a mere support in the idyll—beginning to stir, *stringendo* (mm. 307–14), rising out and away (*hinaus und fort*) from the stasis, driving toward the refocussing of the masculine voice. But this voice is no longer that of the initial rondo; it is the *Heldenthema* (another peripeteia) sounded in unison by the four horns (mm. 315ff.). As mentioned above, its melody is determined primarily by the rhythms and contours of the Mistress-Three theme, and yet one might argue that its (upbeat)-descent-ascent shape, reinforced with extraordinary intensity of timbre, concludes in a manner likely to strike us as

158   James Hepokoski

Example 3.

more potently masculine than anything presented thus far. This is the moment announcing the advent of the Durchbruch, Lenau's Blitz aus Höh'n—Don Juan in some sense unexpectedly transformed by Mistress Three—and the theme is underpinned with "her" tonic pitch, G, now functioning as a powerful dominant of C major. Since the Heldenthema expresses the dominant, not the tonic—potentiality, not actuality—we are now presented with the possibility of a transformed tonic, a telos or utopian tonic to which Episode 3, it now appears, has been pointing. Thus just as Don Juan is given a new theme at this point, he is also given a potentially new tonic. And although it is as yet unrealized, indeed scarcely envisioned, he will also be offered a new structural sign: that of the Durchbruch sonata deformation.

Such an interpretation also addresses one of the (only seemingly minor) puzzles of the piece: why did Strauss fail to provide key signatures for the entire middle section of Don Juan (mm. 197–456; the outer sections, of course, are in four sharps)? Curiously, the signature change to no sharps or flats occurs at the outset of Episode 3, although that moment launches an extensive stretch of "two-flat" music followed by an even longer one of "one-sharp" music (mm. 197–231, 232–313). (All of this, of course, is intended to raise the much-neglected issue of the poetic content of pure notation—in this case, of "wrong" key signatures.) One presumes that Strauss is notationally suggesting that from its beginning he conceives the G area of Episode 3— that is, Mistress Three—as striving by stages to attain the redemptive C major. Thus the G-minor/major episode followed by the clearly dominant function of the *Heldenthema* can be seen as a long-range potential cadence in C major. It is the function of the *Heldenthema* to usher in the *telos*, C major—a *telos* cleverly foreshadowed in such spots as the pseudo-"C^6" implication of measure 1, the first, "innocent" appearance of the feminine (mm. 44–45), and the "C^6" of the rondo recurrence of DJ at m. 169.

But the potential for transformation is not accepted. Instead of resolving the G dominant, Strauss confounds it by bringing it onto a common-tone, C-sharp diminished seventh chord (m. 337). This triggers the return of the old "libertine" impulse in the cellos and basses (DJ^{int}, *rapidamente*), and it is followed by a brief, developmental representation of the struggle between the two *personae* of Don Juan: the traditional libertine (DJ^{int}) and the newly transfigured (perhaps potentially domestic) *Held* (mm. 337–50). At stake is the continued viability of Don Juan's old signs: DJ^{int} and DJ, E major, and the rondo structure.

The composer now leads Don Juan into a fourth episode, the Carnival "scherzo" beginning in D major but lacking a key signature (m. 351: that is, the music is notationally branded by the remembered possibility of C major).[74] Strauss's poetic logic, parallel to the musical logic, would appear to suggest that in rejecting the transformation offered to him, Don Juan believes that, as before, he will be able to get back onto the rondo track. But in Episode 4 Don Juan is identified primarily by the new Hero Theme. He is not who he was: he is now marked by Mistress Three, and the *Heldenthema* is subjected to a developmental, decentering process that leads from frivolity (glockenspiel, m. 358) to increasing distortion and attempts to reassert the rondo theme (DJ^{int} and DJ variants, *vivo*, mm. 386ff.), to ultimate crisis, nonresolution, and collapse (mm. 421–24). The fourth episode is unsuccessful; the rondo game is liquidated.

In the famous shattered-review of episodes (mm. 424–57)—Mistresses One, Two (the possession figure as a sign of Don Juan's original persona), Three, and Two again—Strauss brings the rondo narrative to a halt. What is created here is something of a corridor connecting two areas grounded in differing formal categories—rondo and sonata deformation. Everything preceding this corridor is mainly in dialogue with the rondo principle; everything following it will invite us to revise our hearing in the direction of a sonata deformation. The poetic metaphor would seem to be that of Don

Juan weighing the alternatives of the two personae available to him as expressed in the past episodes. In this famous "Katerstelle" (Hangover Passage) as Strauss called it,[75] the ordering 1, 2, 3 (the new persona), and 2 must be significant, and the second reevocation of the possession figure from Episode 2 (mm. 448–57) conjures up Don Juan's realization that the former rondo persona (the libertine) holds no more pleasure for him (Lenau's *plötzlich ward die Welt mir wüst, umnachtet . . . der Brennstoff ist verzehrt*, and so on). Along with the rondo structure, the DJ themes themselves and their E-major tonic key will ultimately have to be abandoned.

For the present, however, the moment of decision (m. 457, the "snap" V^7 of E major, *a tempo primo*) prepares a sonata-deformation reprise of the Durchbruch type. Both structurally and poetically, this "recapitulation" holds the key to the meaning of *Don Juan* and is simultaneously the most difficult portion of the work to interpret. The composer's decision to have the subject "rebegin" here—after the preceding collapse—can be understood in a number of ways, and I shall suggest three. First, the adoption of a deformation of the sonata principle suggests above all a jettisoning of the rondo, coupled with an acceptance of architectonic rounding and more or less symmetrical resolution, all of which must be understood to be antithetical to the original Don Juan persona. To accept the reprise-and-resolution aspect of the sonata here is decisively to accept the transformation wrought by the peripeteias of Episode 3 and the *Heldenthema*. Thus, from one perspective the energetic rondo theme, now the principal theme of the sonata, is brought back as a sign of embracing sonata activity. (This is no trite argument, I hope, that the recapitulation exists for "purely musical reasons." In some senses this is accurate, but the semiotic point is that those reasons constitute a "negative sign" of what is abandoned—here, the poetic idea of the abandonment of the rondo and the persona with which it is identified. In other words, one way to abandon a rondo is to show the listener that it has become a sonata.)

Second, one may argue that Strauss's narrative task is now to extinguish the signs of Don Juan as libertine in as emphatic a manner as possible. The dialectic established thus far is essentially this: on the one side, E major, rondo deformation, DJ themes, and libertinism; on the other, a potential C major as *telos*, sonata deformation, *Heldenthema*, and abandonment of libertinism and *Erlösung* via Mistress Three. This argument would maintain that the rondo theme and its key are being "set up" in the recapitulation primarily to be destroyed (that is, in the coda). This return of the rondo theme, now the principal theme of a sonata, may be heard as the first stages of the propping up of the target.

Third, the rondo theme may be reevoked to serve as a pointer or pathway to something beyond itself, namely the triumphant reappearance of the *Heldenthema* (mm. 510ff.). The recapitulation would thus summarize the old-persona/new-persona trajectory that characterizes the entire work. One notices that the DJ theme itself now differs from its version in the "exposition": it is far briefer (functioning primarily now as an intensification leading to the *Heldenthema*), and it is no mere restatement of the opening—rather, it is imprinted with traces of the catastrophic Episode-4 experience (for example, the fleeting shift through D in m. 486, suggesting also an unstable E major; the brass motives in mm. 490ff., beginning on V of C-sharp minor; and so on). The actual moment of passage into the *Heldenthema* apotheosis also seems significant: the bass line of the two measures preceding it (mm. 508–9) reevoke the d^1-b chromatic descent characteristic of the accompaniment of the opening of the G-major idyll (cf. mm. 232–37, which, as I have suggested earlier, is the first indication of Don Juan's acceptance of a passive, static role).

As for the *Heldenthema* apotheosis itself (mm. 510ff.), it seems to have a double function. Considered from the side of symmetries and balances, it confirms the sonata deformation, and hence the negation of the rondo, by replacing the themes of the earlier mistresses with the *Durchbruch* idea in E major. But more importantly, the *Heldenthema* expresses V, not I: underpinned by a pedal dominant, it is still unresolved at the moment of its appearance in the recapitulation and represents promise, not fulfillment. In measure 526 the bass dominant begins its 5-4-3-2-1 descent to the tonic, but when the E tonic is reached (m. 529), a ♮7 above veers away from closure on E and begins a process of further intensifications and sequences that push instead into a triumphant C major (m. 543).

In short, Strauss drives the *Heldenthema* not to a cadence in E, but to one in C, the *telos* key promised in Episode 3. I take this attainment of root-position C major (a harmonic and chordal stability that the *Heldenthema* proper never attains) to be both the central "tonal point" of the symphonic poem's key patterns, and, ultimately, the point that I believe unlocks the poetic content of the whole. The E-major tonic (the "rondo"-Don Juan's tonic) is not to be the true locus of the new persona: that E major, too, will have to be liquidated. At this point the composer opens up an escape hatch, so to speak, to permit the new persona to "leap out of" E major into C major—to abandon the E-major piece that has been created thus far.[76]

The C-major passage, the final peripeteia or transfiguration (mm. 543ff.), introduces an exultant, quasi-pentatonic (and again, somewhat Wagnerian)

mm. 543-47

Example 4.

Jubelruf, itself derived from a portion of the *Heldenthema* (example 4).[77] Notwithstanding its function as the redemptive space or the true goal, the C-major passage itself is brief. Strauss now leads the *Jubelruf* through ascending sequences and locks it onto an F-major chord (mm. 556–67), which clearly is to be heard as IV of C. Its function here, however, is to serve as the setup for the E-major cadence that launches the coda (m. 567), whose goal it is to destroy that E major, that is, the old persona. With the F-chord setup comes the return of the ascending "libertine" figures, and with the E cadence that "libertine" key, along with the DJ themes, is propped up as the target for liquidation: the destruction of these things is to be dramatized, made patently audible. (And if we have concluded that the "real content" of the piece has been abandoned with the leap into the C-major *Jubelruf* passage, what remains here on E is a mere shell, a set of empty gestures vulnerable to collapse—that is, transformation into E minor.)

In the "suicide-duel" coda, that E major is extinguished, brought down to E minor with what is usually interpreted as the sword thrust of Don Pedro (mm. 586–87). Once again the penetrator is penetrated (only now literally), in a gesture parallel to that of Episode 3. All of the prior buoyancy and *élan* of the tonic now deflates to its parallel minor—here, as all commentators have noted, a death symbol.[78] Thus the poetic structure of the entire work follows the reverse of the pattern found in Strauss's next symphonic poem: here, instead, we have a *Verklärung und Tod*.

4

That all of the above suggests things beyond the thirty-two lines of Lenau selected by Strauss (in fact, beyond the actual content of the entire Lenau poem or the Don Juan tradition) is obvious. This need not invalidate the poetic idea proposed here. Rather, it raises the issue of whether a musical work may go beyond the concreteness of its avowed program—whether a piece can be in dialogue with its paratext rather than remaining bound to it. The point, ultimately, lies not so much in the verifiability of my programmatic suggestions (short of discovering a note from Strauss mapping out the "secret program" of *Don Juan*, how could one be certain of the details?) than in the exercise itself. I am less concerned with issues of argumentative closure than I am with illustrating a process that founds the symphonic poem as a genre.

But we are still left with some puzzles: which Don Juan story is Strauss telling, and what is its larger significance? Any answer would have to begin by reconfronting the issue of whether the death of Don Juan at the work's end is to be understood literally. If so, in Strauss's version Don Juan ceases to exist as Don Juan at the point of the G-major idyll, the quelling of the ever-renewable potency of his *Feuerpulse*. Strauss leads his hero to confirm this in the Durchbruch and subsequently decentering fourth episode, and after permitting him a last embrace of his beloved destroyer (the *Heldenthema* and *Jubelruf* in the recapitulation) the composer brings his subject to a literal death, the physical realization of the spiritual death suffered earlier. This is a recasting of the common, nihilistic version of the story, variants of which were expanded by Rolland in 1908 into an image of a technically invincible but purposeless German military machine (which "clasps the world in its great arms and subjugates it, and then stops, fatigued by its conquest, and asks: 'Why have I conquered?' "),[79] and, more recently, by Adorno into a metaphor for what he perceives as the emptiness of Strauss's music itself:

> Senile and infantile, his music responds through mimesis to the universal domination of the calculated effect in which it becomes ensnared; it thumbs its nose at the censors. It does not take part, however, in the process of self-preservation. The life which celebrates itself in this music is death; to understand Strauss would be to listen for the murmur beneath the roar, which, inarticulate and questioning, becomes audible in the final measures of *Don Juan* and is his truth-content. Solely in decline, perhaps, is there a trace of what might be more than mortal: inextinguishable experience in disintegration.[80]

But yet, as Lenau suggests in the most telling phrase in the extracts quoted by Strauss, "And perhaps not" (*Vielleicht auch nicht*). Another interpretation, one that seems more likely to me, although it is hardly less unsettling, is that Strauss dramatized the rejection of one traditional masculine persona (the libertine) through the acceptance of another (the sharer of middle-class "heroic" domesticity with the "intended" partner). The suicide-duel at the end of this superficially positive version of the tale, one of the wholehearted acceptance of *bürgerlich* stasis and conformity, would signify not the destruction of the physical individual, but rather the abandonment of an earlier, rakish persona, all cast in somewhat overinflated, mock-heroic terms, but terms that after all are not unrelated to Strauss's life situation in the late 1880s.

In this reading the transformed subject would survive (somewhere outside of the actual piece, one supposes, but in the sharpless and flatless land of C major, having bailed out through the redemptive window opened by the composer near the end of the recapitulation), and the logical poetic sequels to *Don Juan* would be the "bourgeois" conclusion to *Ein Heldenleben* and the whole of the *Symphonia Domestica*. To the degree that one entertains the possibility of the domestic denouement as opposed to the nihilistic one, one might argue that in a broader sense Strauss's radicalism in *Don Juan* is deceptive: a dazzling technical façade conceals far more conventional attitudes that he would reveal more overtly in some of his later tone poems and then embrace even more fervently in the second decade of the next century.

Such considerations suggest larger issues of historical content and meaning. Within the sphere of technique, Strauss situated *Don Juan* within a historical paradigm whose validity was intertwined with issues of artistic innovation and obsolescence, that is, with an aesthetically "correct" intersection with (to borrow Adorno's concept) the "state of the material."[81] His overriding concern was to be perceived as engaging in a progressive dialogue with a complex set of historically determined default attitudes, genres, and formal traditions.

Still, within a working out of these technical problems one may perceive some of the growing historical tensions between "realism" and "modernism," and notwithstanding the slipperiness of these terms and the complexity of the issues they raise, we might conclude by sketching out some of these larger concerns. It could be argued, for example, that the category of realism seems particularly active in the first two thirds of the work. Here in the rondo we encounter a mimetically representational content that seems to be a larger concern than form per se.[82] The mere impulse toward representation, of course, cannot define a work as realistic. As Dahlhaus has warned us, nineteenth-century music's relationship to realism is problematic. Instrumental music more often represents a prolonged adherence to romanticism in an otherwise increasingly realistic world: "The simplistic equating of 'realistic' and 'programmatic' . . . is too primitive to make discussing the instances where it is propounded worthwhile."[83] The larger point, though, is that here the specific rondo program, a mere sequence of sexual encounters altogether unconcerned with defining itself in terms of shape and proportion, is extraordinarily flat, emphatically physical, and (certainly by the onset of the third episode) both repetitively ordinary and seemingly pointless.

More broadly, then, traces of realism may be discerned not in the mere representational intention but in the music's underlying aesthetic stance and

Weltanschauung. As Fredric Jameson has argued, one of realism's key features is to desacralize experience previously overcoded through myth or metaphysics; this is a realism whose represented objects belong to a "desacralized, postmagical, common-sense, everyday, secular reality."[84] In its embracing of some sort of nontranscendent, everyday concreteness and secularized representation, much of Strauss's *Don Juan* (and the later tone poems even more) subjects the prevailing concept of a mystical, autonomous music to a rigorous critique. This aspect of Strauss, which we may now regard as the principal challenge of his work, was not lost on those of his critics who continued to uphold the Schopenhauerian-Wagnerian belief in a music that transcends the merely phenomenal. For any true believer—Mahler, Schoenberg, Bloch, Adorno, and others—the all too easy link between Strauss and the acceptance of everyday experience poisoned the composer's oeuvre and tilted dangerously at the seriousness of music itself: as one of the defenders of the faith, Bloch would refer to Strauss as "the master of the superficial."[85] Strauss's music invites us to ponder the disproportion between the generic promise of his apparatus—the full-blown symphony orchestra, developed by believers to become the bearer of a sacrament—and the often mundane or emphatically negative "realities" that Strauss uses it to convey. All of this would seem to be connected with the sociohistorical concerns of realism and desacralization. To what extent Adorno's charge of Strauss's "technification" of music is relevant here remains to be explored.[86]

The concept of turn-of-the-century musical modernism, too, needs further investigation. Although this "modernism" (in a specifically narrow sense of the term, as opposed, say, to the far broader concept of "modernity" that many writers in the Germanic tradition would see as extending back at least to the eighteenth century)[87] is one of the chief categories of Dahlhaus's system, it remains curiously undeveloped in his writings, existing mostly as something to be posited, following Hermann Bahr, as a "breakaway mood of the 1890s."[88] The literature on literary and artistic modernism, however, is enormous, and although I wish to steer as clear as possible from the impulse to reduce the term to any one of its competing definitions, once again, for our more limited purposes Fredric Jameson provides some helpful remarks. To Jameson this more specifically delimited modernism (which flourished especially in much of the radical art of the earlier twentieth century) is the "dialectical counterconcept" of realism, one with an "emphasis on violent renewal of perception in a world in which experience has solidified into a mass of habits and automatisms."[89] This articulation seems tailored to describe the events of *Don Juan*: the merely sequential, "pointless" rondo, capable of replicating itself ad infinitum (*Sie kann nur sterben hier, dort neu entspringen*); the *Heldenthema Blitz aus Höh'n*; the subsequent decentering of Don Juan's initial persona; the corridor of self-reflection (in which Don Juan acquires a history by reflecting on and thus problematizing the emptiness of merely habitual, "realistic" experience); and the "renewal of perception" made available by retrojecting the category of a breakthrough sonata deformation over past events and then proceeding in suit.

In short, in *Don Juan* Strauss brings into tension three historical categories: the de facto, "neo-Romantic" ideology of the metaphysics of instrumental music; the "realistic" desacralization and the initial embrace of the merely material or the everyday, whose function is to critique the neoromanticism; and the recourse to such "modern" structural processes as breakthrough and attempted resacralization, which, in their turn, critique the realism. It is difficult to ascertain which of the three categories is ultimately decisive. Rather, they seem suspended in an unresolved tension, and it is in that tension that the heart of the piece resides. Such considerations begin to account for the ambiguity of *Don Juan*'s form—a provocative set of possibilities rather than a trim, solvable narrative. And, as the Strauss of 1888 would remind us, all of this is grounded in the "poetic idea" itself ("the musical-poetic content that I want to convey")—which is why, for Strauss, the appeal to older sonata models and "purely formalistic, Hanslickian music-making will no longer be possible."

The crux of the *Don Juan* problem, or network of problems, will always reside in its most ambiguous portion: the altered reprise with its drive out of an ecstatic E major into the temporary, even more ecstatic C major. The recapitulation is the section that most clearly conveys the constellation of tensions at the core of the work. Our preferred individual solutions to these problems (if we need them to be solved at all) will depend largely on the set of assumptions that we bring to them, that is, on our own set of myths that we shall want reinforced. But perhaps we should be content not to fix these meanings too closely. All that is certain is that, as Strauss wants us to hear the tale, the actual subject of *Don Juan* allows his own integrity as indefatigable seducer to be breached. The rules of the game have been broken, and the Don Juan myth distorts, despairs, and ultimately, grudgingly, disappears. (*Vielleicht auch nicht.*)

Notes

1   Carl Dahlhaus, "Schreker and Modernism: On the Dramaturgy of *Der ferne Klang*" [1978], in *Schoenberg and the New Music*, trans. Derrick Puffett and Alfred Clayton (Cambridge: Cambridge University Press, 1987), p. 192; and *Nineteenth-Century Music* [1980], trans. J. Bradford Robinson (Berkeley: University of California Press, 1989), p. 330. For Dahlhaus, the onset of musical "modernism"—a period later maligned for polemical reasons as "late Romanticism" or "post-Romanticism" by the adherents of New Music—is linked to the 1889 premieres of *Don Juan* and Mahler's First Symphony, and it proceeds with its own aesthetic goals and assumptions until around 1914.

2   Theodor W. Adorno, "Cultural Criticism and Society," in *Prisms* [1955], trans. Samuel and Shierry Weber (Cambridge, Mass.: MIT Press, 1981), p. 32.

3   Theodor W. Adorno, "Thoughts on a Theory of the Art Work," *Aesthetic Theory* [1970], ed. Gretel Adorno and Rolf Tiedemann, trans. C. Lenhardt (London: Routledge & Kegan Paul, 1984), p. 252.

4   Gérard Genette, "Structure and Functions of the Title in Literature" [1987], trans. Bernard Crampé, *Critical Inquiry* 14 (1988): 692–720. Cf. Françoise Escal, "Le titre de l'oeuvre musicale," *Poétique* 69 (1987): 101–18.

5   Particularly helpful here is Jean-François Lyotard's concept of agonistics—an adaptation of Wittgenstein's theory of language games—as elaborated in *The Postmodern Condition: A Report on Knowledge* [1979], trans. Geoff Bennington and Brian Massumi (Minneapolis: University of Minnesota Press, 1984), pp. 10–11, 16–17.

6   Cf. Carl Dahlhaus, "The Idea of the Musically Absolute and the Practice of Program Music," in *The Idea of Absolute Music* [1978], trans. Roger Lustig (Chicago: University of Chicago Press, 1989), pp. 128–40. Related writings of Dahlhaus that help to focus the program problem are: "Schoenberg and Programme Music" [1974], *Schoenberg and the New Music*, p. 95; "The Twofold Truth in Wagner's Aesthetics: Nietzsche's Fragment 'On Music and Words,'" [1974], in *Between Romanticism and Modernism*, trans. Mary Whittall (Berkeley: University of California Press, 1980), pp. 19–39; *Realism in Nineteenth-Century Music* [1982], trans. Mary Whittall (Cambridge: Cambridge University Press, 1985), pp. 37–40; and "Program Music and the Art Work of Ideas," in *Nineteenth-Century Music*, pp. 360–68.

7   For a discussion of the classic "chronological" case, see Andrew Bonner, "Liszt's *Les Préludes* and *Les Quatre Élémens*: A Reinvestigation," *19th-Century Music* 10 (1986): 95–107. An "aesthetic" response may be extrapolated, e.g., from Dahlhaus, "Schoenberg and Programme Music," p. 95.

8   Otto Klauwell's discussion in *Geschichte der Programmusik* (Leipzig: Breitkopf & Härtel, 1910), pp. v–vi, which legitimizes only those programmatic works that can also be grasped by a purely "musical logic" or by musical principles alone, may be taken as paradigmatic.

9   Ernst Krause, *Richard Strauss: The Man and His Work*, trans. John Coombs (Boston: Crescendo, 1969), p. 216.

10   Michael Kennedy, *Richard Strauss* (London: Dent, 1976), p. 127.

11   The issue has been effectively touched upon by Carolyn Abbate, "What the Sorcerer Said," *19th-Century Music* 12 (1989): 221–30. Note especially pp. 223–24, wherein she critiques the "interpretive escape route" of explaining puzzling passages of otherwise descriptive music as occurring for "some wholly musical reason": "When a motif's appearance seems contradic-

tory in terms of its symbolic force, it will be stripped of its symbolic meaning. Its recurrence is written off to the exigencies of purely musical logic."

12   Dahlhaus, "Program Music and the Art Work of Ideas," in *Nineteenth-Century Music*, p. 361. See also n. 6 above.

13   Dahlhaus, "The Twofold Truth," in *Between Romanticism and Modernism*, p. 22.

14   Liszt, "Berlioz und seine Harold-Symphonie" [1855], in *Gesammelte Schriften*, vol. 4 (Hildesheim: Georg Olms, 1978), pp. 1–102. See also the excerpt in Constantin Floros, *Gustav Mahler*, vol. 2 (Wiesbaden: Breitkopf & Härtel, 1977), p. 54.

15   *Hans von Bülow and Richard Strauss: Correspondence*, ed. Willi Schuh and Franz Trenner, trans. Anthony Gishford (London: Boosey & Hawkes, 1955), pp. 82–83.

16   For a discussion of the term "musical logic" (which by the end of the nineteenth century was intertwined with Hanslick's concept of the "purely musical") see especially Dahlhaus, *Klassische und romantische Musikästhetik* (Laaber: Laaber, 1988), pp. 282–84, and the chapter devoted to it, "Musical Logic and Speech Character," in *The Idea of Absolute Music*, pp. 103–16.

17   The term *Tonbilder* (tone pictures) is common enough with regard to the Strauss symphonic-poem repertory; one notes its usage (*Tonbilderfolge*) even in Gerlach (see n. 26 below), a writer unconcerned with "extramusical" content. For the important term *Seelenzustände*, the use of which goes back at least as far as A.B. Marx in the 1820s, see Arno Forchert, "Adolf Bernhard Marx und seine *Berliner Allgemeine musikalische Zeitung*," in *Studien zur Musikgeschichte Berlins im frühen 19. Jahrhundert*, ed. Carl Dahlhaus (Regensburg: Bosse, 1980), pp. 381–404, esp. pp. 390–91. See also Leon B. Plantinga, *Schumann as Critic* (New Haven, Conn.: Yale University Press, 1967), p. 120. One may also find the term in Lorenz's 1936 commentary on *Don Juan*, p. 454.

18   Rollo Myers, ed., *Richard Strauss & Romain Rolland: Correspondence* [1951] (Berkeley: University of California Press, 1968), p. 29.

19   Strauss, "Aus meinen Jugend- und Lehrjahren," trans. as "Recollections of My Youth and Years of Apprenticeship," in *Richard Strauss: Recollections and Reflections*, ed. Willi Schuh [1949], trans. L. J. Lawrence (London: Boosey & Hawkes, 1953), p. 139. A ca. 1940 dating is provided in *The New Grove*. Also quoted (along with a few other, similar remarks) in Krause, pp. 179–80, and Dahlhaus, "Program Music and the Art Work of Ideas," pp. 361–62 (see also *The Idea of Absolute Music*, pp. 137–38). The translations above are taken from those of Krause and Schuh. For further collections of Strauss's remarks about programs and musical structures, see also Krause, pp. 214–23, and Constantin Floros, *Gustav Mahler*, vol. 2, pp. 55–56.

20   Krause, pp. 221–22, quoting reminiscences of Strauss by Albert Gutmann and Stefan Zweig. Cf. p. 72; and cf. Schoenberg on Strauss's "pictorial" concerns in "Human Rights" [1947], in *Style and Idea: Selected Writings of Arnold Schoenberg*, ed. Leonard Stein [1975] (revised and reprinted, Berkeley: University of California Press, 1984), p. 511.

21   Krause, p. 217.

22   In Myers, *Richard Strauss and Romain Rolland*, pp. 27–28. For his part, Rolland was eager to accept Strauss's explanation, and we see him offering it on behalf of various tone poems in his essay, "Richard Strauss," in the 1908 *Musiciens d'aujourd'hui*: "[In *Tod und Verklärung*] if all suggestion of a programme is taken away, the symphony still remains intelligible and impressive by its harmonious expression of feeling" (*Musicians of To-day*, trans. Mary Blailock [New York: Henry Holt, 1914], p. 145).

23   For our purposes, an adequate summary of these issues—and of the Lenau poem itself—is provided in Norman Del Mar, *Richard Strauss: A Critical Commentary on His Life and Works*, vol. 1 (1962; reprint, Ithaca: Cornell University Press, 1986), 65–69.

24 Brecher, "Richard Strauss als Symphoniker," [part 2], *Leipziger Kunst* 1 (1 June 1899): 418; Klauwell, *Geschichte der Programmusik* (see n. 8 above), p. 230; Steinitzer, *Richard Strauss* (Berlin: Schuster & Loeffler, 1911), pp. 229–30; Waltershausen, *Richard Strauss: Ein Versuch* (Munich: Drei Masken, 1921), p. 49; Muschler, *Richard Strauss* (Hildesheim: Borgmeyer, [1924]), pp. 262–69; Del Mar, *Richard Strauss*; Kennedy, *Richard Strauss* (London: Dent, 1976), pp. 129–30; Michael Kennedy and Robert Bailey, "Richard Strauss," in *The New Grove Dictionary of Music and Musicians* [1980], revised and reprinted in *The New Grove Turn of the Century Masters* (New York: Norton, 1985), p. 218; Levy, *Music: A Listener's Introduction* (New York: Harper & Row, 1983), pp. 265–69. Donald Francis Tovey also seems to acknowledge at least a sonata exposition in *Essays in Musical Analysis*, reprinted in *Symphonies and Other Orchestral Works* (Oxford: Oxford University Press, 1989), p. 510.

25 Nodnagel, *Jenseits von Wagner und Liszt* (Königsberg: Ostpreußischen Druckerei, 1902), pp. 75–77; Specht, *Richard Strauss und sein Werk*, 2 vols. (Leipzig: Tal, 1921), vol. 1, 183–93; Abraham, *A Hundred Years of Music*, 3d ed. (Chicago: Aldine, 1964; reprint, 1966), p. 209; Goléa, *Richard Strauss* (Paris: Flammarion, 1965), pp. 58–60; Edward Murphy, "Tonal Organization in Five Strauss Tone Poems," *The Music Review* 44 (1983): 223–33; and Heinz Becker, "Richard Strauss," in *The Heritage of Music*, ed. Michael Raeburn and Alan Kendall, vol. 3, *The Nineteenth-Century Legacy*, ed. Martin Cooper and Heinz Becker (Oxford: Oxford University Press, 1989), pp. 281–82.

26 Gerlach, "Analyse und Interpretation der Tondichtung für Grosses Orchester Don Juan Op. 20 von Richard Strauss," in *Don Juan und Rosenkavalier: Studien zu Idee und Gestalt einer tonalen Evolution im Werk Richard Strauss'* (Bern: Paul Haupt, 1966), pp. 13–65. Forchert, "Zur Auflösung traditioneller Formkategorien in der Musik um 1900: Probleme formaler Organisation bei Mahler und Strauss," *Archiv für Musikwissenschaft* 32 (1975): 85–98, esp. pp. 94–96. Cf. Leon Plantinga, in *Romantic Music: A History of Musical Style in Nineteenth-Century Europe* (New York: Norton, 1984), p. 448: "The structure of Don Juan bears some resemblance to both sonata-allegro and rondo form."

27 Gerlach, pp. 46–47.

28 Mauke, "Don Juan: Tondichtung nach N. Lenau: Op. 20," in *Richard Strauss: Symphonien und Tondichtungen* [*Meisterführer* Nr. 6], ed. Herwath Walden (Berlin: Schlesinger [Lienau], 1908), p. 49. Earlier in the essay (again p. 49) Mauke claims that the work subdivides into a beginning, a "calm *Mittelsatz* with three beautiful themes," and a "powerful *Conclusio*" that is followed by an ending in a "gloomy E minor." Cf. Urban, *Richard Strauss* (Berlin: n.p., 1901), p. 19, concerning the early symphonic poems in general: "Here occurs the break with all traditions. One no longer recognizes symphonic forms," etc.

29 Lorenz, "Neue Formerkenntnisse, angewandt auf Richard Straussens 'Don Juan,'" *Archiv für Musikforschung* 1 (1936): 452–66. In brief, according to Lorenz, the bar form's second *Stollen* begins with m. 163, the transition out of Don Juan's B-major encounter with the second of the three mistresses evoked by the music; its *Abgesang* begins with the inbreaking of the *Heldenthema* in the horns, m. 315. While the details of Lorenz's analysis seem largely untenable and uncomfortably schematic today, his reason for arguing on behalf of the bar form rests ultimately on the significance of the appearance of the *Heldenthema*—the arrival of something new midway through the piece. Among the analysts Lorenz alone adequately judges the radical importance of this musical event, and he deals with it by relating it to his concept of *Abgesang* as spiritual transcendence: the bar form itself springs from "processes within the human soul; . . . the attainment of an increase [*Steigerung*] of the soul's power, which as a rule only succeeds after two similar starts" (p. 453).

30   Green, *Form in Tonal Music*, 2d ed. (New York: Holt, Rinehart and Winston, 1979), pp. 299–303. Green's *A'* is very brief: it is the seemingly developmental return of the Don Juan motive, mm. 168–96. His B begins with the G-minor episode (mm. 197–231) and continues through the G-major oboe idyll, mm. 232–314. The final A comprises everything from the onset of the *Heldenthema* in the horns (m. 314) up to the coda (mm. 567–606). The primary sticking point for Green with regard to the sonata issue is the G-minor/major section (his B), for, in the manner of a nondevelopmental episode, it "has all the characteristics of a part in itself." Thus what would have been a sonata-like work in two parts (that is, following the "continuous binary" concept of sonata form) becomes a "unique form" in four parts, the whole governed by its patterns of tonal closure.

31   See especially Hans Robert Jauss, "Literary History as a Challenge to Literary Theory" [1970] and "Theory of Genres and Medieval Literature" [1972], in *Toward an Aesthetic of Reception*, trans. Timothy Bahti (Minneapolis: University of Minnesota, 1982), pp. 3–45 (esp. pp. 20–24) and 76–109. A helpful introduction to the subject of genre is provided by Heather Dubrow, *Genre* (London: Methuen, 1982).

32   Jauss, "Literary History."

33   Dubrow, pp. 1–4.

34   Hepokoski, "Genre and Content in Mid-Century Verdi: 'Addio, del passato,' (*La traviata*, Act III)," *Cambridge Opera Journal* 1 (1989): 249–76. See also the brief discussion and categorization of late nineteenth-century sonata-deformation families provided in the first chapter of Hepokoski, *Sibelius: Symphony No. 5*, forthcoming from Cambridge University Press.

35   In "Mahler: Second Symphony, Finale," in *Analysis and Value Judgment* [1970], trans. Siegmund Levarie (New York: Pendragon, 1983), pp. 82–83.

36   Lorenz, p. 463.

37   The earliest commentators, Mauke (1908, p. 56) and Steinitzer (1911, p. 230), established the tradition of identifying the horn theme as the "second Don-Juan theme," and subsequent writers have in one way or another agreed. The term *Heldenthema* occurs influentially in Specht (1921, p. 187) and, varied, in Lorenz ("Heldenmotiv," 1936, p. 459); it, too, has been adopted by several subsequent commentators. Cf. Becker's identifying of it as Don Juan's pride, n. 38 below.

38   E.g., implied in Specht, pp. 187–88, and stated most clearly in Becker, p. 282: "the hero's theme [DJ, m. 9], which recurs as a rondo and is later replaced by a second theme—a theme on the horn often described [sic] as Don Juan's pride."

39   See, e.g., Specht, p. 185; Abraham, p. 209; and note the characteristic ambiguity of the diagram provided in Murphy, p. 224, in which this passage is denoted as "Transition" and "Female 1," and the first episode proper is deferred until "Female 2" (Murphy's B).

40   Mauke, p. 57; Lorenz, p. 459 (Lorenz may be recalling Mauke, p. 57: "Da wirft sich ihm gleich eine Dirne an den Hals").

41   Abraham, p. 209. Even more to the point, the four episodes, if we are to include the initial transition episode, are grossly unequal in length—19, 70, 118, and 73 measures respectively—and the longest of these is also the slowest. As will be argued in Section 3 below, the interweaving of themes is programmatic.

42   Lorenz, p. 463. Abraham's letter scheme for the work (p. 209), a slight expansion of Specht's, seems designed to demonstrate Lorenz's point: "It might be represented graphically by some such formula as this: A, B, A, Ca, Cb, D, A (+ D), E (+ A and D), B (+ C), A, D, A." Within Abraham's scheme B and C are Mistresses Two and Three, D the *Heldenthema*, E the "Carnival."

43 Waltershausen, p. 49; Muschler, *Richard Strauss* (Hildesheim: Borgmeyer, [1924]), p. 266. Cf. the remarks on Muschler in Abraham, p. 209.

44 Each episode in *Siegfried-Idyll* is marked by its own theme: the first with what might be identified as the Siegfried "Hort der Welt" theme, measures 148–258 (very possibly, within this eminently personalized idyll, a direct reference to the recent birth of Siegfried Wagner as a welcome addition to the "domestic" representations of the exposition); and the second, measures 259–75, with the theme associated in act 3 of *Siegfried* with the words "Sie ist mir ewig, ist mir immer Erb' und Eigen Ein." Both themes—and especially the "Hort der Welt" theme—recur prominently in the recapitulation, beginning at measure 286. Another way of hearing the *Siegfried-Idyll* would be as a large *ABA'* structure in which *A* and *A'* recall aspects of exposition and recapitulation, and in which *A'* incorporates (as an *Aufhebung* of *A* and *B*?) elements of the diptych provided in the *B* section. The latter description, however, also meshes with that of a sonata deformation conceived in the late-nineteenth-century "ternary" manner. Cf. Del Mar's description of *Don Juan*, mentioned in the text almost immediately below.

45 Del Mar, vol. 1, 69. Cf. Kennedy, *The New Grove Turn of the Century Masters*, p. 218: "Like *Macbeth*, *Don Juan* is a sonata movement with self-contained episodes. . . ."

46 Such a plan might have been behind Reinhold Muschler's somewhat unclear remarks in 1924 (p. 266) linking *Don Juan* not only with *Siegfried-Idyll* (see n. 43 above) but also with the structure of the Prelude to *Die Meistersinger*. In the latter case he maintains that both pieces offer us a "broad presentation of themes [in the exposition] with a surprisingly short development"; taken together, the "broadened" exposition and the "minimized" development account, "*ganz logischerweise*," for the "shortened" reprise and coda, "because a repetition of this impressive utterance would weaken the whole [structure]." It may be that Muschler considered the exposition of *Don Juan* as continuing through the G-minor/major episode, although in that case it would have presented its contrasting themes in essentially three keys, E, B, and G. The exposition of the *Meistersinger* Prelude, while certainly multithematic, articulates primarily two keys, C (for a broad complex of themes) and E (the beginning of the "second theme" proper, although before long this material modulates away from that key and soon merges into the developmental space, occupied largely by a "scherzo episode").

47 Levy, pp. 265–69. Continuing one of the most curious available descriptions of the work—albeit within the context of an "appreciation" textbook—Levy also appears to contend that the recapitulation begins toward the end of the Carnival Episode (if so, he may be thinking of the *Vivo* passage, mm. 387ff., beginning in C-sharp minor) and that the entire reprise, mm. 457–566, is actually a coda devoted largely to the "glorification" of an already-dead Don Juan. The catastrophe in mm. 421ff., he argues (apparently following Tovey, who also misunderstood this point), is "the fatal sword thrust" and it is followed by his death, apparently in the *sul ponticello* bars before m. 457. All of this lies far outside the interpretive tradition, and none of it seems tenable.

48 Once again, cf. the differing—but highly unlikely—explanation in Levy (and Tovey), n. 47 above.

49 Forchert, pp. 94–96. "[For Strauss] the procedure is already fully formed in *Don Juan* . . . insofar as *Don Juan* may be considered to be written in first-movement sonata form. But already here the stringency in the succession of these sections is so greatly weakened—because of the individual weight given to each—that it is difficult to decide to what to attribute this: to the logic of musical coherence or to the stations of a represented program" (p. 94).

50 Lorenz, p. 464. See also Green's objections to the sonata interpretation, n. 30 above.

51   Forchert, p. 95.

52   Theodor W. Adorno, Mahler: Eine musikalische Physiognomik (Frankfurt: Suhrkamp, 1960), for example, pp. 60–66. Adorno's other principal Mahler categories are Weltlauf, Suspension, Erfüllung, and Absturz (or Katastrophe). The term Durchbruch may ultimately stem from a passage of analysis of Mahler's First Symphony, first movement, in Paul Bekker, Gustav Mahlers Sinfonien [1921] (rpt. Tutzing: Hans Schneider, 1969), p. 39.

53   Sponheuer, Logik des Zerfalls: Untersuchungen zum Finalproblem in den Symphonien Gustav Mahlers (Tutzing: Hans Schneider, 1978), and especially the extract from the book revised as "Der Durchbruch als primäre Formkategorie Gustav Mahlers: Eine Untersuchung zum Finalproblem der Ersten Symphonie," in Form und Idee in Gustav Mahlers Instrumentalmusik, ed. Klaus Hinrich Stahmer, Taschenbücher zur Musikwissenschaft, no. 70, ed. Richard Schaal (Wilhelmshaven: Heinrichshofen, 1980), pp. 117–64.

54   Adorno's paradigms for the breakthrough effect are those of the trumpet call in the Dungeon Scene of Fidelio—the announcement of salvation from a different, outside world—and in Beethoven's Seventh Symphony the a-natural four bars before the trio that causes a "caesura" in the scherzo (see Adorno, Mahler, p. 12). As Sponheuer points out, however, the clearest symphonic paradigms are the interconnected first and last movements of Mahler's First Symphony, which received its premiere in the same year as Strauss's Don Juan.

The historical roots of the category would seem to go back at least to such works as Schumann's Fourth Symphony. Here the lucid exposition schema of the first movement is abandoned during the development with the double announcement of two new "breakthrough" themes that will play a larger role later in the symphony. Their immediate effect on the first movement's expected recapitulation is to shrink it into a brief, nonsymmetrical, and inconclusive tonic reprise in which the thematic schema of the exposition is replaced by a breakthrough variant of the development's second new theme. The further implications of the breakthrough are pursued later in the work: the development's first new theme becomes the theme of the finale, and so on. The breakthrough strategy in the first movement is an impulsive, Romantic gesture—a peripeteia—that jettisons the original, orthodox exposition in order to pursue a highly unorthodox, four-movement-in-one plan.

55   Sponheuer, "Der Durchbruch," pp. 119–20. The passage quoted from Adorno may be found in Mahler, p. 11.

56   The relevant lines, lines 28–31 of the thirty-two quoted by Strauss, also appear at the beginning of this essay: "Perhaps a thunderbolt from the heights which I contemned, struck fatally at my power of love, and suddenly my world became a desert and darkened. And perhaps not. . . ." Trans. from Del Mar, p. 68, n. 12.

57   Cf., for example, the structural transformation discussed in Anthony Newcomb, "Once More 'Between Absolute and Program Music': Schumann's Second Symphony," 19th-Century Music 9 (1984): 233–50.

58   Arguing principally for the category of a sonata, however fragmentarily realized and however intermixed with other genres, Gerlach proposes a novel idea at this point: the "forgotten themes" recur here, and, in particular, "The [sonata's] 'second theme' in B major and the G-major-section's theme both file a suit on behalf of their right to be 'developed,' to remain within the piece's construction; they file suit on the grounds of infidelity" (p. 43).

59   This is hardly the place to launch a more generalized discussion of the relationship of peripeteia structures to that of "organic" motivic-thematic unfolding, but such a discussion would involve issues central to the aesthetic of both Mahler and Strauss, and probably to

other modern composers as well. We may note here, however, that Strauss, like Mahler, has been careful to ground the breakthrough in the thematic material of the preceding episode.

All of this bears on—and to some extent begins to formulate a response to—Adorno's central criticism of Strauss, namely the charge that the principal aesthetic category of the composer is "the glorification of contingency which is supposed to be the same as a life of freedom (whereas in truth it is nothing but the anarchy of commodity production and the brutality of those who run it)," *Aesthetic Theory*, p. 306. See also Adorno, "Richard Strauss," trans. Samuel and Shierry Weber, *Perspectives of New Music* 4 (1965): 14–32, 113–29.

60   Lorenz, p. 464; Green, p. 301.

61   The basic discussions are Dahlhaus, "The Symphonic Poem" and "Program Music and the Art Work of Ideas," in *Nineteenth-Century Music*, pp. 236–44 and 360–68; and "Liszt, Schönberg und die grosse Form: Das Prinzip der Mehrsätzigkeit in der Einsätzigkeit," *Die Musikforschung* 41 (1988): 202–13.

62   Another option would be to investigate Strauss's sketchbooks for additional clues. The programmatic sentences transcribed in Franz Trenner's *Die Skizzenbücher von Richard Strauss* (Tutzing: Hans Schneider, 1977), p. 2, tantalize but, in the final analysis, offer little concrete help. They seem to belong to an early stage of composition and although they provide some provocative, if maddeningly generalized, labels for themes—*Wonnethema, l. Don Juanthema, leichtfertigen Thema, Schmerzens u. Wonneseufzern, Liebes u. Freudenthemen*, and so on—the musical details and the process they sketch, while certainly recognizable, differ from what actually happens in the final *Don Juan*.

A rough translation of the sketch comments (which seem to begin at a point analogous to the G-minor/major Episode 3) is as follows: "Then connect C-sharp minor. NB! the Delight Theme [*Wonnethema*] again on C-sharp major cantilenas, which, with the appearance of the climax [*Erschöpfung*] will be interrupted in the violas by the first Don Juan theme. At first this [theme] sounds with a jolt and rises up with a bold leap of the first theme onto the C-dominant [and] from there further into a frivolous theme—from which it proceeds into increasingly madder activity, joyful, rejoicing—but interrupted by pain and sighs of delight [*Wonneseufzern*]. Development with ever-increasing *fortissimo*, to the highest intensification. Sudden disenchantment [*Ernüchterung*]. English-horn solitude, the Love and Joy Themes interpenetrate in a purposeless way, interrupted by new yearning and shivers of delight. Finally it connects with a new love-motive, very gushing [*schwärmerisch*] and tender. Then suddenly the new appearance of the first theme. A large, dashing coda. Stormy close."

63   Muschler, p. 265.

64   Mauke, pp. 48–49. Cf. Del Mar, pp. 69–75.

65   Specht, pp. 183–84. Cf. Muschler, p. 266: "It has nothing more in common with it than the initial glimpse of the artistic impulse being liberated out of the merely human. Hence this music lacks anything of the literary; hence it is purely musical [*rein musikalisch*]."

66   Lorenz, p. 464.

67   Tenschert, "Versuch einer Typologie der Richard Straußchen Melodik," *Zeitschrift für Musikwissenschaft* 16 (1934): 282–87.

68   Gilliam, "Strauss's Preliminary Opera Sketches: Thematic Fragments and Symphonic Continuity," *19th-Century Music* 9 (1986): 179.

69   Mauke, pp. 53–54; Specht, pp. 186–87; Lorenz, p. 458; Del Mar, pp. 71–72.

70   Mauke's wish to identify this heroine with the traditional figure of Doña Ana (pp. 55–56, "[Anna], die ihm hätte ein rettender Engel werden können") is based on the central mono-

logue of the Lenau poem, cited by Mauke but not by Strauss, in which Don Juan confesses: "Zum erstenmal bei diesem Weibe / Ist in der Liebe mir zu Mut, / Als sollte meine heiße Glut / Auslöschen nie in ihrem Götterliebe. . . . Und selig scheiternd hängt an Klippen / Der letzte Wunsch an ihren Lippen. / Wenn ich den holden Leib umranke, / Des Himmels Inbegriff und Schranke, / Möcht' ich vergötternd ihn verderben, / Mit ihr in eins zusammen-sterben" (Nikolaus Lenau, *Werke in einem Band* [Hamburg: Hoffmann und Campe, 1966]), pp. 460–61. Cf. the translation of the last two lines in Hugo Schmidt, *Nikolaus Lenau* (New York: Twayne, 1971), p. 151: "While deifying her body, I would like to destroy it and reach union with her in death." Anna is clearly the vision of the Ideal Woman for whom Lenau's Don Juan is striving (cf. "Die Einzle kränkend schwärm' ich für die Gattung"—lines cited by Strauss), but it is unclear whether she actually exists. The immediate link of this idealized love with death may be relevant to Strauss's poetic idea behind the symphonic poem. The G-major section, however, is shadowless, and its pairing with the subsequent, and surely positive, *Heldenthema* is difficult to reconcile with the lurking negative content in Don Juan's apostrophe to Anna in Lenau.

Lenau's version pays homage to the tradition in some retellings of the Don Juan legend of Anna being the only woman with whom Juan actually falls in love—but always with tragic results. This happens, for example, as early as in Alonso Córdoba's *La venganza en el sepulcro* (1660–70), but it is most characteristic of Germanic tellings of the story after E. T. A. Hoff-mann's influential tale, *Don Juan* ("Donna Anna is Don Juan's female counterpart . . . Suppose Anna had been destined by Heaven to make Don Juan recognize the divine nature within him through love . . . and to rescue him from the despair of his vain striving. But it was too late; he saw her at the moment when he had reached the height of wickedness"). See Leo Weinstein, *The Metamorphoses of Don Juan* (New York: AMS, 1967), esp. pp. 69–70, from which the above Hoffmann quotation is taken.

71   Specht, p. 187; Del Mar, p. 72.

72   Perhaps significantly for Strauss, this Brünnhilde melody (or Cosima melody?) is texted in its original appearance in *Siegfried*, "Ewig war ich, / ewig bin ich, / ewig in süss / sehnender Wonne, / doch ewig zu deinem Heil."

73   Del Mar, pp. 150–51.

74   Notice also, however, the motivic relationship with a passage from the Mistress One Epi-sode, mm. 52ff.

75   Richard Strauss, letter of 8 November 1889, in *Briefe an die Eltern 1882–1906*, ed. Willi Schuh (Zurich: Atlantis, 1954), p. 119.

76   Again, the C-major goal of the *Heldenthema* in the recapitulation articulates a possibility that had been present from the beginning, as with, for example, the pseudo-"C^6" implication in mm. 1 and 169. While these early appearances of the potentially redemptive C fall under the actual power of the overriding E, the tonic of libertinism or erotic desire, one of the tonal points of the recapitulation is that the E in the bass has been exorcised and replaced by C.

77   Cf. Brünnhilde's Slumber Motive at the end of *Die Walküre* and, of course, elsewhere in the *Ring*. *Ring* allusions abound elsewhere in the reprise: compare the violin figures in mm. 528ff. with the "Love Motive"; and the horn timbre of the *Heldenthema* itself is not without its Sieg-fried resonances. Cf. the Wagnerian allusions in the triplet anacruses in the trumpets at the move to C major, mm. 542–45. One notices that all of the allusions carry connotations of love, masculine triumph, the ideal partner, etc.

78   In one of the nicest touches of the piece, this E-minor "death" is foreshadowed by the E-minor-chord image of sexual climax in the second episode (mm. 149ff.). The ultimate source of the E minor, of course, is the e⁶ chord at the end of m. 2, a chord that immediately restabilizes onto the "proper" tonic, E major, at the beginning of m. 3. Considered along with the phallic imagery of the opening, the poetic content of the initial measures becomes self-evident: a springing past the possibility of C-major stasis and resolution (attainable, as we eventually learn, only through a fusion with the feminine principle), an arrogant brushing aside of the possibility of E-minor peril or death, and a leaping into the embrace of the erotic E major, the world of libertinism.

79   Rolland, *Musicians of To-Day*, pp. 167. Rolland sees in Strauss's music in general the overturning of a central Beethovenian theme, "the triumph of a conquered hero," into "the defeat of a conquering hero" (p. 166).

80   Adorno, "Richard Strauss," *Perspectives of New Music* 4 (1965): pp. 128–29.

81   See, for example, the standard discussion in Adorno, "Inherent Tendency of Musical Material," *Philosophy of Modern Music* [*Philosophie der Neuen Musik*, 1948], trans. Anne G. Mitchell and Wesley V. Blomster (New York: Seabury, 1980), pp. 32–37; and *Aesthetic Theory*, pp. 300–308.

82   See, however, Dahlhaus's discussion of the problematics of the political and methodological issues involved in claiming that musical content can take precedence over form; *Realism*, p. 3.

83   Dahlhaus, *Realism*, pp. 37, 120.

84   Jameson, "Beyond the Cave: Demystifying the Ideology of Modernism," in *The Ideologies of Theory: Essays 1971–1986* (Minneapolis: University of Minnesota, 1988), vol. 2, 122.

85   Ernst Bloch, "The Exceeding of Limits and the World of Man at Its Most Richly Intense in Music," [from *Das Prinzip Hoffnung*, 1938–1959], trans. Peter Palmer, *Essays on the Philosophy of Music* (Cambridge: Cambridge University Press, 1985), p. 222.

86   Cited in Dahlhaus, *Realism*, p. 39.

87   A prominent example is Jürgen Habermas, *The Philosophical Discourse of Modernity: Twelve Lectures*, trans. Frederick Lawrence (Cambridge: MIT Press, 1987). For a useful discussion of some of the principal issues involved in defining modernism, see Jochen Schulte-Sasse, "Foreword: Theory of Modernism versus Theory of the Avant-Garde," in Peter Bürger, *Theory of the Avant-Garde* [1974], trans. Michael Shaw (Minneapolis: University of Minnesota, 1984), pp. vii–xlvii. Cf. the issues raised in Matei Calinescu, *Five Faces of Modernity* (Durham, N.C.: Duke University Press, 1987). A rather different view is provided in Michel Foucault, *The Order of Things* (New York: Vintage Books, 1973).

88   Dahlhaus, *Nineteenth-Century Music*, p. 334. Cf. "Schreker and Modernism," n. 1 above.

89   Jameson, "Reflections on the Brecht-Lukács Debate" [1977], in *The Ideologies of Theory*, vol. 2, 147.

The Concerto for Oboe and Small Orchestra (1945): Remarks about the Origin of the Work Based on a Newly Discovered Source

Günter Brosche

▼

The National Socialist dictatorship and the Second World War, catastrophes that brought suffering to millions, also had the effect of plunging Richard Strauss, by then an old man, into a state of profound melancholy and despair. While his chief concern was for his Jewish daughter-in-law and his grand-children (deemed "half-breeds" [Mischlinge] by the racist regime)—a reason for repeated evasive tactics in dealing with Nazi authorities and a source of continuous nervous strain—it was the inferno of the last months of the war that thrust him into a mood of deepest depression.

The hail of bombs demolished entire German cities and along with them irretrievable cultural riches. That Goethe's house in Weimar ("Goethe's sacred house," according to the composer) and "the opera houses in Dresden and Vienna that [he] so especially loved should have had to be reduced to heaps of ash and rubble"[1] represented a particularly severe blow, one that, to Strauss, was tantamount to the destruction of his entire life's work. Overcome by a feeling of profound resignation, he turned his back to the world; reading Goethe seemed, above all else, to afford him a sense of inner stability. He considered his creative powers to be exhausted, although he could never stop committing musical ideas to paper.

Thus, in the worst days of February 1945, he wrote a new version of an older composition he called *Munich: A Memorial Waltz* (AV 140); one passage of the work, headed "Mourning for Munich," is clearly reminiscent of the funeral march in Beethoven's *Eroica*. Between March and April 1945 he wrote the *Study for 23 Solo Strings: Metamorphoses* (AV 142); in the final section, headed "In Memoriam," he quotes the original theme of the Beethoven funeral march note for note. Though he composed several works between the years 1945 and 1949, Strauss seemed reluctant to acknowledge their true artistic value, claiming that his life's work had already been completed. Hence, in his well-known comment to Willi Schuh, he affirmed that "since *Capriccio*, I have not been writing any 'novelties,' only some competent studies for our worthy instrumentalists and devoted *a cappella* choirs—studio works, so that the wrist does not become too stiff and the mind prematurely senile; for posterity, Horatio, for posterity!"[2]

Indeed, posterity has shown that Strauss greatly underestimated these late works. The concert hall has shown that they include a number of real masterpieces. Moreover, they belong to a phase that in fact began before the end of the war; the final catastrophe may simply have established more firmly the stylistic traits common to them. Schuh, Strauss's close friend during the late years in Switzerland and his biographer of choice, commented on Strauss's late style in an essay written during the last year of the composer's life.

> The late works of Richard Strauss are marked by a refinement of the stylistic devices he employs. Characteristic of them all—the late operas (we particularly think of the last three: *Daphne*, *Die Liebe der Danae*, and *Capriccio*), as well as the most recent instrumental works (the concertos for horn, for oboe, for clarinet and bassoon, the *Metamorphoses*, two sonatinas for 16 wind instruments) and the four songs for voice and orchestra, based on texts by Eichendorff and Hermann Hesse—is a certain grace and lucidity that depend on simplicity honed to the kind of delicacy and fluidity more typical of chamber music. Another quality common to them all is their noble dignity, the reflection of a deeper affinity with his beloved classical composers—above all Mozart—and, hence, with an artistry capable of the most inventive expression in elegant and restrained forms, artistry that can resolve even the greatest difficulty with apparent ease. Carefree gaiety, a wise and buoyant detachment from the material world he has long since viewed from a remote distance, is a distinctive feature of these exquisite late works. They confirm that Strauss never repeats himself, although (as Hofmannsthal once wrote) "he never relinquishes anything completely, but returns, by a more circuitous route, to the same point"—to opera based on mythological themes, where figures from realms of classical antiquity are shown time and again in a new light; to the classical form of the concerto; to the piece for wind players, which he was already cultivating at the age of sixteen, and, ultimately, to the songs for voice and orchestra.[3]

Origins of the Oboe Concerto

Strauss's Oboe Concerto (AV 144) belongs to this series of late works that culminate in the so-called Four Last Songs (AV 150), which were composed between May and September 1948 and no doubt represent the acme of his late period. In an undated Garmisch sketchbook (Tr. 135)—one of the types of small-format pocket-sized books (ca. 8 × 13 cm. and usually bound in black oilcloth) that Strauss always carried with him so that he could immediately jot down musical ideas—a note in ink on the inside front cover reads: "Oboe Concerto 1945/suggested by an American Soldier/(oboe player from Chicago)" (see figure 1).[4]

For Strauss, the immediate postwar period turned out to be better than expected, for on 10 May 1945 he wrote Schuh:

> Eight days have now gone by since our poor, ravaged, ruined Germany was liberated from twelve years of slavery . . . Today, I am taking advantage of the first available opportunity to let you know . . . that Garmisch was spared any bombing attacks, and since, thank God, no resistance was offered when the Americans marched in, it has remained unscathed; it has simply been occupied. The very next day, some high-ranking offi-

Figure 1. Title notice in the Garmisch sketchbook Tr. 135: "Oboe Concerto 1945/ inspired by an American soldier/ (Oboist from Chicago)." (Richard-Strauss-Archiv, Garmisch)

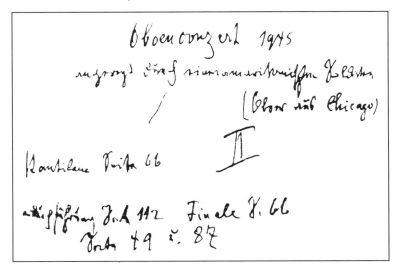

cers turned up and, in the most polite and respectful way, exempted my house (the residence of Richard Strauss) from any kind of requisitioning by putting up a large sign which said "Off Limits." The commanding general himself paid me a special visit. . . . In any case, the Americans are being extremely kind and friendly, and I can hardly get away from all the autograph-hunters—many's the time I have to note down the waltz from *Rosenkavalier*, and, on one occasion, the Don Juan motif.[5]

One of the many American soldiers who called on the composer was John de Lancie, a young oboe player, only twenty-four years old at the time. Accompanied by Alfred Mann, the two visited Strauss's Garmisch villa in May 1945. In his recollections about the meeting with Strauss, preserved in a photograph of the two men on the terrace of the Strauss home (figure 2), de Lancie wrote:

> I must confess that I was overcome by shyness and a feeling of great awe in the presence of this man, and I remember thinking, at the time, that I would have nothing at all to contribute to the conversation that could possibly be of interest to the composer. Once, though, I summoned up all my courage and began to talk about the beautiful oboe melodies one comes across in so many of his works—in *Don Quixote*, *Don Juan*, the *Sinfonia Domestica* and many others besides. I wanted to know if he had a special affinity for that particular instrument, and, since I was familiar with his Horn Concerto, I asked him whether he had ever thought of writing a concerto for oboe. His answer was a plain "No!" That was about the most I could get out of him, so I assumed the whole subject was either of no interest at all, or of no further interest to him.[6]

Despite the apparently terse and negative response by the composer, the timid question evidently fell on fertile ground, for by 6 July Strauss was writing Schuh: "In the studio of my old age, a concerto for oboe and small orchestra is being 'concocted.' The idea for this [work] was suggested to me by an oboe player from Chicago."[7] On 11 October 1945, when Strauss moved to Switzerland (where he would remain until May 1949), he took with him the short score he had completed in "Garmisch, 14 September 1945." He finished writing the fair copy of the full score, according to his note at the end, on 25 October at the Hotel Verenhof in Baden. The concerto premiered on 26 February 1946 at the eighth concert in the Tonhalle Society's subscription series in the Tonhalle in Zurich. The soloist, Marcel Saillet, was accompanied by the Zurich Tonhalle Orchestra conducted by Volkmar Andreae. Strauss, incidentally, wrote a letter in French to de Lancie,[8] inviting him to attend the

Figure 2. Richard Strauss and John de Lancie in Garmisch, May 1945. (Richard Strauss-Archiv, Garmisch)

concert, but by that time he was back in the United States and had to decline the invitation.[9]

The Sources

Five autograph sources are known to exist; with the help of these it is possible to trace the origin and evolution of the oboe concerto quite clearly. The earliest autograph is, of course, the small sketchbook already mentioned. Strauss jotted down his early ideas for each of the three movements (in pencil and ink) on 124 pages (see figure 3). Also in the Garmisch archive are the aforementioned short score and full score, which number twenty and forty-two pages, respectively. The estate of Strauss's London publisher, Ernst Roth of Boosey and Hawkes, includes a single folio ("Montreux, 1 February 1948") containing a revision for the ending of the concerto, which was incorporated in the printed score published in 1948 (Boosey and Hawkes) as both full and piano scores. In 1986, a private Viennese collector donated a hitherto unknown source to the music department of the Austrian National Library (Mus. Hs. 39.546).[10] Chronologically, this source lies somewhere between the sketchbook and the short score. The loose double folio with sketches for the Oboe Concerto was purchased from Hans Schneider (Tutzing) in 1970 by Friedrich Zeileis; thereafter he bound the manuscript.[11]

Figure 3. Two pages from the sketchbook (Richard-Strauss-Archiv, Garmisch)

The Austrian National Library Sketches

Strauss wrote these pencil sketches in a two-staff piano format, although he occasionally employed a three-staff format in the last two movements. The paper shortage during these austere postwar years accounts for the fact that he reused a discarded sheet of paper on which he had already made a hand-written copy of Till Eulenspiegel. During these financially troubling times for Strauss, he made manuscript copies of several older works, which he considered a kind of capital for his family; some of them were, in fact, sold by middlemen in the United States. Strauss made two copies of Till Eulenspiegel—one in 1944 and the other in 1945. The first of these, described as a "copy, in my own hand, for my beloved children and grandchildren, 1 October 1944. To dear old Till, in honor of his 50th birthday," remains in the family archive in Garmisch[12] because the original 1895 score had long since passed into private Swiss ownership (it is now in the Bavarian State Library, Munich).

In the course of his work on the two copies, Strauss evidently discarded this double folio because of mistakes he had made in the instrumental layout and in the viola part. In the left-hand margin of the first page (see figure 4), we see specifications for the scoring of Till and a single measure for strings (fourth bar after reh. 31).[13] The mistakes were the designations for divided violins (which only come after reh. 33) and the last two notes of the viola

Figure 4. The newly discovered source, fol. 1r, with the figures from the printed score. (Austrian National Library, Music Department, Mus. Hs. 39.546)

part, which should have been written as rests. The original page number "41" (also in black ink) in the top right-hand corner refers, of course, to the Till copy. Strauss's pencil repagination from "41" to "2" (in pencil) refers to the concerto sketches, and indicates that there must have been another double (or at least single) folio now lost or in private hands. In short, these four pages, which contain sketches solely for the second and third movements, represent only the latter portion of the original manuscript.

A fascinating aspect of these sketches is that although entire passages clearly correspond with the final version, they nonetheless are not arranged in what would be their ultimate sequence; indeed, by comparison they appear to have been thrown together higgledy-piggledy (see figures 4 and 10). This curious layout suggests an intermediate stage of evolution somewhere between the sketchbook and short score. The passages themselves may have been worked out musically to their final shape, but their actual sequence would not be determined until later. At the top of fol. 1 one finds sketches for reh. 24 ("un poco più mosso") in the second movement (the "Andante" above refers to the whole movement).

It is possible to discern the musical progression precisely: mm. 1–2, two horns; mm. 3–6, clarinets; mm. 7–10, solo oboe and flute; mm. 11–16, first violins and first clarinet. Measures 2 and 3 in the third system comprise a bridge passage to reh. 25, which is arrived at in m. 4, albeit in different harmony (see figure 5). The beginning of the fourth system shows a continuation of the syncopated violin motive, but this was not adopted in the end. The same applies to the second half of the system, which, to judge by the general appearance of the writing, is part of the third movement. By the beginning of the fifth system (reh. 42) we have already come to this movement. Up to m. 5 (see figure 6) one can trace precisely the dialogue between cellos and contrabasses on the one hand and first violins on the other, but from that moment onward Strauss seems at a loss as to how to proceed; it is, moreover, impossible to identify the second group of five measures. In the next system (the sixth system) we find reh. 43, and this passage continues (despite differences in mm. 5 and 6) through the beginning of the following system (two bars after reh. 44). Here the sketch breaks off just where the cue for the oboe is indicated (the three quarter notes on f^2). After a brief gap in notation, we find ourselves at a point a bit earlier in the score: five bars after reh. 36 (see figure 7). Here again we find an easily discernible dialogue between various instruments: flute/violin, cello/contrabass/bassoon, English horn/ second violin. This dialogue continues in the next system (the fourth from the bottom of the page), right next to the measure from Till, and at the end of

Figure 5. The first three systems of the sketch together with corresponding pages of the printed score: minor differences are marked with ↓ or ↑

this system (six bars after reh. 37), the idea suddenly breaks off. The last three systems on this first page show the musical progression from reh. 46 up to four measures after reh. 47 quite clearly (see figure 8).

The four systems at the top of fol. 1v (see figure 9) suggest that the transition between reh. 47 and 48 posed a problem for Strauss, for little corresponds with the final score. Nonetheless, here one finds individual brief motives

Figure 6. Systems 5–7 of the sketch = score, reh. 42–44

that only appear later on in the score. In measures three through five of the upper part of system one there is, for example, a motive in the first violins that is found two bars after reh. 48 in the printed score; similarly, a closely related passage in bars five through seven in the second system begins, in the

Figure 7. Systems 7 and 8 = score five measures after reh. 36 to six measures after reh. 37

final score, six bars after reh. 49. In figure 9 both of these passages are marked with ⌈ ⌉. In the fifth system—where Strauss has written "Coda" in the left-hand margin—reh. 48 has obviously been reached. The further evolution is plain to see: by the end of the page the development (right to the end of the

Figure 8. Systems 9–11 = score from reh. 46 to four measures after reh. 47

cadenza) has been noted down, although some of it (reh. 50, for instance) only in string harmonies.

Certain details offer some insight into how Strauss went about his work: in bars five through eight of the fifth system—a three-staff system for first violins, oboe, and cello (later bassoon)—the composer indicates a passage for solo oboe, an idea he later abandoned. The end of this solo passage coincides with reh. 49, and here the entry of the oboe is indicated; in the final score this does not occur until four bars later. These extra four bars are not sketched anywhere on this document.

The bridge passage leading to the cadenza may be found in the sixth system, beginning with measure six, and in the seventh and eighth systems in string harmonies only. The harmonic ideas correspond, by and large, to the ones adopted in the printed score, but they appear in a more condensed

Figure 9. Fol. 1v of the source with rehearsal numbers and instrumentation from the score

form—either four measures were telescoped into one (marked with open brackets in figure 9), or enharmonic changes (for example, A♯ = B♭) were made in the final notation. Here one also finds the cadenza written out in full, with the exception of four measures (a repeat on the dominant in a sequence) that were inserted later. After the double bar lines at the bottom of

Figure 10. Idem, fol. 2r

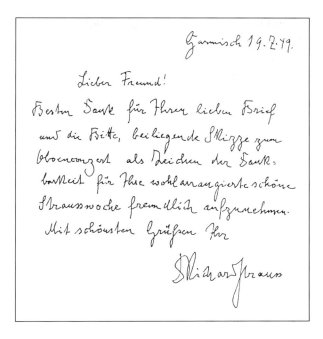

Figure 11. Richard Strauss's letter to Gustav Samazeuilh

the page, Strauss indicates the time signature ($\frac{6}{8}$) for the third movement. Strauss sketched an alternate, longer ending for the cadenza; this was the one he ultimately used.

Folio 2 (see figure 10) contains sketches for this ($\frac{6}{8}$) closing Allegro, which —with the oboe solo indicated—lead up to the conclusion of the work on the verso side. Once again, the order of individual passages does not correspond to the final sequence, namely reh. 53 to 56, 52 to 53, and 56 to the end. Strauss added measure numbers (after two deleted measures) as well as letters [(a) and (b)] for the sake of clarity for future work. He made some other amendments as well, as can be seen at (a) for the final reh. 53 and at (b) for reh. 54.

This fascinating double folio was originally presented to Gustav Samazeuilh, Strauss's loyal champion in France, as a token of his gratitude for his help in organizing a Strauss Festival. The upper right-hand corner bears the date of the composer's 85th birthday: 11 June 1949. This gift was accompanied by a short letter (now affixed on the inside front cover) of 19 July 1949 (see figure 11):

Dear Friend,

Many thanks for your lovely letter and my hope that you will accept the enclosed sketch to the Oboe Concerto as a friendly token of my appreciation for your delightful well organized Strauss Week.

With best wishes

Yours,

Dr. Richard Strauss

This brief note to Samazeuilh is of special significance in that it is among the last letters Strauss wrote; the composer died just over six weeks later.

Notes

1   Letter to Willi Schuh (10 May 1945) in *Richard Strauss–Willi Schuh Briefwechsel* (Zurich: Atlantis, 1969), pp. 78ff.

2   Ibid., p. 87.

3   Willi Schuh, "Zum Melodie- und Harmoniestil der Richard Strauss'schen Spätwerke," *Schweizerische Musikzeitung* 89 (1949): 236.

4   Franz Trenner, ed., *Die Skizzenbücher von Richard Strauss aus dem Richard-Strauss-Archiv in Garmisch* (Tutzing: Hans Schneider, 1977), pp. 135ff.

5   Letter to Schuh, *Strauss-Schuh Briefwechsel*, pp. 78ff.

6   Stephan Kohler, ed. and trans., "John de Lancie: Im Gespräch mit Richard Strauss. Neues über die Entstehung des Oboekonzertes," *Richard Strauss Blätter* 11 (1984): 36–40.

7   Letter to Schuh, *Strauss-Schuh Briefwechsel*, p. 84.

8   *Der Strom der Töne trug mich fort. Die Welt um Richard Strauss in Briefen*, ed. Franz Grasberger (Tutzing: Hans Schneider, 1967), p. 446.

9   Kohler, "John de Lancie," p. 40.

10 The Austrian National Library owns twenty-one musical autographs and more than six hundred letters in Richard Strauss's hand. As far back as 1924 and 1928, the autograph scores to *Der Rosenkavalier* and *Die ägyptische Helena*, respectively, were presented to the library by the composer in connection with the construction of his house in Vienna. But over the past eight years other valuable additions have been made to the collection. The bequest of Clemens Krauss and Viorica Ursuleac deserves particular mention. From this bequest eight original musical manuscripts—most notably the short score to *Capriccio*—were transferred to the ownership of the library. The collection has recently been further supplemented by donations from Hans P. Wertitsch (a Viennese private collector) and by individual purchases, such as two early and two late songs, as well as sketches for the Oboe Concerto and the *Duett Concertino*. The large collection of letters includes correspondence with Ludwig Karpath, Franz Schalk, Clemens Krauss and Viorica Ursuleac, and Roland Tenschert.

11 At some earlier date a strip of paper (1.3 cm. wide) had been attached to the top.

12 *Richard Strauss Thematisches Verzeichnis*, ed. Erich H. Müller von Asow, Alfons Ott, and Franz Trenner (Vienna, 1964–74), p. 156.

13 First edition (Vienna: Joseph Aibl, 1904), pp. 44–45; Eulenburg Study Score, p. 77.

The Metamorphosis of the
Metamorphosen: New Analytical and
Source-Critical Discoveries
Timothy L. Jackson

▼

Man is a great deep, Lord. You number his very hairs and they are not lost in Your sight: but the hairs of his head are easier to number than his affections and the movements of his heart.
—Augustine, Confessions, *IV, 14*

Shostakovich's music . . . thanks to his preference for pragmatic survival over principled martyrdom, is extensive and, to say the least, multifaceted. . . . The music itself, being beyond the notes, can only be heard if the listener is in tune with the composer's intentions—*for to attribute inappropriate meaning to a piece of music is to experience not the music itself, but a sort of self-hypnotic dream one is having about it.* —Ian MacDonald, The New Shostakovich, 1990

Introduction

Since the immediate postwar era, musicologists, performers, and general audiences alike have believed the subject of Richard Strauss's *Metamorphosen* to be the destruction of Munich, the "Bavarian Pompeii," in the Second World War. For Germany, a country that badly needed to mourn its own innocent victims and martyrs, Strauss's music seemed an indigenous and appropriate expression of grief. The *Metamorphosen* was frequently used as maudlin background music for documentary footage of German cities reduced to rubble. This view of the *Metamorphosen* as an elegy for a Munich in ruins received support from an early (1951) study of the *Metamorphosen* sketches, which concluded from the close chronological and physical proximity of sketches for Strauss's 1945 revision of the waltz *München* (originally composed in 1939 as background music for a documentary film about Munich), that the destruction of Munich must also be the subject of the *Metamorphosen*.[1] The authors of this article asserted that Strauss discovered the snap rhythm of the *Metamorphosen* in a sketch that Strauss himself labeled *Trauer um München*, "definitive proof" in their eyes that the subject of the *Metamorphosen* was the destruction of Munich. Because full disclosure of Nazi atrocities immediately after the war threatened to delegitimize any perception of Germany as victim, convincing symbols of German anguish and suffering were in short supply. Thus, the myth that Strauss's *Metamorphosen* mourned a destroyed Munich fulfilled a deeply rooted contemporary need. Since the early fifties, the association of the *Metamorphosen* with *München, ein Gedächtniswalzer* through the *Trauer um München* sketch has been accepted uncritically by Strauss scholars and general audiences worldwide. The *Trauer um München* sketch, in turn, is supposed to adumbrate and explain Strauss's quotation of the *Eroica* "Trauermarsch" at the end of the *Metamorphosen*.

An arch was once described as two weaknesses leaning against one another to form a strength. In this article, two investigations, analytical and musicological, buttressing each other, lead to a single conclusion: the current view of the *Metamorphosen* as an elegy to a postwar Munich is untenable. From a reconstruction of compositional chronology, it will become apparent that Strauss discovered neither the subject nor the snap rhythm of the *Metamorphosen* in the *Trauer um München* sketch, which was intended solely for the *Gedächtniswalzer*. The *Trauer um München* sketch probably postdates a great deal of intense work on the *Metamorphosen*; therefore it could hardly be the source sketch for the essential compositional idea in the *Metamorphosen*. Rather, careful investigation suggests that the seminal idea for the *Metamorphosen* may have come from quite a different source, namely a sketch for a choral setting of a Goethe poem, *Niemand wird sich selber kennen*, a project which Strauss seems to have put aside in August 1944 as soon as he received the *Metamorphosen* commission. However, the essential poetic and motivic idea of the *Niemand wird sich selber kennen* sketch was not abandoned; it was reworked in the *Metamorphosen*, which was, from the outset, conceived as a Goethean work, although the title "*Metamorphosen*," with its allusion to Goethe's *Die Metamorphose der Pflanzen* and *Die Metamorphose der Tiere*, probably occurred to Strauss only late in the compositional process.

While it is indisputable that the *Metamorphosen* relates in a general sense to the war, there appears to be no factual basis to the assertion that Strauss intended the *Metamorphosen* as a memorial to the destroyed Bavarian capital. The work that unequivocally responds to the bombing of Munich is the *Gedächtniswalzer*. The original *München* (the *Gelegenheitswalzer* of 1939) was built around *Feuersnot* material: the waltz that we hear when the hearth fires of Munich have been restored (rehearsal 190ff.). In the 1945 version, with the additional *minore* section, Strauss adds more *Feuersnot* material, specifically the music corresponding to the extinguishing of Munich's flame. The symbolism is overt.

Compositional and historical evidence suggests that the *Metamorphosen*, unlike the *Gedächtniswalzer*, is a philosophical rather than a tone-pictorial work. The *Metamorphosen* is a Goethean probing of the underlying cause of war, namely of the bestial in man. In the *Metamorphosen*, Strauss is concerned with the inversion of the classical concept of metamorphosis rather than with the outward physical destruction wrought by Allied bombing. According to the classical metamorphosis tradition, by discovering the divine within, man could metamorphose into the godly. This idea forms the background against which Goethe's poem *Niemand wird sich selber kennen* and Strauss's choral sketch must be understood. But in Strauss's instrumental treatment of the classical theme in the *Metamorphosen*, the outcome of transformation through self-knowledge is inverted. In Strauss's essentially tragic view, self-knowledge reveals the bestial, not the divine, in man. Thus, in the *Metamorphosen*, the end result of metamorphosis is not man's attainment of the divine but his descent into bestiality. In subject matter and technical construction, München, ein *Gedächtniswalzer* is less weighty than the *Metamorphosen*, and it is hardly surprising to find evidence suggesting that composition of the *Gedächtniswalzer* was a diversion while Strauss struggled to break the serious compositional impasse he encountered while working on the *Metamorphosen*.

The *Metamorphosen* was composed during a period (August 1944–March 1945) when it had become painfully clear to all Germans that, in spite of Goebbels's megalomaniac declaration of "total war," Germany must lose and be destroyed in the process. Documentary evidence suggests that Strauss's personal and financial relations with high-ranking Nazis continued into 1944, and that it was only at this late juncture that the full enormity of Nazi criminality may have finally dawned upon the composer. Sadly, it may have taken the cancellation of the premiere of *Die Liebe der Danae* in line with Goebbels's declaration to pull the wool completely off Strauss's eyes. Indeed, it was not until hostilities in Europe had ceased that Strauss could articulate his antipathy to the Nazis, and then only in the privacy of his diary. In May 1945, he apparently entered in his diary: "Germany 1945. 'So, although the body is indeed dead, the spirit is alive. Luther.' On 12th March the glorious Vienna Opera became the victim of bombs. But on 1st May ended the most terrible period for mankind—12 years of the rule of bestiality, ignorance and illiteracy under the greatest criminals. . . ."[2] One may assert that Thomas Mann and Strauss exemplify two opposite and contrasting reactions to the Nazis. Mann and other prominent intelligentsia who had left early on found consolation in an uncompromised moral stand, in spite of the hardship of uprooting. In

Strauss's defense, it should be noted that he collaborated with the regime not simply to pursue his own agenda, but in the sincere if ultimately misguided hope of preserving the great German cultural tradition from within. Like Shostakovich, Strauss clearly preferred "pragmatic survival over principled martyrdom." However, the genesis of the *Metamorphosen* through the setting of Goethe's implicitly self-critical *Niemand wird sich selber kennen* may have co-incided with a change in Strauss's private opinion of the Nazis in late 1944— an opinion that he could not articulate verbally even in his private diary for fear of discovery by the Gestapo. The emphasis on self-examination and self-judgment in Goethe's *Niemand wird sich selber kennen* suggests that both the sketch and composition of the *Metamorphosen* out of the sketch could be connected with Strauss's increasingly critical perception, not only of the Nazis, but of his own involvement with them.

While some have sought to exonerate Strauss of all wrongdoing by suggesting that he was interested only in artistic and musical matters and not in politics, there are many indications that he was politically alert. In June 1939, Strauss's seventy-fifth birthday was celebrated in Vienna with a special *Festkonzert* at which the Suite from the *Bürger als Edelmann* and the *Symphonia Domestica* were played, with the Strauss family in attendance. Otto Strasser, recalling this occasion overshadowed by the gathering clouds of war, reports that he found Strauss standing alone in the corridor immediately after the performance with tears in his eyes mumbling "Jetzt ist alles aus! Alles ist vorbei!" ("Now everything is over! Everything is past!") Then Strauss's son Franz appeared and comforted his father, and soon the composer again became an affable bourgeois.[3] This incident aptly illustrates Strauss's Janus-faced personality in which bonhomie screened profound sensitivity to world events. The "other" Strauss, momentarily visible in the incident reported by Strasser, emerges in some of the last works, especially in the *Letzte Lieder* and the *Metamorphosen*.

According to Strasser's memoirs, Strauss was unusually communicative about musical matters during his birthday celebrations. Among the topics of discussion was the famous question of "die absolute Musik." Strauss's response was, "Ich kenne sie nicht!" ("I do not know what it is!") For Strauss, music was always bound up with a precise concept ("immer mit irgendeiner prezisen Vorstellung verbunden") and had its origins in a "real background" ("in einer realen Hintergrund").[4] This "precise concept" does not have to be indigenous to the particular composition; rather, it can trace its ancestry back to an earlier work. Indeed, all aspects of Strauss's oeuvre existed for him in an eternal present. The meaning of compositions within the oeuvre may be elucidated by a web of interrelationships that are sometimes overt and sometimes concealed. This assessment is confirmed by accounts of Strauss's capacity to remember and reactivate compositional ideas regardless of their time of origin. Strauss's friend Ernst Roth reports that "he always carried a sketchbook with him. But he could first use sketches from the year 1900 twelve years later."[5] Systematic investigation of Strauss's self-references sheds new light on the "precise concepts" behind the masterpieces of his last period. In the works of the 1940s, the "precise concept" may not simply derive from self-quotation, but even extend to resolution, or—as I shall demonstrate in the case of the *Metamorphosen*—to inversion of the "precise concept" in the earlier work or sketch. Generally speaking, this reevaluation is relevant to Strauss's and Europe's postwar circumstances.

There are, for example, strong links between the so-called *Four Last Songs* (1946–48)—not Strauss's title—and an early song, *Ruhe, meine Seele!* (1894).[6] A musical-poetical connection is created through resolution of a motive from *Ruhe meine Seele!*, the so-called *Notmotiv* ("need-motive"), in the more recently composed *Im Abendrot*. To underscore the connection between the songs through the *Notmotiv*—which represents both the *Not* of Europe's postwar agony and Strauss's impecunious Swiss exile—Strauss orchestrates *Ruhe, meine Seele!* immediately after orchestrating *Im Abendrot*, but before composing the remaining *Letzte Lieder*. There is an analogous musical-poetical connection between the *Metamorphosen* and the abandoned choral setting of Goethe's poem *Niemand wird sich selber kennen*.

In the aforementioned study of the *Metamorphosen* sketches, Ludwig Kusche and Kurt Wilhelm conclude that the snap rhythm was taken from the sketch for the revision of München labeled *Trauer um München*.[7] At first glance, chronology, subject matter, and proximity in the sketchbooks seem to support this generally accepted hypothesis. The dates of the Particells of the *minore* section of the *Gedächtniswalzer* and of the *Metamorphosen*, 23 January 1945 and 8 March 1945 respectively, show that the revision of the waltz München, newly subtitled *ein Gedächtniswalzer*, was conceptually finished about six weeks before the *Metamorphosen*, leaving open the possibility that the waltz could have been influential. The *minore* section of the *Gedächtniswalzer* is subtitled *in memoriam*, as is the quotation in the coda of the *Metamorphosen* (mm. 502–6) of the slow movement from Beethoven's *Eroica*.

Subsequent Strauss researchers have uncritically accepted the corollary hypotheses that: first, the *Trauer um München* sketch is for both the *Gedächtniswalzer* and the *Metamorphosen*, and second, the *Trauer um München* sketch contains the first adumbration of the *Eroica* citation in the coda of the *Metamor-*

phosen. In the *Richard Strauss Werkverzeichnis,* Franz Trenner includes the *Trauer um München* sketch under the *Metamorphosen* rather than under the *Gedächtniswalzer* entry with the following remark: "The conclusion [of the *Metamorphosen*] with its exact quotation of the theme from the [*Eroica*] *Trauermarsch* grows out of this original motivic cell, which is then marked with the words 'In memoriam!'"[8] In *Richard Strauss Autographen in München und Wien,* sketches for the *Metamorphosen* are twice labeled "Trauer um München," although this caption is never found in the sketchbook itself.[9] Most recently (1988), according to John Williamson, "a contemporary sketch labeled *Trauer um München* grew into the idea that is introduced by two solo violas in the ninth bar of the *Metamorphosen.* As the work germinated, this figure revealed an affinity with the opening idea of the funeral march from Beethoven's *Eroica* Symphony. This led Strauss to quote Beethoven's theme in the closing bars of the complete work accompanied by the words 'In memoriam.'"[10]

Two fundamental questions must be addressed. Is the programmatic allusion of *München, ein Gedächtniswalzer*—the destruction of Munich by allied bombing—also that of the *Metamorphosen?* Are the *Gedächtniswalzer* and the *Metamorphosen* compositionally related by effectually sharing the *Trauer um München* sketch? Analysis and reconstruction of compositional chronology through the sources gainsay any positive response.

Since none of Strauss's sketches are dated, chronology has to be determined by a study of both the sketches' disposition in the host sketchbooks and their musical content. The source-critical part of this study presents evidence that: (1) the sketch for Goethe's *Niemand wird sich selber kennen* immediately antedates the earliest sketches for the *Metamorphosen* (all of which date from August–September 1944);[11] (2) by 30 September 1944, the date of a "progress-report" letter to Karl Böhm, Strauss had already entered some eighteen sketch drafts for the *Metamorphosen* into his sketchbooks; (3) Strauss determined the central motivic issues in the *Metamorphosen* in August–September 1944 before interrupting its composition in October–January 1945 to work on other projects, including the revision of *München* (to which the *Trauer um München* sketch properly belongs); and (4) the last sketches for the *Metamorphosen* date from between late January and late February 1945. According to this chronology, Strauss first arrived at the musical-poetical idea of the *Metamorphosen* well before encountering a compositional impasse and interrupting work to turn to other projects, including the *Einleitung und Walzer aus dem Rosenkavalier* and the revision of the waltz *München.* Discovery of the role of the incomplete setting of Goethe's *Niemand wird sich selber kennen* in the genesis of the *Metamorphosen* sheds new light on Strauss's "precise concept." The subject of the *Metamorphosen* is not the outward physical destruction of Munich, which is portrayed in the new *minore* section of *München*, but the much more subtle reworking of the Goethean concept in the *Niemand wird sich selber kennen* sketch.

Toward the end of the war, Strauss was personally affected by the general catastrophe. As the conduct of the regime became more hysterical, he began to fear for the safety of his previously spared Jewish daughter-in-law, Alice, and grandchildren, who according to the Nazi racial laws, were *Mischlinge* 1. *Klasse* ("halfbreeds, first class") and therefore subject to deportation and liquidation. To cope, he buried himself in Goethe, whose works he owned in the huge *Propyläenausgabe*. According to Alice Strauss, the composer read virtually everything with the exception of the *Farbenlehre*.[12] For Strauss, Goethe represented the pinnacle of German culture. Through Goethe, he sought continuity with a tradition that appeared to be dissolving.

It was under these circumstances, just prior to commencing work on the *Metamorphosen* in the late summer of 1944, that Strauss came upon two short poems by Goethe, *Niemand wird sich selber kennen* and *Wie es aber in der Welt zugeht*, which he copied onto the front cover of one of his pocket sketchbooks. He set the first poem, which comes from a collection of "Sprüche" ("Sayings") entitled *Zahme Xenion* ("Tame Invectives"):

> Niemand wird sich selber kennen,
> Sich von seinem Selbst-Ich trennen;
> Doch probier' er jeden Tag,
> Was nach aussen endlich, klar,[13]
> Was er ist und was er war,
> Was er kann und was er mag.

> [No one can know himself,
> Detach himself from his Self-I;
> Yet, let him put to the test every day,
> That which is objectively finally clear,
> What he is and what he was,
> What he can and what he may.]

Perhaps Strauss intended combining both poems in a single choral work, but only the first poem was set, ending inconclusively on the dominant. Recomposition of the incomplete setting of Goethe's *Niemand wird sich selber kennen* in the *Metamorphosen* seems to coincide with Strauss's ultimate disillusionment with the National Socialists. The emphasis in the poem's final lines on accepting limitations is especially significant when viewed in the context of Nazi megalomania and where it had led. It has often been said that Strauss never expressed remorse for his accommodation with the regime. Perhaps, anticipating accusations of guilt by association, Strauss himself was surprised by his own previous actions and was affected personally by the line "No one can know himself." By reworking the Goethean piece in the *Metamorphosen*, he may also have affirmed, if only to himself, the rectitude of Goethe's assertion that a man must finally "put himself to the test" and take responsibility for "what he was." Thus, by expanding the *Metamorphosen* out of the setting of *Niemand wird sich selber kennen*, Strauss may have privately confessed, in strictly musical terms, his personal culpability. The confessional aspect of the *Metamorphosen* may have prevented Strauss from attending its premiere. Paul Sacher has informed me that "Strauss did not want to attend the concert [premiere] but asked whether he could be present at the last rehearsal [24 January 1946]. When driving to the concert hall, he expressed the wish to conduct [the last rehearsal of] his *Metamorphosen*. He did so without interruption, thanked the musicians, turned round and left."[14] Schuh describes this momentous, single run-through in the almost empty hall under the composer's direction: "Strauss knew above all how to achieve magnificently the great sweep of development through powerful increase of dynamic and tempos—an unforgettable experience for the conductor [Sacher], the players of the Collegium, and the very few listeners present."[15]

The fundamental theme, the "precise concept," of the *Metamorphosen* is thus poetic, philosophical, and possibly autobiographical: the negation of the traditional affirmation of self-knowledge as a means of discovering the divine within. In the Middle Ages, the motto of the Delphic oracle, *Nosce te*, was reinterpreted in a Christian sense. Since man is created in the image of God, to know God, man must know himself. In *Niemand wird sich selber kennen*, while maintaining self-knowledge to be theoretically impossible, Goethe paradoxically urges its practical attainment. Clemens Heselhaus suggests that the "Erkenne dich selbst" and the "Metamorphose" concepts have been traditionally linked.[16] According to both classical and biblical lore, by penetrating to the core of being, the human soul is transfigured or metamorphosed by its discovery of the divine within.[17]

At what point in the compositional process did Strauss associate Goethe's treatment of the problem of self-knowledge with his theory of metamorphosis? Unless further evidence comes to light, the answer must remain speculative. But the fact that Strauss neither labels any of the individual *Metamorphosen* sketches "Metamorphosen" nor refers to the evolving work by name in the "progress report" to Böhm (he simply speaks of an adagio) suggests that the title could well have been a late inspiration postdating the sketches altogether. The motivic link with the *Niemand wird sich selber kennen* sketch suggests that the adagio was probably conceived as a Goethean work from the outset. Only when Strauss had perceived the composition in its entirety, with its peculiar physiognomy of obsessive foreground motives superimposed on continuous middleground transformation, could he associate the idea of "Erkenne dich selbst" in *Niemand wird sich selber kennen* with the concept of "Metamorphose" presented in *Die Metamorphose der Pflanzen* and *Die Metamorphose der Tiere*.

Goethe's view of metamorphosis, like the classical notion, is essentially optimistic; it is a view of "order in motion." The "holy Muse" brings this concept "harmonically" to man ("die heilige Muse/ Bringt harmonisch ihn dir").[18] But in Strauss's instrumental meditation, Goethe's concept is violently inverted; through self-knowledge, man regresses from the divine to the bestial. With this inversion, Strauss's *Metamorphosen* has a great deal—though probably inadvertently—in common with Kafka's, where the human protagonist awakens as a giant beetle.[19] While the analytical portion of this article will examine in detail the musical means Strauss employs to represent the inversion of Goethe's classical metamorphosis concept, one overriding musical indication may be immediately apprehended: the negation of background C major by C minor. Since C major is, surprisingly, the anomaly in this piece, one wonders why Strauss insists on notating the work as a whole in C major when he could have easily avoided so many accidentals simply by changing the key signature to C minor. Why does he persist with the C-major key signature right to the bitter C-minor end? The answer concerns Strauss's tonal symbolism for the negation of the divine in man. The origin of man's being is indeed divine, represented by "perfect" C major. But this background, divine C major is obfuscated, distorted, and finally annihilated by man's C minor. Once the thin veneer of civilization has been stripped away, man's animalism is quickly revealed.

At least one critic who heard the work shortly after its premier seems to have sensed Strauss's program, although he completely misinterpreted Strauss's intentions. In 1947, Dutch critic Matthijs Vermeulen claimed the work to be a *Grabgesang* for the Hitler regime.[20] His review was considered important enough to be immediately translated into German and published by a major Swiss newspaper.[21] In a pair of related articles, Willi Schuh, who had been involved with the work from the beginning, vehemently denied the claim, pointing out that since the *Metamorphosen* was finished before Germany's defeat it could hardly refer to Hitler's death and to the regime's demise.[22] He also reported that Strauss became conscious of the connection between the snap rhythm in his work and Beethoven's *Marcia funebre* in the *Eroica* only once the *Metamorphosen* was almost finished.[23] According to Schuh, Strauss's caption "In memoriam!" above the *Eroica* citation refers not to Hitler but to Beethoven. Virtually all subsequent Strauss scholars have supported Schuh's interpretation.

But one should not dismiss Vermeulen's claim out of hand. The caption "In memoriam" could refer to Hitler, not as a true hero, but as a false hero who aspired to greatness but descended to bestiality. The *Eroica* quote could well tie in with Strauss's rejection of the Nazis at the time of composition. Schuh's objection that Hitler was still alive while Strauss was writing the *Metamorphosen* if anything reinforces this contention. We recall that Beethoven, when he became disillusioned with Napoleon, furiously rededicated the *Eroica* "per festeggiare il *sovennire* di un grande Uomo" ("*to the memory* of a great man") while Napoleon was still alive and in power. Strauss was fond of oblique references and layered connotations; thus, the caption "In memoriam" could have manifold meanings. It could refer to the victims of the war, fallen heroes, the fact that Strauss has only "remembered" the connection with Beethoven at the end of composing the *Metamorphosen*, and finally, Beethoven's ironic, premature "burial" of the still-living Napoleon. By citing Beethoven's angry rejection of Napoleon in the *Eroica* dedication, Strauss could also have been pointing to a famous precedent for his own repudiation of a tyrant, whom he, like Beethoven, had once supported.

Analytical Evidence

The texture of the *Niemand wird sich selber kennen* sketch suggests a choral medium, probably four-part men's choir (example 1). This voicing is not specified in the sketch but is indicated by the spacing, which would be most awkward without the downward octave displacement of the two upper voices.[24] Cursory analysis reveals parallels between the *Niemand wird sich selber kennen* sketch and the *Metamorphosen*. Like the sketch, it is in C major, but a C major heavily overlaid with elements of E minor and C minor. In the first four measures of the Goethe sketch, the effect of the tonic C-major chord is weakened by E-minor chords. The key of E minor is further suggested by the cadence on its dominant in measure 4. Turning to the first four measures of the *Metamorphosen*, one finds the same E/C ambiguity (example 2). The first chord is an E-minor triad, and the last chord of the phrase, the C-flat-major chord, is enharmonically equivalent to the dominant of E minor. C is not established

Example 1. Realization of *Niemand wird sich selber kennen* for men's choir (TTTB)

as a tonal center until mm. 7–10, and even then it is C minor rather than C major that is suggested.

In the *Metamorphosen* entry in the Strauss *Werkverzeichnis*, the *Keimzelle* ("seminal idea") of the Beethovenian quotation is alleged to have been first appropriated in the *Trauer um München* sketch (example 3). Closer analysis of this

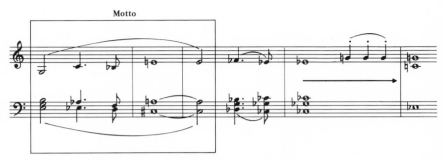

Example 2. Beginning of the *Metamorphosen*

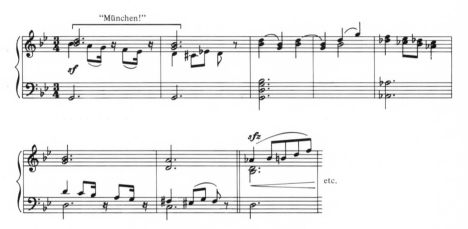

Example 3. Beginning of the *Trauer um München* sketch

sketch, however, fails to show any significant musical connections with the *Metamorphosen*. Neither its $\frac{3}{4}$ time signature nor its G-minor tonality appear anywhere in the final version or in any of the sketches for the *Metamorphosen*. Moreover, it is untrue that the snap rhythm characteristic of both the *Metamorphosen* and Beethoven's *Marcia funebre* first occurs in the *Trauer um München* sketch. In that sketch, an eighth note followed by a sixteenth note and a sixteenth rest create a portamento, while the different and harsher effect of the snap rhythm in the *Metamorphosen* and the *Eroica* is produced by a sixteenth note followed by a dotted eighth note or the reverse.

When most musicians speak of "metamorphosis," they generally mean a motivic transformation whereby a motive metamorphoses into another. But in Strauss's *Metamorphosen*, the primary motives (six in all) are, paradoxi-

Example 4. Six invariant foreground motives in the *Metamorphosen* (at right)

cally, reiterated again and again in their original forms (example 4). Wilfried Brennecke concludes that with "Strauss's *Trauermusik* it is impossible to speak of a new form, 'metamorphosis,' a form which can be distinguished as an architectonic scheme or general compositional model from other forms. . . . The theoretical definition of musical metamorphosis . . . —namely, 'specific thematic material conceived in constant flux'—cannot, therefore, be applied to Strauss's work. One can hardly speak of a 'living transformational process' and 'continuous remodelling' of the themes, since the form of the . . . themes remains completely unaltered."[25] While accurately describing part of the phenomenon, Brennecke misses the essential point. The foreground themes remain unchanged in order to focus attention on the middle and

Example 5. Form of the *Metamorphosen*: final version and initial concept

Measure	1	82	130	145	187	213	246
(a) Final Version — Formal section	**Exposition**					**Development**	
	Group 1 Adagio	Group II Subsidiary theme I (G)	Transition I	Subsidiary theme II (E)	Transition II	Group I Part I	Part II
Tempo indication	"Adagio ma non troppo"	"etwas fliessender"	"poco piu mosso"	"appassionato"		"Agitato"	"noch etwas lebhafter"
Comment			Motive 5 (e)			Motive 5 (c)	
(b) Initial Conception — Formal section	**Exposition**		**Development**			**Recapitulation**	
Tempo indication	"Adagio"		"Agitato"			"Allegro"	
Comment			Motive 5 (e)				

background transformations of a single, underlying motive, a motive derived from the *Niemand wird sich selber kennen* sketch. I do not think it specious, given the antagonism of many Strauss scholars towards Schenker and Schenker's harsh critiques of early Strauss, to highlight the congruence between Strauss's Goethe-inspired compositional emphasis on subsurface transformation in the *Metamorphosen* and Schenker's discovery of precisely this kind of transformation through his analytical application of Goethean concepts.[26]

Previous commentators on the *Metamorphosen* have offered differing interpretations of its form. Del Mar sidesteps the issue, simply describing the work as "symphonic."[27] Brennecke leans toward a fantasy interpretation, while also admitting the possibility of "free-sonata form."[28] Schuh maintains

278	299	345	391	433	437	449	487	502
			Recapitulation	**Overlap of recapitulation and coda**				
Part III	Transition III	Group II Recapitulation of subsidiary theme I (C)	Adagio	Beginning of coda	Transition IV	Recapitulation resumes	Coda resumes	'Coda to the coda'
	"Piu allegro"		"Adagio tempo primo"					
							Deceptive cadence on Fb	Eroica citation V–I cadence bridged over
								Eroica

that, while it shows fantasy-like freedom, the work is nevertheless in sonata form. He organizes the six invariant motives within the exposition into three groups: the first spans the introductory Adagio (motives 1–3, mm. 1–81), the second encompasses the G-major theme (motive 4, mm. 82–133), and the third includes the E-minor/major themes (motives 5–6, mm. 134–212).[29]

Example 5a presents my analysis of the form of the finished work. While I agree with Schuh's view of a sonata form where the exposition comprises mm. 1–212, the development mm. 213–390, and the recapitulation and coda mm. 391 to the end, I divide the exposition into two large groups (rather than the three proposed by Schuh), separated by the cadence in m. 81.[30] Group I, the Adagio proper (mm. 1–81), presents motives 1–3, while group II comprises two subsidiary themes: subsidiary theme I in G major (motive 4, mm. 82–130), and subsidiary theme II in E major (motive 6, mm. 145–86). Unlike Schuh, I identify two transitions within the exposition. The first, transition I (theme 5, mm. 130–44), leads from subsidiary theme I to subsidiary theme II, and the second, transition II (mm. 187–212), from subsidiary theme II into the development.

The development divides into two large groups, the first of which, group I (mm. 213–345), subdivides into three parts. Within group I, part I (mm. 213–45) focuses on motive 5. Part II (mm. 246–77) begins with a recomposition of the opening motto and culminates in part III (mm. 278–98), a recomposition—in E-flat minor—of the tonal structure of subsidiary theme II.[31] A long transition, transition III (mm. 299–344), leads to group II (mm. 345–86)—a recapitulation of subsidiary theme I within the development.[32] Because of this premature recapitulation, only a brief restatement (mm. 425–31) is necessary within the recapitulation proper.

The recapitulation (mm. 391–486) and coda (mm. 433–501) overlap for over fifty measures. The coda begins after the dramatic pause in m. 432, but then an intense transition, transition IV (mm. 437–48),[33] leads back to the recapitulation, which continues until the F-flat major deceptive cadence in m. 486.[34] At this point, the coda resumes until it approaches a cadence in m. 502, which is also evaded and there follows a short but extremely important "coda to the coda" containing the Eroica citation (m. 502 to the end).[35]

This sonata form does, of course, exhibit fantasy-like features that blur its main structural divisions: four substantial transitions, insertion of part of the recapitulation into the development, and an unusual overlap of recapitulation and coda. Another remarkable formal aspect unmentioned in the literature is the ambiguity concerning the true beginning of the development. Since motive 5 has a strongly developmental character, the listener

Example 6. The *Metamorphosemotiv*

tends to confuse its first appearance in transition I (m. 134) with the beginning of the development. However, if transition I really were the beginning of the development, the development would encompass music of the exposition, namely subsidiary theme II (mm. 145–86) and transition II (mm. 187–212). As my reconstruction of the sketches will show, in Strauss's initial conception of the form, the development begins in measure 134 and the recapitulation in m. 213 (example 5b). Only relatively late in the compositional process does Strauss decide to make the material of subsidiary theme II and transition II part of the exposition rather than part of the development. As a result of this decision, the development, rather than the recapitulation, commences in measure 213.

Since any two diatonic triads a third apart hold two notes in common, one triad is easily destabilized by or transformed into the other (example 6). In this case, the C-major and E-minor triads hold E and G in common, and the distinction between them depends entirely on the semitone B-C (the stemmed notes in examples 6 and 9–11). I believe that the uncertainty of C major in the face of E minor in the first measure of the *Niemand wird sich selber kennen* sketch represents the elusiveness of the "Self-I." I shall call this putative analogue for the "Self-I" the *Metamorphosemotiv*.

In the sketch, the *Metamorphosemotiv* is subjected to three transformations, labeled a, b, and c (example 7a–c). Example 8a and b shows these transformations in the middleground of the setting. When Strauss abandoned the *Niemand wird sich selber kennen* sketch to work on the *Metamorphosen*, he did not abandon the *Metamorphosemotiv*. Three transformations of this figure (labeled x, y, and z forms) and their transpositions determine the tonal structure of

Example 7. Transformations of the *Metamorphosemotiv* in the *Niemand wird sich selber kennen* sketch

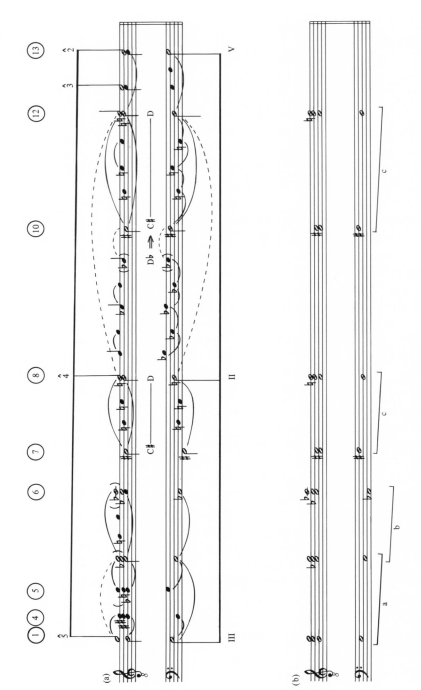

Example 8. Linear analysis of the *Niemand wird sich selber kennen* sketch showing transformations of the *Metamorphosemotiv* in the middleground

Example 9. x forms of the *Metamorphosemotiv*

Example 10. y forms of the *Metamorphosemotiv*

Example 11. z forms of the *Metamorphosemotiv*

the *Metamorphosen* (examples 9–11). The y-forms in the *Metamorphosen* restate *a* from the *Niemand wird sich selber kennen* sketch at exactly the same transpositional level.[36]

X forms: C in the B-C semitone is displaced by C-sharp or its enharmonic equivalent, D-flat (example 9a–e). Example 9a is the basis for the *Metamorphosen*'s motto (example 2). Y forms: the B-C semitone is preserved while E and G are chromatically altered (example 10a–c). Z forms: B is sustained or enharmonically transformed into C-flat (example 11a–c). In example 11a, the triad is simply shifted from first inversion to root position.

Examples 12 and 13 show enlargements of x, y, and z forms of the *Metamorphosemotiv* in the middle- and background of the work. The ultimate background of the *Metamorphosen* is an enlargement of z in diatonic C major (examples 11a, transposed to C, and 12a). At the next level, the C-major chord is displaced by the initial E-minor chord (m. 1) and by the final C-minor chord (m. 506) transforming z into y (compare examples 10a and 12b). By inserting the great C-sharp-major seventh chord at the end of the develop-

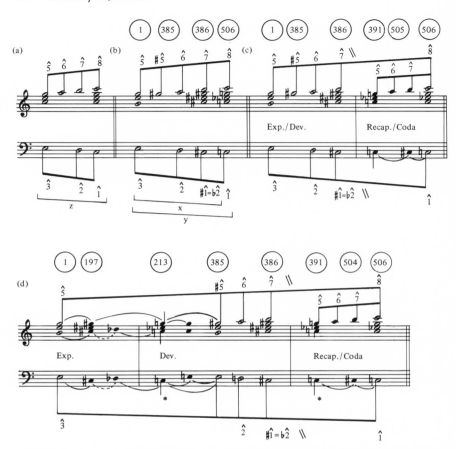

Example 12. Linear analysis of the *Metamorphosen*; background and middle-ground

ment (m. 386) into this underlying chord progression, *x* is nested within *y* (examples 9d and 12b).

Here, as in conventional sonata form, interruption on $\hat{2}$ occurs at the end of the development. But this interruption is transferred to the bass and $\hat{2}$ is only intelligible through an enharmonic reinterpretation in which C-sharp or $\sharp\hat{1}$ is reconstrued as D-flat or $\flat\hat{2}$. The upper voice, which unfolds an ascending fourth, $\hat{5}$-$\hat{6}$-$\hat{7}$-$\hat{8}$, is simultaneously interrupted on B or $\hat{7}$ (example 12c).[37]

Tonal ideas taken from the *Niemand wird sich selber kennen* sketch are not simply reused in the *Metamorphosen*—they are revalued. In the poem, Goethe asserts paradoxically that man can and must experience elevating self-transfiguration through self-knowledge, an idea that finds its musical counterpart in the triumph of "pure," that is, "divine" C-major diatonicism, at the end of Strauss's sketch. In the *Metamorphosen*, on the other hand, the colossal struggle between background C major and more foreground E minor and C minor ends with the previously discussed displacement of C major by C minor, representing annihilation of the divine (C major) by the bestial (C minor) in man. Man's ultimate defeat, while foreshadowed by emphatic tonic-minor chords at the beginning of the development and recapitulation (marked with asterisks in example 12d), is definitively achieved only in the final tonic-minor chord because it is only in this chord that the largest-scale structural lines resolve. Strauss's negation of the metamorphosis tradition results in his recomposition of a further aspect of the *Niemand wird sich selber kennen* sketch: the redemptive D-flat-becoming-C-sharp enharmonic. In the sketch, D-flat, redeemed through its transformation into C-sharp, ascends to D as man, transfigured, ascends to the divine (example 8a). But in the *Metamorphosen*, C-sharp's right to rise is denied at critical junctures; man is incapable of redemption (example 13a).[38]

A late, seemingly insignificant change to the *Eroica* citation itself underscores the genetic connection between the *Metamorphosen* and the *Niemand wird sich selber kennen* sketch through the *Metamorphosemotiv*. The first and only sketch of the citation is to be found on pages 93–94 in S (draft XLIII).[39] The lateness of this sketch confirms Strauss's remark to Schuh that the motivic connection between the *Metamorphosen* and the *Eroica* only became obvious to him once the work was almost finished.[40] Example 14a–b compares the sketch and final versions of the citation. Strauss initially contemplates slightly altering the beginning of the citation (example 14a) but opts for a literal quotation (example 14b).

A striking feature of Beethoven's theme is the rhythmic shift of the initial C. Example 15a shows the theme before the shift (how it "should be") and example 15b after the shift (how it is). By sustaining the initial G an extra quarter note, thereby delaying the arrival of the C, Beethoven draws out the initial fourth, G-C (compare the brackets in example 15a–b). This elongation has the effect of a slowed-down *Schleifer*, evoking the slow tread of the funeral cortege—an effect heightened by its contrast with the fast *Schleifer* in the bass (a diminution of the rising fourth, example 15c). When Strauss initially transferred Beethoven's theme into the bass, he apparently wanted a strong perfect cadence on the downbeat of m. 502. Instead of literal quotation, he eliminated the rhythmic shift in Beethoven's theme so that the C would fall on the downbeat of m. 502 (compare examples 14a and 15a). In the

214

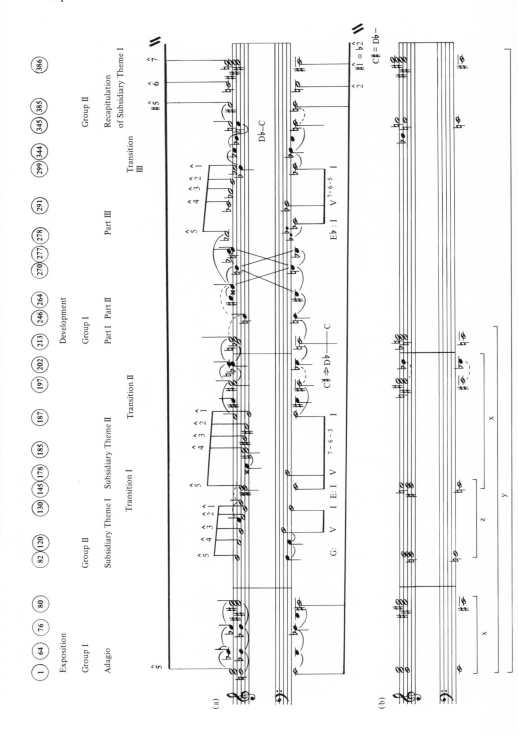

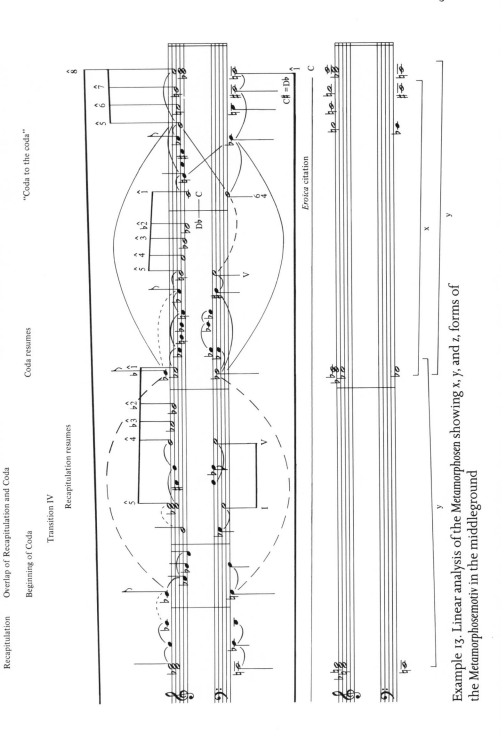

Example 13. Linear analysis of the *Metamorphosen* showing *x, y,* and *z,* forms of the *Metamorphosemotiv* in the middleground

Example 14. Comparison of mm. 500–end in the sketch and in the final version

Example 15. The rhythmic shift in the *Eroica* theme

final version, however, by using the literal quotation with the rhythmic shift, he creates an unstable six-four chord on the downbeat of m. 502, frustrating the anticipated cadence (compare examples 14b and 15b).

The ultimate elimination of the sketch's strong perfect cadence in m. 502 has a profound effect not merely at the local level but also on the largest scale. Example 16a–b compares the effect of nonliteral and literal quotations of the *Eroica* motive on the voice leading in the recapitulation, coda, and "coda to the coda" (m. 391 to the end). In the sketch version, the voice-leading arch extends only to the perfect cadence in m. 502, while in the final version it extends from the F-flat-major chord at the end of the recapitulation (m. 487) through the voice exchange (mm. 502–5) to the final C-minor chord (m. 506). In the final version, then, the motion from F-flat major (m. 487) to C minor (m. 506) creates a colossal enlargement of the y form of the *Metamorphose-motiv*, which, as noted above, is a restatement of the *a* form of the motive discovered in the *Niemand wird sich selber kennen* sketch. In short, it was only after writing out the *Particell* that Strauss realized the possibility of creating an enlargement of the *Metamorphosemotiv* through the rhythmic shift in the *Eroica* theme (compare examples 7a, 8b, 10c and 16b).

Source Evidence

Strauss thought of himself primarily as an opera composer. After completing his last stage work, *Capriccio* (1941), he maintained that his career was effectively over, ironically referring to all subsequent works (including the *Metamorphosen*) as *Handgelenksübungen*, or "wrist exercises." One of the most intriguing aspects of late Strauss is the dichotomy between works in a cheerful pseudo-Mozartian style and those in a more serious Wagnerian-

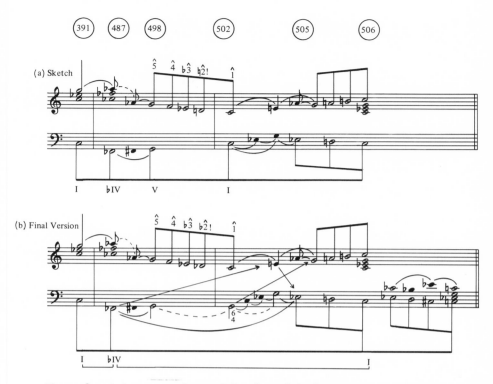

Example 16. Linear analysis of sketch and final versions of recapitulation, coda, and "coda to the coda"

Brahmsian late-Romantic vein. Given the contrasting moods and styles of these "wrist exercises," the overlap in compositional chronology and proximity in the sketchbooks seem especially remarkable. Perhaps the lighter Mozartian pieces, the second *Symphonie für Bläser*, the *Konzert für Oboe*, the *Duett-Concertino*, and the song *Malven* are best understood as the alter egos of the serious Wagnerian-Brahmsian pieces—the *Metamorphosen*, the orchestral versions of *Ich liebe dich* and *Ruhe, meine Seele!*, the *Letzte Orchesterlieder*, and the unfinished choral work *Besinnung*.[41]

Sketches for the *Metamorphosen*, the *Symphonie für Bläser*, and the *Gedächtniswalzer* are found in four pocket sketchbooks dating from 1943–45: Trenner Sketchbook 133 (Tr. 133), Trenner Sketchbook 134 (Tr. 134), a sketchbook in a private collection (PS [Privatsammlung]), and a sketchbook in the Bayerische Staatsbibliothek (S [Staatsbibliothek], Mus. MSS. 9986).[42] The complete sketches for the *Metamorphosen*, comprising at least forty-five individual drafts and some 140 sketchbook pages, are divided between Tr. 134, PS, and S, while sketches for the *Symphonie* are found in Tr. 133, Tr. 134, and S, and sketches for the *Gedächtniswalzer* in PS.

Example 17 shows the distribution of *Metamorphosen*, *Symphonie*, and *Gedächtniswalzer* sketches in Tr. 133, Tr. 134, PS, and S. One might expect Strauss to fill a sketchbook systematically by starting at the beginning and proceeding to the

Example 17. Distribution of *Metamorphosen*, *Symphonie*, and *Gedächtniswalzer* sketches in sketchbooks Tr. 133, Tr. 134, PS, S

Tr. 133 "Rondo Es dur"	Tr. 134 "Bläser Suite"	
Einleitung und Allegro (*Symphonie*, IV) Before 6 December 1943	*Allegro* (*Symphonie*, I) Before 14 February 1944	p. 70
Menuett (*Symphonie*, III) May–June 1945	*Niemand wird sich selber kennen* First *Metamorphosen* sketches August–September 1944 *Andantino* (*Symphonie*, II) May 1945	
Einleitung und Allegro	*Allegro*	p. 101

PS	S "Rondeau Es dur"
Metamorphosen September 1944– January 1945	"*Allegro*" (Eb, 4/4) Miscellaneous sketches Before February 1944
München, Ein Gedächtniswalzer October 1944–January 1945	*Metamorphosen* January–February 1945 "*Allegro Bläser*" (Eb, 4/4) Before February 1944

end. However, he often enters sketches at the front of the book and, leaving a block of blank pages in the middle (room to expand on material already entered), leaps to the end. An overview of chronology suggests that all of the sketchbooks under consideration, with the exception of PS, are filled in precisely this way.

While a detailed analysis of the sketches for the *Symphonie* would take us beyond our present topic, some discussion of these sketches is necessary in order to date the *Niemand wird sich selber kennen* sketch and the earliest sketches for the *Metamorphosen*. As shown in example 17, the *Niemand wird sich selber kennen* sketch and the first *Metamorphosen* sketches in Tr. 134 are surrounded by *Symphonie* sketches. Pages 1–70 and 101–end of Tr. 134 contain sketches for the

Example 18. Detailed view of the contents of Tr. 134, pp. 71–100

Page	Title/tempo	Key	Time signature	Comment	Date
71		Bb	2/4	Early idea for Symphonie, II?	May 1945?
72		F	2/4	Sketch for Symphonie, II	May 1945
73					
74					
75					
76					
77					
78	"Andante"	G	4/4	Early idea for Symphonie, II?	May 1945?
79					
80	"Niemand wird sich selber kennen"	C	4/4		August–September 1944
81					
82		f	4/4	Early idea for Symphonie, II?	May 1945?
83					
84					
85	"Moderato"	C	4/4	Concordance with S, p. 90. Early idea	May 1945?

first, Allegro, movement of the *Symphonie*. Since the Particell for this movement is dated 14 February 1944, all of these Allegro sketches must antedate February 1944.

Example 18 presents a detailed view of the contents of pages 71–100 in Tr. 134. The *Niemand wird sich selber kennen* sketch and the first *Metamorphosen* sketches occur on pages 80–81 and pages 86–88 respectively. Pages 71–79 and 82–85 contain early ideas for the second, Andantino, movement of the *Symphonie*. Since Strauss worked on the Andantino in May 1945—after completing the *Metamorphosen* in April 1945—these Andantino sketches must be the last to have been entered into Tr. 134. As of February 1944, while the rest of the sketchbook was already filled with sketches for the Allegro of the *Symphonie*,

Page	Title/tempo	Key	Time signature	Comment	Date
				for *Symphonie*, II?	
86	"Adagio"	C	4/4	First sketches for *Metamorphosen*	August–September 1944
87					
88					
89	[blank]				
90		C	4/4	*Metamorphosen* sketches	August–September 1944
91					
92					
93					
94					
95					
96					
97					
98					
99					
100	[blank]				

the middle thirty pages of Tr. 134 (pp. 71–100) were still blank. Strauss must have entered the *Niemand wird sich selber kennen* sketch and the first *Metamorphosen* sketches on those blank pages in August–September 1944.

Example 19 shows the chronology of the *Metamorphosen* sketches in Tr. 134, PS, and S. In August–September 1944, Strauss begins working in Tr. 134, entering the *Niemand wird sich kennen* sketch and the earliest *Metamorphosen* sketches on pages 80–81 and 86–88 (drafts I–II). At this time, PS is still completely empty. In PS, Strauss then enters preliminary ideas for the *Metamorphosen* on pages 35–37, 16–17, and 117–19 (drafts III–V). After entering two more drafts in Tr. 134 on pages 90–98 (drafts VI–VII), Strauss turns definitively to PS. Twenty drafts (drafts VIII–XV, XVIII–XXII, and XXIV–XXX) are then entered in the first ninety pages of PS.

As of October–December 1944, S is already partly filled with "Rondeau Es dur" sketches for the *Symphonie* and other miscellaneous ideas. These sketches, however, are distributed primarily at the beginning and end of the book, with a large block of empty pages remaining in the middle (pp. 34–83). Twice while working in PS Strauss switches over to S, entering short drafts on pages 50, 35–36, and 1–3 (drafts XVI–XVII and XXIII). The definitive turn to S occurs after draft XXXI, the thirteen drafts (drafts XXXI–XXXVII and XL–XLV) filling up the large block of blank pages in the middle of the sketchbook.

Returning now to example 17, the sketches for the *Metamorphosen* in Tr. 134 are earlier than those in PS, which in turn are earlier than those in S. Conversely, the sketches for the *Symphonie* in S are possibly earlier than those in Tr. 134. In other words, Strauss probably entered sketches for the *Metamorphosen* and the *Symphonie* in Tr. 134 and S in inverse chronological order: while Tr. 134 contains the first sketches for the *Metamorphosen* (August–September 1944), it also contains late sketches for the second Andantino movement of the *Symphonie* (April–May 1945); and while S contains early "Rondeau Es dur" sketches for one of the outer movements of the *Symphonie* (January–February 1944), it also contains the last sketches for the *Metamorphosen* (February 1945).

The situation of the *Niemand wird sich selber kennen*, *Metamorphosen*, and *Symphonie* sketches places the *Niemand wird sich selber kennen* sketch in chronological proximity to the first *Metamorphosen* sketches. But how far had Strauss progressed in composing the *Metamorphosen* before he entered the *Trauer um München* sketch in PS?

While composing the *Metamorphosen*, Strauss definitively switches from PS to S at draft XXXI. This switch establishes the relative chronology of *Gedächtniswalzer* sketches in PS and *Metamorphosen* sketches in S. Strauss's turn to S

Example 19: Disposition of *Metamorphosen* sketches in Tr. 134, PS, and S

Draft		Tr. 134	PS	S
I	Niemand wird sich selber kennen	80–81		
II		86–88		
III			35–37	
IV			*17–16	
V			*119–117	
VI		90–95		
VII		95–98		
VIII			1–15	
IX			19	
X			42–45	
XI			39–41	
XII			29–30	
XIII			*21–20	
			22	
			22	
XIV			23–28	
XV			18	
XVI				50
XVII				35–36
XVIII			85–88	
XIX			4–5	
XX			57	
XXI			61–71	
XXII			72–74	
XXIII				1–3
XXIV			56	
XXV			38	
XXVI			48–51	
XXVII			51–52	
XXVIII			46–47	
XXIX			75–77	
XXX			58–60	
XXXI				37–48

Draft	Tr. 134	PS	S
XXXII			87
XXXIII			51
XXXIV			49
XXXV			52–75
XXXVI			76–79
XXXVII			80–81
XXXVIII		60	
XXXIX		61	
XL			unnumbered page opposite 35
XLI			82–83
XLII			95–96
XLIII			92–94
XLIV			97–98
XLV			128–120

*Pages filled in reverse order

was probably motivated by a lack of free pages in PS. The first half of PS was probably already filled with Metamorphosen sketches and the second half with Gedächtniswalzer sketches. It follows, then, that these latter sketches in PS probably antedate drafts XXXI–XLV for the Metamorphosen, which were entered in S after PS was filled. Since the Particell for the Gedächtniswalzer is dated 23 January 1945, sketches for the waltz in the second part of PS probably date from December 1944 to early January 1945; and since the Particell for the Metamorphosen is dated 8 March 1945, drafts XXXI–XLV for it in S probably date from late January–February 1945.

There is no indication that Strauss began working on the revision of the Gedächtniswalzer before writing the "progress report" letter to Böhm dated 30 September 1944; on the contrary, this report reveals intense work on the Metamorphosen until that date. To establish the chronological relation of the Trauer um München sketch for the Gedächtniswalzer to the Metamorphosen sketches one must determine how many of the twenty-three Metamorphosen sketches in PS had been set down by the date of the letter. The following discussion coordinates information gleaned from the letter with an analysis of the compositional genesis of the Metamorphosen and the disposition of the Metamorphosen and Gedächtniswalzer sketches in PS.

In the Böhm letter, a typically Straussian mixture of bonhomie and sarcasm disguising pessimism, the composer reports: "I have been working for some time—so that Schneiderhan can start practicing the wrist exercise—on an Adagio for some 11 solo strings, which will probably develop into an Allegro, so that I do not drag it out too long in Brucknerian fashion [*Brucknerscher Orgelruhe*]. Please convey my good Swiss friends my thanks for their friendly request that the work, when it is finally finished (these days, one can hardly be sure!), will be placed at their disposal for the desired premiere."[43]

Strauss reports that the work is an "Adagio that will probably develop into an Allegro" ("[ein] Adagio . . . , das sich wahrscheinlich zu einem Allegro entwickeln wird"). The word "wahrscheinlich," which may be translated as "probably" (or perhaps "evidently"), implies that this development is already in the process of being realized, almost of itself—note the reflexive "sich . . . entwickeln"—but at the same time has not yet been fully achieved. Schuh cites this statement as proof that composition on the *Metamorphosen* has "not yet progressed very far." But the evidence shows that between the first proposal in August 1944 and the letter to Böhm on 30 September 1944, Strauss had progressed much further than Schuh realized.[44]

As described in the Böhm letter, the final version indeed witnesses a steady increase in tempo from the opening "Adagio ma non troppo" to the "piu allegro" of the last section of the development (mm. 345ff.). The sketches, however, indicate that as late as draft XXXI the acceleration was to have extended through to a climactic allegro recapitulation—rather than to an adagio recapitulation, as in the final version. It is only in a final revision to draft XXXI that Strauss opts for an adagio in place of the previously intended allegro recapitulation, hence his note on page 47 in S: "landet in früherer G dur Melodie aber in C dur [mm. 345ff.] aber plötzlich abbrechen, von da auf tragisch Adagioschluss in Wehmut!" While Strauss's progress report could have originated in the same period that he sketched draft XXXI (i.e., just before the above-quoted note revising the allegro recapitulation to an adagio), other indicators reveal that the letter was written at a less advanced stage in the compositional process.

Compelling page-analytic evidence indicating that the *Trauer um München* sketch antedates draft XXIX leads one to conclude that the letter to Böhm must also antedate draft XXIX. The basic principle of page analysis is space availability: sketches which interrupt or block other sketches must be earlier. Example 20 shows the disposition of sketches in PS. Draft XXIX is broken off on page 77 because it is blocked by the *Trauer um München* sketch already in place on pages 78–79; therefore, it must antedate draft XXIX. Since the letter to Böhm also antedates the *Trauer um München* sketch, the letter must have been penned earlier in the compositional process than draft XXIX.

At what point in the composition of the *Metamorphosen* did Strauss write his letter of 30 September 1944 to Böhm? If the "Allegro" mentioned in the letter refers to a planned allegro recapitulation, it was probably not written before draft XX, which is the first sketch to clearly project an allegro recapitulation (example 21a). Once Strauss has secured the allegro recapitulation, his

Page	Draft	Sequence in PS	Page	Draft	Sequence in PS	Page	Draft
1	VIII	Fourth	23	XIV	Tenth	46	XXVIII
2			24			47	
3			25			48	XXVI
4	XIX	Thirteenth	26			49	
5			27			50	
6	VIII	(Fourth)	28			51	XXVII
7	(continued)		29	XII	Eighth	52	
8			30			53	Waltz
9			31	*Metamorphosen*		54	
10			32	transposition of		55	
11				measure 95f.		56	XXIV
12			33	Waltz		57	XX
13			34			58	XXX
14			35	III	First	59	
15			36			60	
16	IV	Second	37			61	XXI
17			38	XXV	Eighteenth	62	
18	XV	Eleventh	39	XI	Seventh	63	
19	IX	Fifth	40			64	
20	XIII	Ninth	41			65	
21			42	X	Sixth	66	
22			43			67	
			44			68	
			45			69	
						70	
						71	

Region I ———
Region II — —

* The *minore* of the *Gedächtniswalzer* quotes *Feuersnot*.
** Drafts xxxviii–xxxix entered in ink on free staves

Example 20. Detailed view of *Metamorphosen* and *Gedächtniswalzer* sketches in PS, pp. 1–127

drafts XXI–XXII (example 21c–d) sketch a development that leads from draft XIX (example 21b) to the climactic allegro recapitulation already sketched in draft XX.

But now a serious compositional problem arises. In earlier projections of the development (prior to draft XXI), E-major material clearly belongs to

Sequence in PS	Page	Draft	Sequence in PS	Page	Draft	Sequence in PS
Twenty-first	72	XXII	Sixteenth	97		
	73			98	"Klage"	
Nineteenth	74			99		
	75	XXIX	Twenty-second	100		
	76			101	"Langsam"	
Twentieth	77			102	"Coda"	
	78	"Trauer um Munchen"		103	Waltz	
				104		
	79			105	Waltz	
	80	"Allegro"		106	Waltz	
Seventeenth	81			107		
Fourteenth	82			108		
Twenty-third	83	"Feuersnot"*		109		
	84	"Finale Allegro"		110	"Wals"	
				111		
Fifteenth **	85	XVIII	Twelfth	112		
	86			113		
	87			114		
	88			115		
				116	"Marschartig"	
	89	"Moderato"		117	V	Third
	90			118		
	91	"Agitato"		119		
	92	Blank		120	"Allegro moderato"	
	93			121		
	94			122		
	95	"Coda"		123		
	96			124		
				125		
				126		
				127		

Example 21.

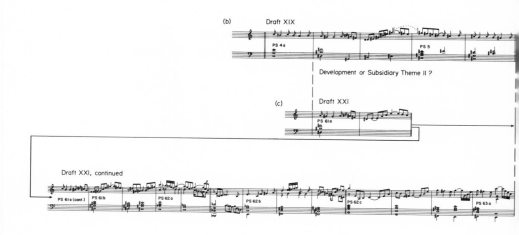

the development, which begins with music corresponding to measure 134 in the final version. However, as this material coalesces in drafts XXII–XXIII (example 21d–e), it starts to assume the characteristics of a subsidiary theme within the exposition; in other words, ideas destined for the development are "drifting" into the exposition. A dividend of this process is that the acceleration, which originally encompassed only the development, now extends back into the exposition. But if the E-major material is assimilated into the exposition, the music that used to be the beginning of the development (which corresponds to measure 134ff. in the final version) can no longer be the beginning of the development but must also become part of the exposition. Where, then, is the beginning of the development? Strauss has reached an impasse.

The point at which Strauss wrote the letter seems to fall somewhere after draft XX, the first draft to show an allegro recapitulation, but before draft XXIX, the draft blocked by the *Trauer um München* sketch, which the letter also antedates. According to the letter, Strauss has decided upon an acceleration from the adagio exposition through to the allegro recapitulation. But his uncertainty about the ultimate path from the adagio to the allegro recapitulation (the path is not yet worked out, hence his comment "an Adagio . . . which will probably develop into an Allegro") bespeaks the compositional impasse encountered in drafts XXI–XXII.

When Strauss encounters a compositional problem of this nature, he generally puts the work aside and concentrates on other projects until a solution emerges. The composer himself mentions these hiatuses in the essay "Vom melodischen Einfall" (c. 1940): "Work progresses in such a way, that it comes to the first stage [Linie] to wait for the time when imagination is capable and ready to help me further. But the readiness is mostly evoked and facilitated by a great compulsion, after long reflection, also . . . deep excitement (even rage and anger). This spiritual process belongs not only to the realm of in-born talent, but to self-criticism and self-development. 'Genius is hard work,' Goethe is supposed to have said. But industriousness and the desire to work is inborn and not instilled."[45] And again: "Musical ideas must, like young wine, be aged, and only after one has allowed them to ferment and mature should one return to them. I often write down a motive or a melody and then lay it aside for a whole year. When I take it up again, I find that almost unconsciously, something in me—the imagination—has worked on it."[46]

My hypothesis of a hiatus in the composition of the *Metamorphosen* accords with the chronology of Strauss's various compositional projects from October 1944 to March 1945. Up to the point of writing to Böhm, Strauss has worked intensively on the *Metamorphosen*, but having reached an impasse he now turns to other projects: the potpourri of waltzes from the *Rosenkavalier* (finished in November 1944) and the revision of the waltz *München* (finished in January–February 1945).

Table 1 summarizes, in the form of a time line, a hypothetical reconstruction of Strauss's compositional activity from August 1944 to early March 1945. In August 1944, Paul Sacher proposes to Strauss (through Böhm and Schuh) a possible work for string orchestra to be premiered by the Collegium Musicum under Sacher. Around the time of receiving the commission, Strauss enters a choral setting of Goethe's *Niemand wird sich selber kennen* in Tr. 134. The setting of the Goethe poem is abandoned as Strauss turns to

Table 1. Chronology of Strauss's compositional activity
from August 1944 to March 1945

Date	Compositional event
August–September 1944	*Niemand wird sich selber kennen* entered in Tr. 134. Approximately twenty drafts for the *Metamorphosen* entered in Tr. 134 and PS
30 September 1944	Letter to Böhm, a "progress report" on composition of the *Metamorphosen*. Strauss has probably reached draft XXII in PS
early October 1944	Impasse in composition of the *Metamorphosen*. Strauss turns to other projects, the *Einleitung und Walzer aus dem Rosenkavalier* and *München, ein Gedächtniswalzer*
15 November 1944	*Einleitung und Walzer aus dem Rosenkavalier* finished
October 1944–January 1945	Early sketches for the *Gedächtniswalzer* in PS, including *Trauer um München*. Strauss sets down drafts XXIV–XXVIII in PS
23 January 1945	Particell for the *Gedächtniswalzer* finished
late January–February 1945	Strauss reaches draft XXX. PS now full of sketches for the *Metamorphosen* and the *Gedächtniswalzer*. Strauss switches to S for the remaining *Metamorphosen* sketches drafts XXXI–XLV
8 March 1945	Particell for the *Metamorphosen* completed

the new project entering the first Metamorphosen sketches in Tr. 134. Through September, Strauss works intensely on the Metamorphosen, developing the musical-poetical idea (the Metamorphosemotiv) first expressed in the Niemand wird sich selber kennen sketch. By draft XXII (the twenty-second of forty-five drafts for the Metamorphosen), Strauss reaches a compositional impasse. He pauses, writes the letter to Böhm dated 30 September 1944, and then turns to other projects. From early October 1944 to early January 1945, while still tinkering with the relatively unproblematic exposition of the Metamorphosen in drafts XXIV–XXVIII, Strauss arranges the Einleitung und Walzer aus dem Rosenkavalier, the score of which is dated 15 November 1944, and enters the Gedächtniswalzer sketches—including the Trauer um München sketch—in PS. The Particell for the Gedächtniswalzer is ready on 23 January 1945. Strauss does not resolve the problem concerning the demarcation of the development in the Metamorphosen until late January. Work now proceeds intensely. The remaining Metamorphosen sketches are set down in S in February and the Particell is ready on 8 March 1945.

Strauss specialists have traced the origins of the snap rhythm in the Metamorphosen to the Trauer um München sketch, but the sources clearly indicate that this sketch postdates early October 1944 and is contemporaneous with drafts XXIV–XXVIII for the Metamorphosen. The earliest Metamorphosen sketch to contain the snap rhythm, which appears in all later sketches, is draft XIII. Thus, the snap rhythm is a characteristic motivic idea of the Metamorphosen well before Strauss interrupts its composition to work on other projects, including the revision of München.

The notion that the Metamorphosen derives from Trauer um München has become so firmly entrenched that the description of S by Dachs and Brosche places the caption Trauer um München in parentheses next to entries for sketches on pages 35–36 and 50 (drafts XVI–XVII).[47] This designation is highly misleading, since these two Metamorphosen sketches bear no relation whatsoever to the Trauer um München sketch for the Gedächtniswalzer. A further indication of the conceptual independence of the Metamorphosen and München, ein Gedächtniswalzer projects can be found on page 37 in S (figure 1). In the top left-hand corner of the page, Strauss writes, in ink, "Münch[en]" without entering a sketch for München. (Indeed, no sketches for München ever found their way into S.) At a later date, probably February 1945, Strauss emphatically crosses out this heading and, working entirely in pencil, enters a sketch for the Metamorphosen (draft XXXI). Strauss's cancellation of the incorrect caption clearly indicates his concern not to mislabel and thereby confuse sketches intended for two separate, independent projects.

Figure 1. Strauss has crossed out the caption "Münch[en]" above a sketch for the *Metamorphosen*, sketchbook S, c. February 1945

Conclusion

München, ein Gedächtniswalzer exhibits overt and rather facile tone-painting of the bombing of Munich and the frantic efforts to put out the flames. The *Metamorphosen*, by contrast, is a deeply philosophical, meditational work, a Goethean investigation, not of the manifestations, but of the underlying cause of war. Strauss subtitles the *Metamorphosen* a "Studie" for twenty-three solo strings. As a study of *homo homini lupus* it is, in the words of Alan Jefferson, "possibly the saddest piece of music ever written."[48]

This revised chronology forces one to question whether both general audiences and Strauss scholars have been fully "in tune with the composer's intentions," or whether, colored by superficial, hypothetical linkage with *München, ein Gedächtniswalzer*, our hearing of the *Metamorphosen* has not been falsely colored in "a sort of self-hypnotic dream." It has been asserted that Strauss discovered the motivic cell of the *Eroica* quotation in the *Trauer um München* sketch. This claim is on chronological and analytical grounds impossible, notwithstanding Strauss's comment that he was quite unconscious of any motivic connection between the *Metamorphosen* and the *Eroica* "Trauermarsch" until late in the compositional process.

The question of Strauss's intentions in the *Metamorphosen* finds a compelling parallel in Shostakovich's wartime compositions. In the case of the Seventh Symphony, the so-called "Leningrad Symphony," a closer look at chronology also bears upon subject matter, casting the work in a completely new light. In memoirs intended for posthumous publication (which, after much debate, have finally been acknowledged as substantially genuine), Shostakovich himself debunks the propagandistic misrepresentation of the Seventh Symphony by pointing to compositional chronology: "The Seventh Symphony had been planned before the war and consequently cannot be seen as a reaction to Hitler's attack. The 'invasion theme' has nothing to do with the attack. I was thinking of other enemies of humanity when I composed the theme. . . . I've heard so much nonsense about the Seventh and Eighth Symphonies. It's amazing how long-lived these stupidities are. . . . Everything that was written about those symphonies in the first few days is repeated without any changes to this very day, even though there has been time to do some thinking."[49]

The widely disseminated interpretation of Strauss's *Metamorphosen* as depicting the destruction of Munich circulated in "the early days" of the post-war period and has similarly been repeated up to our own time without serious question. On analytical and musicological grounds, this study proposes that Strauss's "precise concept" in the *Metamorphosen* can only be discovered in the metamorphosis of his abandoned setting of Goethe's *Niemand wird sich selber kennen*.

Notes

Research for this article was conducted with support from the following scholarly institutions: the Social Sciences and Humanities Research Council of Canada (SSHRCC), the Deutscher Akademischer Austauschdienst (DAAD), and the Österreichischer Austauschdienst (ÖAD). In undertaking the research, the author gratefully acknowledges the assistance of many people both in Europe and in North America. I would especially like to thank the late Frau Alice Strauss for her hospitality on my several research trips to Garmisch. To Dr. Franz Trenner (Munich), who arranged for me to consult Strauss documents in Garmisch and various private collections, a very special thank-you. I am indebted to the anonymous owners of one of the *Metamorphosen* sketchbooks, who permitted me to work in their home and showed me every kindness. The late Dr. Schuh also took the trouble to receive me in spite of the difficult circumstances surrounding his last illness. Special thanks must be given to the staff of the Bayerische Staatsbibliothek, Musikabteilung, and especially to Dr. Helmut Hell, who occasionally helped in deciphering Strauss's handwriting. Dr. Clemens Hellsberg and Prof. Otto Strasser at the Archiv der Wiener Philharmoniker kindly made available the unpublished letters from Strauss to Böhm. Finally, I would like to thank Prof. Bryan Gilliam

(Duke University), Prof. Jean-Michel Boulay (University of Ottawa), Mr. Donald Anderson (Royal Conservatory of Music, Toronto), Mr. Thomas Green (University of Windsor) and Prof. Thomas Stoner (Connecticut College) for their many valuable comments and suggestions. This article is dedicated to Deborah Mariashe Estrin.

1   Ludwig Kusche and Kurt Wilhelm, "Die *Metamorphosen* von Richard Strauss, Zur Entstehungs-geschichte des Werkes," *Schweizerische Musikzeitung* 91 (1951): 19–22.

2   Michael Kennedy, *Richard Strauss* (London: J.M. Dent and Sons, 1976, revised ed. 1988), p. 112. This quotation, presumably made available to Kennedy by the Strauss family between 1976 and 1988, was added in the new edition. An accurate picture of Strauss's private views and feelings will not emerge until the contents of the diaries are made public in their entirety.

3   Otto Strasser, *Und dafür wird man noch bezahlt* (Vienna: Paul Neff, 1974), p. 182.

4   Prof. Strasser graciously discussed his conversations with Strauss in an interview with this author in 1988.

5   Ernst Roth, *Musik als Kunst und Ware. Betrachtungen und Begegnungen eines Musikverlegers* (Zurich: Atlantis, 1966), p. 189.

6   Timothy L. Jackson, "The Last Strauss: Studies of the *Letzte Lieder*" (Ph.D. diss., Graduate Center of the City University of New York, 1988). See "*Ruhe, meine Seele!* and the *Letzte Orchesterlieder*" in *Richard Strauss and His World*, ed. Bryan Gilliam (Princeton: Princeton University Press, 1992), pp. 90–137.

7   Kusche and Wilhelm, pp. 19–22.

8   *Richard Strauss: Thematisches Verzeichnis*, ed. Alfons Ott and Franz Trenner (Vienna: Doblinger, 1974), vol. 3, 1314.

9   *Richard Strauss Autographen in München und Wien*, ed. Günther Brosche and Karl Dachs (Tutzing: Hans Schneider, 1979), p. 26.

10 John Williamson, program notes to Richard Strauss, *Four Last Songs, Metamorphosen, Oboe Concerto* (Deutsche Grammophon, Galleria 423 888–2[10]), p. 4.

11 In a letter from Willi Schuh to Wilfried Brennecke (quoted by Brennecke), "Die Metamor-phosen-Werke von Richard Strauss und Paul Hindemith," *Schweizerische Musikzeitung* 103 (1963): 130, n. 7, Schuh reports that the commission for the *Metamorphosen* was arranged at a meeting between Paul Sacher, Karl Böhm, and himself in Waldhaus Sils-Maria in August 1944. Elsewhere ("Gruelmärchen um Richard Strauss' *Metamorphosen*," *Schweizerische Musikzeitung* 87 [1947]: 418), Schuh explicitly states that the work was proposed in July. I have accepted August as the time when Strauss received and began work on the commission.

12 Kurt Wilhelm, *Richard Strauss persönlich: Eine Bildbiographie* (Munich: Kindler, 1984), p. 383.

13 I have preserved Strauss's punctuation, as shown in facsimile 1. Unless otherwise indicated, all translations from Goethe in this article are mine.

14 Paul Sacher, personal communication.

15 Willi Schuh, "Kompositionsaufträge," in *Alte und Neue Musik: Das Baslerkammerorchester unter Leitung von Paul Sacher 1926–51* (Zurich: Atlantis, 1952), p. 105.

16 Clemens Haselhaus, "Metamorphose-Dichtungen und Metamorphose-Anschauungen," *Euphorion* 47 (1953): 122–23.

17 Haselhaus, p. 123: "[Die Metamorphose] steigt von einem noch ganz urtümlichen und vorliterarischen Fabulieren über den natürlichen Versuch des Menschen, zu einer Erkenntnis über sich selbst zu kommen, bis zu den Inbildung der Verherrlichung und der Verklärung des Menschen hinein."

18 The last stanza of Goethe's *Die Metamorphose der Tiere* reads:

> Dieser schöne Begriff von Macht und Schranken, von Willkür
> Und Gesetz, von Freiheit und Mass, von beweglicher Ordnung,
> Vorzug und Mangel erfreue dich hoch; die heilige Muse
> Bringt harmonisch ihn dir, mit sanftem Zwange belehrend.

> [May this beautiful concept of power and limit, of random
> Venture and law, freedom and measure, of order in motion,
> Defect and benefit, bring you high pleasure; gently instructive,
> Thus, the sacred Muse in her teaching tells you of harmonies.]

Translation by Christopher Middleton, *Goethe. The Poems* (Boston: Suhrkamp-Insel, 1983), p. 163.

19 It is doubtful that Strauss knew Kafka's work.

20 Matthijs Vermeulen, "Een dubbel schandaal: Het Concertgebouw herdenkt Hitler," *De Groene Amsterdammer*, 11 October 1947, p. 7.

21 "Ein doppelter Skandal. Das Concertgebouw gedenkt Hitlers," *National Zeitung*, Basel, 25 October 1947, p. 2.

22 Willi Schuh, "Gruelmärchen," pp. 437–38; "Epilog zu Gruelmärchen um Richard Strauss' *Metamorphosen*," *Schweizerische Musikzeitung* 87 (1947): 455–56.

23 Schuh, "Gruelmärchen," 438.

24 I would like to thank Charles Burkhart (Graduate Center of the City University of New York) for pointing this out to me.

25 Wilfried Brennecke, "Die Metamorphosen-Werke," p. 129: "Von einer neuen Form der 'Metamorphose,' einer Form, die als architektonisches Schema oder ungefähres Modell einer Komposition von anderen Formen abzugrenzen ist, kann bei Strauss' Trauermusik nicht die Rede sein. Auch wird man das Kompositionsverfahren, das ja überwiegend ein melodisch-kontrapunktisches ist, nicht oder nur im akzidentallen Sinne also Metamorphose bezeichen können. . . . Die oben gebrachte theoretische Definition einer Metamorphose in der Musik wird man deshalb auf Strauss' Werk nich beziehen können, weil zwar 'ein bestimmtes thematisches Material in ständigem Fluss begriffen ist,' von 'lebendigem Wandlungsprozess' und 'fortwährender Umgestaltung' der Themen in ihrer Gestalt weitgehend unverändert bleiben."

26 Schenker describes subsurface motivic transformations as "organic." Charles Burkhart provides an eloquent explanation of Schenker's use of this term ("Schenker's 'Motivic Parallelisms,'" *Journal of Music Theory* 22 [1978]: 174): "Surface repetition is effortlessly apprehended and gives instant pleasure. . . . Repetitions of a different sort, less immediately gratifying, but no less genuine and audible, lie concealed beneath the musical surface. These 'hidden repetitions' can range from the tiniest particles to the broadest of tonal spans. When they appear in a composition they give it a more deeply 'organic' dimension." As Jamie Kassler shows ("Heinrich Schenker's Epistemology and Philosophy of Music: An Essay on the Relations between Evolutionary Theory and Music Theory," in *The Wider Domain of Evolutionary Thought*, ed. D. Oldroyd and I. Langham [Dordrecht, n.p. 1984], pp. 221–60), Schenker's concept of "organic" transformation is influenced by, if not indebted to Goethe's theory of metamorphosis (see also William Pastille, "Music and morphology: Goethe's influence on Schenker's Thought," in *Schenker Studies*, ed. Hedi Siegel [Cambridge: Cambridge University

Press, 1990], pp. 29–44). Thus, Goethe's metamorphosis theory is a vital point of contact between Schenker and Strauss. Notwithstanding Schenker's anti-Strauss polemics, many— although not all—of Strauss's compositions are highly organic.

27   Norman Del Mar, *Richard Strauss: A Critical Commentary on His Life and Works*, vol. 3 (London: Barrie & Jenkins, 1978), pp. 425–31.

28   Brennecke, "Die Metamorphosen-Werke," p. 129.

29   Schuh, "Richard Strauss' *Metamorphosen*," *Schweizerische Musikzeitung* 86 (1946): 80–83.

30   Why only two groups within the exposition? There is an unmistakable change of tempo, texture and mood in m. 82, which is much more clearly marked than that between subsidiary themes I (mm. 82ff.) and II (mm. 145ff.), although the latter two are separated by transition I. More importantly, as shown in the graph in example 13a, within measures 1–80, the bass descends E-E♭-D-C♯(=D♭). This bass progression, which is an augmentation of the bass in the motto in mm. 1–2, unifies the Adagio. The same bass progression, through what Schenker calls "transference," determines the bass of the work as a whole, the C sharp definitively resolving as D flat to C only in m. 506.

31   Part III within the development (mm. 278–98) is a structural recomposition of subsidiary theme II within the exposition (mm. 145–86) because, in both cases, the $\hat{5}$ line is supported by I-V-I such that the stretch $\hat{4}$–$\hat{2}$ is supported by V alone (as V^{7-6-5}, see example 13a). Both sections terminate with long, motivically analogous dominant prolongations.

32   The C major of subsidiary theme I's recapitulation within the development is something of an ironic illusion. The C-major root-position chord is never structurally stabilized. Rather, the six-three position in m. 345 ultimately moves to the E-major five-three chord in m. 385 (example 13a). For a detailed explanation of the voice leading in mm. 345–85, see note 37.

33   Transition IV (mm. 437–48) develops an idea that occurs earlier in transition III (mm. 314– 37). All of the transitions in this piece are developmental episodes whose role it is to carry the music forward from one structural node to another. The role of transition IV is to take the music from the beginning of the coda (mm. 433–36) back to the still unfolding recapitulation (mm. 449–86), which had been so dramatically interrupted in m. 432.

34   The music approaches what seems to be a strong cadence on the downbeat of m. 486 (C: V$^6_4$-$^5_3$-I), the dominant intensified by the preceding augmented sixth chord. I construe this cadence as marking the end of the recapitulation. But Strauss frustrates the expected cadence, reharmonizing D flat in the upper voice, which is ♭$\hat{2}$ of C, as $\hat{4}$ of A-flat (the seventh of V^7 in A-flat). This V^7/A♭ then resolves deceptively to ♭VI/A♭ major, F-flat major, which, at the background level, is simultaneously ♭IV of C major. As shown in example 13a, the high a♭^{2} in measure 487 picks up the a♭^{2} of m. 434, the F in the bass of m. 434 being displaced by F flat. The coda then continues to its own cadence in m. 498, which is also subverted, as will be explained in my detailed structural analysis of the *Eroica* citation below.

       One cannot overestimate the importance of the deceptive cadence to F-flat major in m. 487. This importance derives not merely from the structural significance of the F-flat-major chord in m. 487 but from the motivic association of the F-flat-major sonority with E-major sonorities earlier in the piece, especially the E major of subsidiary theme II (mm. 145–86) and the E-major chord of m. 385. F-flat major in m. 487 is a bitter enharmonic parody of these earlier manifestations of E major.

35   The sketches show that Strauss originally intended a perfect cadence in m. 502 (see the discussion of examples 14–16 below).

36   There have been a number of recent studies on tonal symbolism and pitch specificity in

Strauss's music. See, for example, the section on tonal symbolism in Bryan Gilliam's *Richard Strauss's Elektra* (Oxford: Oxford University Press, 1991), pp. 67–75; Derrick Puffett's, "Lass Er die Musi, wo sie ist: Pitch Specificity in Strauss," in *Richard Strauss and His World*, ed. Bryan Gilliam (Princeton: Princeton University Press, 1992), pp. 138–63; and this author's "*Ruhe meine Seele!* and the *Letzte Orchesterlieder*."

37   My analysis of a rising 5̂–8̂ *Urlinie* in the background of the *Metamorphosen*, conceived in Munich in 1986, anticipated publication of David Neumeyer's article "The Ascending *Urlinie*," *Journal of Music Theory* 31 (1987): 275–303. My independent discovery of the ascending *Urlinie* in this work lends credence to Neumeyer's argument.

The reader may ask why I do not read a structural dominant beginning in m. 377 embellished by a cadential six-four and extended through m. 389, the bass moving down a tritone from G to the Neapolitan D-flat and back up to G. While this interpretation would seem to be the obvious reading, it is not necessarily the best. The upper-voice G (m. 345) descends through F (m. 376) to E (m. 377). The bass counterpoints this descent by rising up from E through F to G. Now, at this point, the six-four on G sounds like a cadential six-four embellishing a cadential dominant with scale degree 2̂, D, deflected to ♭2̂, D♭ (example 22a). But

Example 22.

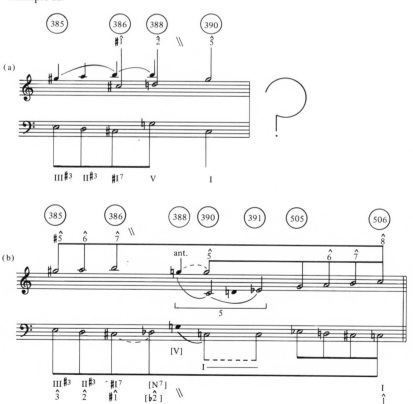

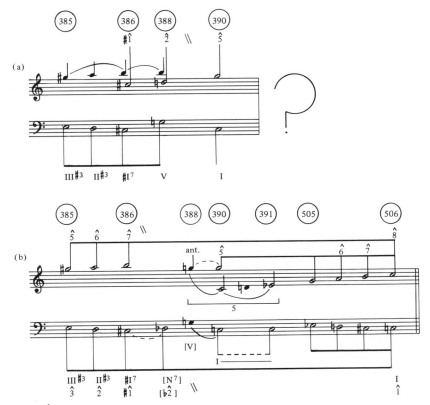

Example 23.

the subsequent path of the upper voice, which ascends F-G (m. 384)-G♯ (m. 385), in conjunction with the bass, which descends back down to the E with which the section began (m. 345), suggests a different reading. In my view, the purpose of the entire recapitulation of subsidiary theme I is to convert the upper-voice G into G sharp through a chromaticized voice exchange (example 22b).

Turning now to the events of mm. 385ff., it would not be implausible to read the G chord in m. 388 as a structural dominant. The structural harmonies would then be III$^{\sharp3}$-$^{\sharp}$I^{7} (= N^{7})-V (example 23a). But I do not subscribe to this interpretation. The B in the upper voice in m. 386 impacts with and is supported by the C sharp in the bass. The B is then arpeggiated up an octave. Thus, the G chord does not support structural $\hat{2}$ in the upper voice, as we generally find at the end of a classical sonata development. Rather, I construe this G chord as an apparent dominant built on the tonic's upper fifth (example 23b). Notice, however, that my interpretation is also supported by motivic considerations: the melody in the violas, celli and basses in mm. 388–92 is a rhythmic enlargement of motive 5. The G in m. 388 is therefore motivically associated with the following C rather than the preceding C sharp. In other words, this G in m. 388 occurs too soon, overlapping the Neapolitan seventh chord and anticipating the tonic in m. 391. Thus, in my reading, the Gs of mm. 377 and 388 are not structurally connected. The former is the upper third of E caught within the voice exchange, while the latter is the upper-fifth of the subsequent tonic (examples 22b and 23b).

It is precisely these local technical and motivic considerations which lead me to my interpretation of the background, not a desire to project large-scale motivic transference. However, one should by no means ignore the colossal motivic transference of the bass progression E-E♭-D-C♯ (D♭), which this interpretation of mm. 345ff. reveals. On the contrary, I believe that Strauss absolutely intends this transference to be heard over ever larger spans: mm. 1–2 become mm. 1–80, which become mm. 1–end (example 13a). The increasingly larger and structurally deeper restatements of this basic progression are essential to Strauss's "metamorphosis" concept.

38 For sustained investigation of the religious and philosophical connotations of transforming a descending tone into its enharmonically equivalent ascending tone, see Timothy L. Jackson, "The Enharmonics of Faith: Enharmonic Symbolism in Bruckner's *Christus factus est* (1884)," *Bruckner Jahrbuch* 1987–88 (1990): 7–20; "Schubert as John the Baptist to Wagner-Jesus: Large-Scale Enharmonicism in Bruckner and his Models," *Bruckner Jahrbuch* 1989–90 (forthcoming, 1992); "Mahler and Bruckner's Wagner-*Rezeption* (read at the ASI/MTSNYS joint conference, Columbia University, 1991, forthcoming); "Bruckner's Metrical Numbers," *19th-Century Music* 14 (1990): 101–31 (especially the analysis of enharmonicism in the motet *Vexilla regis*).

39 For a discussion of the sketchbooks and sketch chronology, see below.

40 Schuh, "Gruelmärchen," p. 438.

41 In a letter to Schuh concerning the *Metamorphosen* (6 December 1945), Strauss writes: "The thought of figuring in a premier concert ruffled me because since *Capriccio* I don't write 'new' works, only 'handwork' study material for our courageous instrumentalists and willing-to-be-sacrificed choirs—studio works so that the wrist does not become entirely stiff and the head not entirely full with up-to-date idiocy: posthumous, posthumous, Horatio!" ["Mich hatte nur der Gedanke etwas froissiert, in einem Novitätenconcert zu figurieren, da ich seit *Capriccio* keine 'Novitäten' mehr schreibe, sondern nur handwerkliches Studienmaterial für unsere braven Instrumentalisten und opferwilligen a cappella Chöre—Atelierarbeiten, damit das Handgelenk nicht allzu steif und der Kopf nicht allzu zeitgemäss verblödet wird: Nachlass-Nachlass Horatio!"]. *Richard Strauss: Briefwechsel mit Willi Schuh*, ed. Willi Schuh (Zurich: Atlantis, 1969), p. 87.

42 The sketchbook numbers refer to Franz Trenner's catalogue *Die Skizzenbücher von Richard Strauss aus dem Richard-Strauss-Archiv in Garmisch.* (Tutzing: Hans Schneider, 1974).

43 "Ich arbeite schon seit einiger Zeit, um das Handgelenk auch Schneiderhan gegenüber in Übung zu erhalten, an einem Adagio für etwa 11 Solostreicher, das sich wahrscheinlich zu einem Allegro entwickeln wird, da ich es in Brucknerscher Orgelruhe nicht allzu lang aushalte. Bitte teilen Sie den braven Schweizer Freunden mit meinem besten Dank für ihr liebenswürdiges Anerbieten mit, dass ich ihnen das Stück, wenn es überhaupt fertig wird (kann man heute nicht mehr mit Bestimmtheit sagen!) gerne zur gewünschten Uraufführung zur Verfügung stellen werde." This letter is preserved in the Archiv der Wiener Philharmoniker. For information on Strauss's relation to Schneiderhan, see Strasser, *Und dafür wird man noch bezahlt.*

44 Schuh's observations in a letter from Schuh to Brennecke (quoted by Brennecke, "Die Metamorphosen-Werke," p. 130, n. 7).

45 "Diese Arbeit geht nun in der Weise vor sich, dass es in erster Linie darauf ankommt, den Zeitpunkt abzuwarten, in welchem die Phantasie fähig und bereit ist, mir weiter zu dienen. Aber die Bereitschaft wird doch meistens bei grösserer Musse, nach längerem Nachdenken, auch . . . durch seelische Erregung (auch Zorn und Ärger) hervorgerufen und gefördert. Diese geistigen Prozesse gehören nicht allein in das Gebiet angeborener Begabung, sondern der Selbstkritik und Selbsterziehung. 'Genie ist Fleiss,' soll Goethe gesagt haben. Aber auch Fleiss und die Lust zur Arbeit sind angeboren, nicht nur anerzogen." In *Richard Strauss, Betrachtungen und Erinnerungen,* ed. Willi Schuh (Zurich: Atlantis, 1949), p. 138.

In his discussion of the chronology of *Elektra,* Bryan Gilliam touches upon Strauss's moment of creative impasse when he got to the Recognition Scene. Rather than struggle with the scene, Strauss chose to spend the next eight months orchestrating what he had sketched up to that point. He also wrote some less ambitious, smaller-scale compositions during that time. See Gilliam's "Elektra Chronology" in *Richard Strauss's Elektra,* pp. 49–66.

46 "Musikalische Ideen müssen, wie junger Wein, gelagert werden und erst, nachdem man ihnen erlaubt hat zu garen und zu reifen, wieder aufgenommen werden. Ich schreibe oft ein Motiv oder eine Melodie nieder und lege sie dann ein Jahr lang weg. Wenn ich sie wieder aufgreife, finde ich, dass ganz unbewusst, etwas in mir—die Phantasie—an ihr gearbeitet hat" (quoted in Trenner, *Die Skizzenbücher,* p. vi).

47 *Richard Strauss Autographen in München und Wien,* p. 26.

48 Allen Jefferson, *The Lieder of Richard Strauss* (New York: Praeger, 1971), p. 11. Bernhard Adamy, acknowledging Strauss's long familiarity with Schopenhauer, describes the *Metamorphosen* as a "Schopenhauerian work" (Bernhard Adamy, "Schopenhauer bei Richard Strauss," *Schopenhauer Jahrbuch* 61 [1980]: 195–98). Perhaps as he penned the "In memoriam" above the *Eroica* citation in the closing days of World War II Strauss remembered Schopenhauer's terrifying description of man: "Man is at bottom a dreadful wild animal. We know this wild animal only in the tamed state called civilization and we are therefore shocked by occasional outbreaks of its true nature: but if and when the bolts and bars of the legal order once fall apart and anarchy supervenes it reveals itself for what it is. For enlightenment on this matter, though, you have no need to wait until that happens: there exist hundreds of reports, recent and less recent, which will suffice to convince you that man is in no way inferior to the tiger or the hyena in pitilessness and cruelty" (*On Ethics*).

"The chief source of the most serious evils affecting man is man himself; *homo homini lupus.* He who keeps this last fact clearly in view beholds the world as a hell, surpassing that of Dante by the fact that one man must be the devil of another. For this purpose, of course, one is more fitted than another, indeed an archfiend is more fitted than all the rest, and appears in the form of a conqueror; he sets several hundred thousand men facing one another, and exclaims to them: 'To suffer and die is your destiny; now shoot one another with musket and cannon!' and they do so" (*The World as Will and Representation*).

49 Solomon Volkov, *Testimony: The Memoirs of Dimitri Shostakovich* (New York: Harper and Row, 1979), pp. xxxiii–xxxiv and 154–57. For a history of the debate surrounding the authenticity of these memoirs, see MacDonald, *The New Shostakovich* (London: Fourth Estate, 1990).

The Element of Time in
Der Rosenkavalier
Lewis Lockwood

▼

In a famous passage at the end of act 1 of *Der Rosenkavalier*, the Marschallin sits alone and sings a long soliloquy. The tumultuous events of the morning had begun with her awakening and breakfast with Octavian and their declarations of love and intimacy. Then Baron Ochs had arrived, as presumptive bridegroom of Sophie von Faninal, bringing the gradual comic revelation of Ochs as lecher, braggart, and embodiment of Austrian rustic nobility at its worst, pursuing the maid Mariandel (Octavian in disguise) as his diversion for the day. It had continued with the colorful swarm of minor characters assembled in the Marschallin's levée.[1] After the departure of the crowd, including Valzacchi, Annina, the Italian tenor and the rest—when all this hubbub is finally over, the Marschallin settles down to quiet contemplation of it all. Looking at herself in her hand mirror, she speculates on the problem of time, identity, and change. She remembers herself as a young girl "fresh from the convent" (like Sophie, the bride-to-be), and as she is now, at the ripe age of thirty-five. She asks herself how it can really be that she, who was once a charming young girl, is now an "alte Frau" but yet is the same person, despite the passage of time and changing personal experience. And why does God not only let this happen, but makes her the witness of her own aging:

> Wie macht denn das der liebe Gott?
> Wo ich doch immer die gleiche bin.
> Und wenn er's schon so machen muss,
> warum lasst er mich denn zuschau'n dabei,
> mit gar so klarem Sinn? Warum versteckt
>   er's nicht vor mir?
> Das alles ist geheim, so viel geheim,
> und man ist dazu da,
> dass man's erträgt.

[How can our dear Lord make it so?
When I am still the same person?
And if He must make it so,
why does He let me see it all
so very clearly? Why does he not hide it from me?
It's all a mystery, so very much a mystery.
And we are here to bear it.]

From here on the issue of time becomes ever more pressing in the plot and text. Once she has voiced her awareness of the problem of time and change, this perception and feeling colors all of the remaining action of the plot. It makes us realize that she has been talking about time from the very beginning of act 1. At breakfast she had said to Octavian, in her worldly-wise manner, that "everything [happens] in its own time" ("Jedes Ding hat seine Zeit"). And after her soliloquy she opens her heart to Octavian, urging him not to hold too tightly to their love, because, as she tells him, "whoever tries to hold too much, holds nothing fast" ("Wer allzuviel umarmt, der hält nichts fest"). And shortly thereafter she says, "Deep in my heart I know how we should grasp at nothing . . . how life and its joys slip through our fingers, how everything changes as we try to grasp it . . . like shadows and dreams." Then comes the famous passage with the text "Time, after all, Quinquin, time leaves the world unchanged . . . While one is living one's life away, it is absolutely nothing. Then, suddenly, one is aware of nothing else" ["Die Zeit im Grunde, Quinquin, die Zeit, die ändert doch nichts an den Sachen . . . Wenn man so hinlebt, ist sie rein gar nichts. Aber dann auf einmal, da spürt man nichts als sie"].[2]

From here on the Marschallin tries to prepare Octavian for their eventual parting, "heut oder morgen," anticipating her eventual acceptance of his choice of a younger woman and thus the later phases of the plot and its ending. And now the subject of time and experience, seen from different vantage points, comes up in direct or indirect ways in the voices of the other main characters, whose differences in age and depth of experience are thrown into relief: the young and easily infatuated Octavian; the innocent but proud Sophie; the coarse and cowardly Ochs, whose "experience" as lover consists of nothing more than brutal domination of servants and peasant girls; and so on through the plot.

So far all that I have said is long familiar in the critical literature. Recently Alan Jefferson has argued that the "three themes . . . of the drama are time, love, and nobility."[3] This is certainly correct from the standpoint of portrayal of character and individuality in the drama. Love, whether poignant or passionate, spiritual or physical—or all of these—is clearly in the foreground. And the theme of nobility, whether seen as a deep or superficial value, is well represented by the ironic opposition of the Marschallin and Baron Ochs. Yet the argument of this study is that the issue of time in the work has even wider ramifications than have been realized heretofore, not only in Hofmannsthal's conception of the plot, meaning, and dramatic development of the work, but also in Strauss's approach to its musical setting. Beyond this, the element of time might serve in part to suggest ways of reconciling the literary and musical sides of this work.

On the dramatic side, I begin with Hofmannsthal's observation to Strauss, in a letter of 1908, that what he was striving for was a "psychological comedy in prose." The key word is "psychological." The aim is not merely to furnish an entertainment, a "festive comedy" as it was eventually called on the title page of the score, but a comic drama with serious overtones in which characters presented in an eighteenth-century Viennese setting reveal themselves in terms of modern sensibility and shades of feeling. The basic plot is simple, but the characters are complex, and the dialogue keeps their responses and feelings constantly in the foreground. Of course this is superficially true of endless numbers of other plays and operas that are set in distant historical time. But here the point is that Hofmannsthal deliberately sets out to arouse a degree of nostalgia in contemporary audiences for the eighteenth-century customs and manners of the Austrian nobility, seemingly celebrating their precious and self-conscious ways. Of this the chief exhibit is the ceremony of the presentation of the rose to confirm a betrothal. Even if this ceremony is Hofmannsthal's invention and is not, after all, borrowed from historical sources, it epitomizes the formality of aristocratic social behavior and thus captures the spirit of the *ancien régime* as background setting for the work. It is no accident that these formalities are stressed especially by Baron Ochs, who constantly reminds everyone that he is a member of the nobility, while at the same time he is comically betraying the fact that he is one of its most degenerate representatives. Even if it is true that the discrepancy in the individual between the titled nobleman and the real, vulnerable person is a dramatic paradox of long standing—for example, in Beaumarchais—this in no way lessens its effect in the modern *buffo* character of Ochs. The point, then, is that the setting of the work "in the time of Maria Theresa" and its basic use of the manners and morals of an old and great period of Austrian history give the drama a strong sense of paradox and anachronism. Hofmannsthal drives this feeling home more strongly by introducing, directly or indirectly, many references to older works of literature and art that in their own time had satirized the foibles of the aristocracy. This may be the reason for his choice of background material in works by Molière, Hogarth, and two late eighteenth-century comic playwrights—Louvet de Couvray and his "Adventures of the Chevalier de Faublas," and Beaumarchais's *Le Mariage de Figaro*. Of these it is Beaumarchais, and especially *Figaro*, that cast the largest shadow over aspects of the plot, not only in obvious character connections but in several other ways.

The real title of *Le Mariage de Figaro* is "La folle journée," the "crazy day." The title tells us that the action takes place in a single day, that the plots and counterplots of masters and servants, of Count and Countess, of Susanna and Figaro, all unfold within a narrow time frame that begins in the morning and ends that same night. In Da Ponte's libretto the secondary title became the only main title—*Le Nozze di Figaro*—but the libretto is filled with references to the issue of time and duration in the plot, and the whole work winds up in its last chorus with words that give the "real title" at the end:

> Questo giorno di tormenti,
> Di capricci e di follia,
> In contenti e in allegria
> Solo amor può terminar.
>
> [This day of torments,
> Of caprices and of madness,
> In joy and happiness,
> Only Love can bring to an end.]

The parallels between *Figaro* and *Der Rosenkavalier* in character portrayal have long been obvious: between the Countess and the Marschallin (both poignant mature female figures); between Cherubino and Octavian (both roles sung by young women who play impetuous young men and who dress up as women in the course of the plot); between Annina and Valzacchi, on the one hand, and Don Basilio, the chief schemer of *Figaro* on the other. Even a partial parallel between the lecherous Baron Ochs and the self-righteous Count Almaviva is not exaggerated, at least insofar as the count pursues all the females of his household and arrogantly defends his ancient lordly prerogative, the *droit du seigneur*. There is more: in both works the male nobleman is tricked into an evening assignation with a young woman in disguise; he is prevented by a masquerade from consummating his desires; and he is confounded at the end by the regal entrance of a noblewoman (in *Figaro* his wife, in *Rosenkavalier* his cousin) in the final climactic moment of the drama.

And beyond all this, the two works share another form-building element: the urgency of dramatic time as a primary element in the drama. Act 1 of *Rosenkavalier* takes place in the morning; act 2 takes place that same day or at the latest the next day (the text is not explicit on this point, but not much time can have elapsed between the two acts); and act 3 takes place on the night of the same day as act 2.[4]

In a drama dealing with historical time and experiential time, as *Rosenkavalier* clearly does, there must also be a strong element of place—not simply the location of the action but its cultural and social setting. Clearly this play is not just set anywhere in the historical Austrian empire; it is firmly located in its capital, Vienna. Again and again this point is made, though mainly by Ochs, the boor from the country, who never tires of noticing how corrupt everything is in the big city. Thus, in act 1, he snubs the appeal for money from the Italian scandalmongers, by saying, "Hm! Fancy what goes on here in Vienna!" ("Hm! Was es alles gibt in diesem Wien!"); and again, after he is wounded in act 2, he exclaims, "What can't happen to a gentleman in this Vienna!" ("Was ei'm Cavalier nit all's passieren kann in dieser Wienerstadt!"). The focus on place has two results. First, it gives the work a strongly defined local context that reinforces its sense of history; second, it provides an element of historical truth, something that Hofmannsthal admired in *Die Meistersinger*, as he wrote to Strauss in an eloquent letter of 1927:

> The truly decisive element, which governs all the others, is Nuremberg. This city, which was still quite unspoiled in the 1830s, offered not merely a mirror, but actually an example of the whole intellectual and spiritual life of the German middle class around 1500; this city world was one of the great decisive experiences of the romantics, from Tieck and Wackenroder . . . through Arnim and E.T.A. Hoffmann down to Richard Wagner. . . . This is what gives the opera its indestructible truth; that it brings to life again a genuine, complete world which did exist—not like *Lohengrin* and *Tannhäuser* or even the *Ring* . . . imaginary or excogitated worlds which have never existed anywhere.[5]

Now I do not claim that Vienna in *Der Rosenkavalier* is as fully present a historical location as Nuremberg is in *Die Meistersinger*. But Vienna is sufficiently important that the dichotomy of old and new—of old Vienna and modern Vienna of the early twentieth century—becomes a further effective element of anachronism. The modern sensibility of the characters, musing on the fragility of their experience, reminds us that their city is in the same condition. In 1910 this Vienna was a hollow shell in relation to its former glories, caught up in the dreams of its past, a bastion of antimodernism frustrated by the modern sensibility by which it felt the manifest contradictions between past and present. As with the Marschallin, who is the best representative of its lost nobility, the question is, how could it once have been so different from what it is now and still be the same place, the same city? And, as with the Marschallin, the question is not one that can be answered.

This dualism of young and old brings us to the musical side of the question of time. Under this heading many different themes could be developed. For example, the element of time in musical terms might center on Strauss's sense of proportions in the structuring of the work—its acts, scenes, continuous segments and set numbers, above all near the end as it reaches its great climactic moments. Another would focus on Strauss's sense of stage time and stage timing, an instinct given to all real opera composers but not at all to others, however great their artistic abilities. But my purpose here instead is to deal with Strauss's achievements in *Der Rosenkavalier* in a different way: by considering in what ways the musical substance of the work responds to the issue of historical and experiential time that I have suggested for the plot, characters, and setting.

We can begin with the familiar claim that *Rosenkavalier* represents a stylistic regression in Strauss's development as a composer; that it returns to a diatonic and essentially tonal framework merely laced with chromaticism, after the sexual pathology and appropriately dissonant language of *Elektra*. From this point of view *Rosenkavalier* is seen as a deliberate attempt by Strauss to draw a line across his own path as a composer in which he deliberately chooses to assure his worldly success by regaining a position well within familiar boundaries, even using Viennese popular elements, such as the waltz, to reassure audiences of 1910, fearful of new music, that all was well in the comfortable sound-world of this period comedy.[6] This view of the work is often reflected in modern criticism, such as that of Charles Rosen: "The operas *Salome* and *Elektra* that he wrote in 1905 and 1908 are daring in their extreme chromaticism and in their representation of pathological states, but after *Elektra* Strauss quickly retreated into eighteenth-century pastiche and the delicious Viennese pastry of *Der Rosenkavalier*."[7]

If we reject this view, we must replace it with something better. Recently Reinhold Schlötterer approached *Rosenkavalier* against the background of Strauss's long-range development as a composer up to this time, including the symphonic poems, in their variety of topics from the heroic to the narrative and comic; and also the songs and the earlier operas, from the post-Wagnerian beginnings with *Guntram* and *Feuersnot* to the full-blooded expressionism of *Salome* and *Elektra*. Strauss's problem, as Schlötterer puts it, was to come to terms with the problem of tradition and innovation in the framework of the problems faced by large-scale operatic and symphonic composition in the wake of Wagner's extensions of the tonal language.[8] And within this broad array of problems, the special difficulty that he confronted in *Rosenkavalier* was whether or not he could put to use his full strength as a composer, at this stage of his development, in the service of a "Spieloper," a "psychological comedy in prose." What many commentators have failed to see is that Strauss's solution to this problem was not merely to design a more conservative tonal language for this work than he had used in the two previous works. He set out to employ it with such subtlety and polish in filling out the details of the opera that any critic should have seen that he was in no way merely borrowing the language of the contemporary Viennese operetta, then in a stage of brilliant success after the triumphant premiere of *Die lustige Witwe*, just five years before *Rosenkavalier*.[9]

Thus the basic language of *Rosenkavalier*, with its diatonic framework, makes extensive and brilliant use of the mature post-Wagnerian method of composition that Strauss had been steadily developing for thirty years. The work is certainly rich in triadic clusters and progressions, and it uses triads as points of stability for departure and arrival; thus the opera glitters with what some commentators have called its quality of *Wohlklang*. Strauss's harmonic method is highly flexible in its rapid motion between chords related closely or distantly on a chromatic spectrum; it revels in distant leaps from temporarily established chords, constantly suggesting full arrivals but mostly postponing them. Yet the primary linear motion, whether in the voice parts or in the orchestral leitmotifs, is more often diatonic than chromatic, and even where polychords and chromatic motion form the basis of a given motif, the total shape of a phrase normally admits of a basically diatonic interpretation. A characteristic sample is the motif associated with the Marschallin and Octavian's awakening in the introduction (see example 1).

Here the entire chromatic chord-progression sequence takes place over a tonic pedal, E, which anchors the motion securely to the bass and keeps the key of E major firm and stable, despite the chromatic harmonies that float above it. If we think for a moment of the much more difficult, truly chromatic harmonic systems of *Tristan*, we realize that the harmonic language of *Rosenkavalier*, and even of Strauss's more difficult works, such as *Elektra*, represents a more eclectic mixture of diatonic and chromatic elements, firmly maintaining large-scale tonal frameworks within which fluctuating motions and progressions can constantly suggest and carry out divergent motions,

Example 1. *Der Rosenkavalier*, act 1, introduction, closing passage

but without bringing down the structural beams of the harmonic scaffolding. This is even more true in *Rosenkavalier* than in *Elektra*, for obvious reasons. Yet why should Strauss be accused of sudden reversion to a conservative idiom in this work, when it appears that his choice of harmonic and other means is deliberately designed to fit the poetic and dramatic content of the drama? The obvious comparison that comes to mind here is of course Wagner's own "reversion" in method from the extreme chromatic of *Tristan* to the brilliant diatonic language of *Die Meistersinger*, his next major work after *Tristan*.[10] What Kurth calls the "intensive alteration style" in *Tristan* and works that follow in its path is clearly avoided or attenuated in *Meistersinger* to a remarkable degree. Yet no serious analyst would claim that *Meistersinger*'s tonal language is a "regression" from that of *Tristan*. Rather, it represents a deliberate decision on Wagner's part to find an idiom that effectively intermingles chromatic and enriched harmonic chords and progressions within a basically diatonic framework, a style not only suitable for a Romantic comedy but even more for a work whose historical setting is rich in implications for the allegories of nineteenth-century art and nationalism that underlie the work. Is it not possible that, as Strauss looked back on these two powerfully contrasting works of Wagner's greatest maturity—the first tragic and powerfully chromatic, the second comic and suitably diatonic, with occasional historicizing moments of reference to older styles—is it not possible that the idiom of *Rosenkavalier* could have taken shape after that of *Elektra* as an approximately comparable artistic progression? All of which, if true, would still in no way lessen the autonomy of his own artistic development, nor would this choice of idiom in *Rosenkavalier*, seen in this light, represent a capitulation to the box-office attractions of the fashionable world of Léhar and the operetta.

And yet the work does undeniably contain elements that the public could immediately associate with music of pure entertainment and enjoyment—the waltzes above all, but also other strains, including the wonderful simplicity of the final duet between Octavian and Sophie. For this, too, the answer lies in Strauss's innate understanding of the significance of Hofmannsthal's libretto: its historical setting, its high sensibility, its stress on time, place, and the fragility of human relationships and human experience. To give the music of the drama something of the same depth as the stage drama —to lend it a sense of engagement with the historical setting and its focus on the long-range and short-range passing of time—Strauss sought first to establish a basic diatonic language and then to populate the work with large-scale references to three different musical styles that could be associated with three different aspects of the drama.

The first and foremost is his own modern style of 1910, full-blooded and richly developed from start to finish, mainly diatonic but containing plenty of room for every type of complex harmonic, linear, rhythmic, and sonorous relationship that his compositional background could provide.

Second, he deliberately cultivates the Viennese waltz as a type of "character piece" within the opera, encrusting the waltz style of his popular predecessors, especially Johann Strauss, with chromatic touches wherever possible, but equally clearly endowing the opera with the one symbolic musical element that clearly evoked nostalgia in his audiences for the Vienna of the 1860s and 1870s. That this had personal meaning for Strauss as well is clear from a memoir he wrote in 1925 on his own encounter with Johann Strauss at least forty years earlier. He revelled in his recollected admiration for Johann Strauss, above all because the latter was "one of the last who had a primary gift for melody . . . yes, the elemental, the original, the most basic elements of melody—that's really what counts . . . [and after recollecting an evening in which Johann Strauss played for him, he writes] . . . and with regard to the waltzes in *Der Rosenkavalier* . . . how could I not have thought of the laughing god of Vienna?" [11]

We can hardly doubt that Strauss was creating a self-consciously "Viennese effect" by spreading the waltzes so prominently through the opera. The historical paradox has been lost on those commentators who only observe that these references in the score are to the Vienna of the wrong century—the late nineteenth rather than the eighteenth. They see the trees but not the woods.

We also find that Strauss at several crucial points in the piece indeed makes use of a third, or quasi-eighteenth-century style, including near-quotations from Mozart—above all in the duet of Octavian and Sophie at the end, with its immediate reminiscence of the duet in *Die Zauberflöte* in which Pamina and Papageno sing of the joys of "friendship's harmony" and "friendly sympathy":

> Könnte jeder brave Mann
> Solche Glöckchen finden!
> Seine Feinde wurden dann
> Ohne Muhe schwinden.
> Und er lebte ohne sie
> In der besten Harmonie
> Mildert die Beschwerden;
> Ohne diese Sympathie
> Ist kein Glück auf Erden.[12]

> [If to every honest man
> Bells like these were given
> All his foes would swiftly then
> Far away be driven.
> He would live contentedly
> In the sweetest harmony
> Only friendship's harmony
> Lessens pain and grieving;
> Without friendly sympathy
> Joy this earth is leaving.]

Strauss's basic decision was to avoid writing a "period piece," and not to create a direct imitation of eighteenth-century style as his basic idiom for the work. Instead, he inserts this Mozart reference as a self-conscious allusion to the century in which the action takes place. Mozart is of course a little later than the time of the drama, "in the early years of the reign of Maria Theresa," but this nevertheless is an unambiguous reference to the classical style, to music from the Vienna of the 1780s and 1790s. Against this the waltzes burst forth as an equally clear reference to the Vienna of the 1860s and '70s, as if compelling our perception of the same place and same culture at a later phase. And finally, Strauss's own mature style of the early twentieth century becomes the vessel that can contain the basic material of the work and also these overt allusions to the musical past. The result of this procedure—a

Example 2a. *Der Rosenkavalier*, act 3, final duet, excerpt

kind of collage—is to give the music, like the drama, a sense of the layering of history. Like the plot and its hypersensitive characters, the music evokes a feeling of the passage of time through a single place, Vienna, in various phases of its existence. And like the Marschallin, who questions her sense of identity across the years of her life and her varied perceptions and identities, the three musical styles evoke three different periods of music history. Thus Strauss finds his own way of creating a layered structure, suggestive of the past in richly allusive ways yet never stooping to direct quotation. The interaction of dramatic and musical material is more than a matter of structural

Example 2b. Mozart, *Die Zauberflöte*, act 1, finale: duet of Pamina and Papageno, beginning

necessity, and the music is more than a vehicle for the text and its declamation and rhetoric. It seeks to be a parallel structure, in which the composer finds the means within his own artistic traditions to mirror something of the range of historical style and sensibility that he found to be so adeptly woven into the text by his master librettist.

The result is that Strauss takes a special place in the long history of twentieth-century composers who have sought to give voice to their sense of the dilemma of history. At one extreme are those works that closely imitate, though with modern phraseology, the styles of earlier periods; an example is Prokofiev's *Classical Symphony*, in which the composer tried an experiment of staying "close to Haydn," but "with a difference," as he put it. Another way is found in the much more subtle transformations of earlier styles we see in *Pulcinella* or *The Rake's Progress*; the latter is a masterly example of the assimilation of the spirit of eighteenth-century operatic forms and methods in a work attuned to modern sensibility. Such an approach, but by a different route, cognizant of what his great librettist had provided, is what Strauss had tried to achieve in *Der Rosenkavalier*. And this aspect of the work is not the least of the ways in which it remains a thoroughly modern achievement.

Appendix: The Waltzes in *Der Rosenkavalier*: A Structural Overview

Beyond providing color, atmosphere, and the evocation of a specific sector of the musical past, the waltzes in *Der Rosenkavalier* also play another and more fully structural role. They represent yet another aspect of the element of time. When we look at the way in which Strauss introduces the waltz sections in acts 1 and 2 of the work, we find the following pattern (see table 1). In act 1, there are five separate waltz segments, all of them before the levée, and each one introduced for a specific dramatic purpose. The first accompanies the breakfast scene for the Marschallin and Octavian; the second characterizes Octavian dressed up as "Mariandel"; the third, a quasi-waltz, occurs when Ochs voices his need for a bearer of the rose; the fourth picks up the implications of the second when Ochs propositions Mariandel; and the fifth concludes the whole first part of the act, before the swarm of the levée.

In act 2, which contains six dramatic sections, there are four principal uses of the waltz: 1) for the dialogue between Sophie and Octavian, as they smell the rose and begin to fall in love; 2) when Ochs preens himself before Sophie and promises her endless delights ("mit mir") just before leaving the room; 3) a quasi-waltz tempo dominates during the comic duel scene between Ochs and Octavian (reh. nos. 197–215); and 4) the end of the act, with Ochs now wounded but consoling himself with wine, dreaming of his assignation with Mariandel.

The function of the waltz segments in acts 1 and 2 is to furnish well-timed, separate interventions into the otherwise continuous prose dialogue and discourse. They create large segments of rhythmic regularity, periodicity, and symmetry of phrase structure and thus almost take on a ritornello function, alternating with the steady conversational dialogue and helping to provide a

Table 1. Layout of waltzes in *Der Rosenkavalier*
Numbers in parentheses refer to rehearsal numbers.

Act 1

Segment 1 (1–48)	Introduction; awakening; morning chocolate; concealment and reappearance of Octavian
Segment 2 (48–88)	*Waltz* I (breakfast of the Marschallin and Octavian) The Marschallin's premonition; expectation of husband's arrival; Octavian flees the room
Segment 3 (88–127)	*Waltz* II (Ochs outside; Octavian as Mariandel) Ochs's arrival; distracted by Mariandel
Segment 4 (127–42)	Ochs needs a Rosenkavalier; *quasi-Waltz* (127ff.); discussion of the Rosenkavalier; Hausmeister
Segment 5 (143–216)	*Waltz* III: Ochs and Mariandel (143–48); Ochs describes his lechery; Ochs, the Marschallin, and Octavian (Terzett) *Waltz* IV (205–16)
Segment 6 (217–268)	*Levée*; to departure of Ochs
Segment 7 (268–283)	Marschallin: monologue
Segment 8 (283–342)	The Marschallin and Octavian embrace; the Marschallin reflects on time and eventual separation; the Marschallin sends after Octavian and sends the rose

Act 2

Segment 1 (1–38) (39–61)	Introduction; Faninal's household; Sophie; expectation and arrival of Rosenkavalier; Octavian and Sophie fall in love; *Waltz* I (dialogue between Sophie and Octavian)
Segment 2 (62–89)	Ochs arrives; his gross behavior; Sophie's anger; Trio
(89–99)	*Waltz* II (Ochs, "Mit mir"; Ochs leaves)
Segment 3 (100–129)	Octavian and Sophie; Ochs's servants pursue girls; Sophie and Octavian embrace; Duet
Segment 4 (129–54)	Surprised by Annina and Valzacchi; call for Ochs; Ochs confronts Sophie + Octavian
Segment 5 (154–215)	*quasi-Waltz* (154–97); Duel; Ochs wounded; Faninal gives Sophie ultimatum, dismisses Octavian; exit Sophie and Octavian

Segment 6 (215–56)	Ochs and Doctor; Ochs suffering; Faninal promises satisfaction; Annina arrives with letter; *Waltz III*: "Mit mir"
Act 3	
Segment 1 (1–59)	*Waltz I* (Pantomime) 30–51; *Waltz II* (With stage music) 51–59
Segment 2 (59–122)	Ochs enters; *Waltz II* continues; more waltzes dominate segment 2
Segment 3 (122–141)	No waltzes (Confusion and deceptions)
Segment 4 (141–209)	Police; Faninal; children; Sophie; more confusion; landlord and waiters; Ochs outraged
Segment 5 (210–46)	The Marschallin enters; answers and solutions
Segment 6 (246–63)	Ochs leaves at last; *Waltz III*
Segment 7 (263–84)	The Marschallin; Sophie, Octavian; Octavian's choice; waltzes becoming integrated into an increasingly serious context
Segment 8 (285–93)	Trio (Sublimation of waltz material into the crowning serious ensemble of the work)
Segment 9 (294–end)	Duets and closing scene.

contrasting means of organization for both acts. In the third act, on the other hand, these waltzes and waltz-tempo segments dominate the texture almost from the beginning. The waltz, indeed, plays a strategic role in segments 1, 2, and 6 (see table 1). The waltz segments are longer than in acts 1 and 2 and have a more continuous role in supporting the dramatic action and dialogue, rather than interrupting it and articulating it.

Notes

1   This scene is well known to have been suggested to Hofmannsthal by Hogarth's *Marriage à la Mode*; its piling-up of characters may also hark back to the great second-act finale of *Le Nozze di Figaro*.

2   Translation by Adele Poindexter and Sabine Steinhausen, copyright Polydor International, 1984.

3   Alan Jefferson, ed., *Der Rosenkavalier* (Cambridge: Cambridge University Press, 1985), pp. 115–19.

4   In Act 1, Ochs tells Mariandel, as he tries to set up his assignation with her, that he is on his way with his retinue to the "White Horse Inn" (the "Weissen Ross") and that he will be there "until tomorrow morning." Accordingly, it is entirely possible that the action of the entire drama should be read as taking place all in one day, from early morning until night—exactly as in *Figaro*.

5   *A Working Friendship: The Correspondence between Richard Strauss and Hugo von Hofmannsthal*, translated by Hanns Hammelmann and Ewald Osers (New York: Vienna House, 1961), p. 433. Apart from this felt similarity between the setting of *Meistersinger* and *Rosenkavalier*, we may note the many differences in tone and emphasis, above all in the treatment of social class. In *Meistersinger* the knight, Walther von Stolzing, is certainly placed in sharp contrast to the city burghers who have constituted themselves as "Masters," but the entire treatment of Walther's knighthood lacks any touch of nostalgia or sympathy for his role as member of a feudal upper class.

6   A characteristic view of Viennese conservatism is provided by Romain Rolland in his diary, published in English as part of *Richard Strauss and Romain Rolland: Correspondence*, ed. Rollo Myers (Berkeley and Los Angeles: University of California Press, 1968), p. 164, entry for 11 May 1924: "Vienna: a big old provincial town. It has no inkling whatever of such people as Stravinsky, Honneger, etc., of this frenzy which we can no longer do with in music, especially operatic music—I feel here that I am with distinguished old people half-asleep and habit-bound."

7   Charles Rosen, *Arnold Schoenberg* (New York: Viking Press, 1975), p. 16.

8   Reinhold Schlötterer, ed. "Komödie als musikalische Struktur," in *Musik und Theater im "Rosenkavalier" von Richard Strauss*, Reinhold Schlötterer et al. (Vienna: Doblinger, 1985), pp. 9–60.

9   See Franzpeter Messmer, "*Der Rosenkavalier* und die Tradition der musikalischen Komödie um 1911," in *Musik und Theater*, pp. 169–210. Messmer sets the work not simply against Léhar and the Viennese operetta but in the tradition of light opera and operatic comedy that includes fairy-tale operas after Wagner, such as Humperdinck's *Hänsel und Gretel* and Leo Blech's *Aschenbrödel*; exotic comedies such as Hugo Wolf's *Corregidor*; and the comic operas of Ermanno Wolf-Ferrari, sometimes reviving eighteenth-century opera buffa traditions, as in *Le donne curiose* (1903), based on Goldoni. The charm and success of these works gave Hofmannsthal a point of departure for attempting a higher level of subtlety and significance; Messmer quotes a letter of Hofmannsthal's of 1928, in which he claims that he was not "so töricht . . . zu denken, man könnte einfachere, naivere Kunstformen erneuren. Das ist Dilettantismus, Spielerei Wolf-Ferraris, usw." (Messmer, p. 185)

10   See Ernst Kurth, *Romantische Harmonik und ihre Krise in Wagners "Tristan"* (1923); reprint (Hildesheim: Georg Olms, 1968).

11   *Neues Wiener Tagblatt*, 25 October 1925; quoted in *Richard Strauss: Dokumente* (Leipzig: Philipp Reclam, 1980), p. 44. On the waltzes in *Der Rosenkavalier* see the excellent study by Roswitha Schlötterer, "Die musikalische und szenische Bedeutung der *Rosenkavalier-walzer*," in *Musik und Theater*, pp. 135–68.

12   Translation by Ruth and Thomas Martin. Of course the two, Pamina and Papageno, have previously sung of the joys of matrimony, and of "Mann und Weib" as loving pair. The reference is to both duets, though musically and directly only to the second.

Strauss's *Intermezzo*: Innovation and Tradition

Bryan Gilliam

▼

Strauss's penchant for juxtaposing the ridiculous and the sublime, the trivial and the exalted, the everyday and the universal, remains a controversial aspect of his musical personality. We find not only some startling juxtapositions of musical thought within a given work (one could name any number of tone poems or operas), but also Strauss's predilection for stark contrasts between chronologically adjacent works. Only some six months separate the completion of *Symphonia Domestica*, with its harmless depiction of bourgeois family life, and the beginning of work on *Salome*, an opera that presents an unsettling combination of oriental exoticism and sexual depravity.

A look at Strauss's trilogy of operas on marriage—*Die Frau ohne Schatten* (1917), *Intermezzo* (1923), and *Die ägyptische Helena* (1927)—reveals this same tendency. On either end of this tryptich the subject of marriage is treated in a deeply symbolic, even allegorical fashion; the centerpiece of this arrangement, however, explores not the metaphysical or even the universal, but rather the prosaic world of the everyday. *Intermezzo* is, in short, an autobiographical, bourgeois sex comedy built around the theme of Strauss's stormy relationship with his own wife, Pauline.

One cannot address the subject of *Intermezzo* and its origins without reference to *Die Frau ohne Schatten*, which served as its catalyst both positively and negatively. In a memoir the composer specifically associates the completion of *Die Frau ohne Schatten* with the First World War and even blamed some of the nervous counterpoint in the last act on certain wartime anxieties.[1] *Die Frau ohne Schatten*, heavily laden with obscure symbolism and occasionally overwrought polyphony, stands as a compelling epitaph for post-Romanticism: it was conceived in peacetime, composed during conflict, and premiered after the Treaty of Versailles.

In the summer of 1916, before completing act 3 of that opera, Strauss had already begun to distance himself from Romanticism; he expressed an overriding wish to get away from myth, allegory, and the supernatural. What he desired more than anything else was a fresh, modern subject. In letters to Hofmannsthal he openly expressed his resolve to shed himself of "the Wagnerian musical armor," and he also declared: "Let us resolve that *Die Frau ohne Schatten* will be the last Romantic opera. Hopefully you will soon have a fine, happy idea that will definitely help set me out on the new road."[2] Strauss would have to embark on that new road without the help of Hofmannsthal, who would have nothing to do with the composer's suggestions, which not only included a modern domestic comedy, but a "diplomatic love intrigue" built around an aristocratic ambassador's wife who betrays her country after falling in love with a secret agent.[3]

Strauss's role as a composer in the musical life of the Weimar Republic has not been fully sorted out, but it is safe to say that his debut in the postwar period as a composer of new works was hardly auspicious. Indeed, the years between *Der Rosenkavalier* and *Intermezzo* saw a series of miscalculations and misfires—witness the premieres of *Josephslegende*, *Die Frau ohne Schatten*, and *Schlagobers*—that were either chronological or aesthetic holdovers from the Wilhelminian era. As a man approaching his sixtieth birthday, Strauss was no longer regarded as a leading progressive figure in German music, a role that he never claimed in the first place. For his sixtieth birthday in 1924, the year of *Intermezzo*'s premiere, the composer was regaled in Germany and throughout Europe with a host of *Strauss-Tage*; but others, such as Adorno, Ernest Newman, and Lazare Saminsky, marked this same anniversary by writing Strauss's musical obituary, proclaiming his talent played out and his future moribund.[4]

Nonetheless, Strauss's desire to set a modern, everyday operatic subject, despite Hofmannsthal's misgivings, anticipates an antiromantic sentiment that would prevail throughout the Weimar Era. The realities of the cultural collapse in the aftermath of World War I catalyzed fundamental changes in German musical life. A younger generation rejected, as symbols of the old regime, both post-Romanticism and Expressionism. Hans Curjel described the new music of the postwar period as part of a "sobering-up process."[5] The new movement sought to celebrate modern society; the fruition of this aesthetic was *Neue Sachlichkeit*. Gustav Hartlaub, who coined the term in 1923, observed that, although the new aesthetic resulted in part from postwar cynicism, it nonetheless "[expressed] itself in the enthusiasm for the immediate reality as a result of the desire to take things entirely objectively on a material basis without immediately investing them with ideal implications."[6]

Numerous manifestations of this new aesthetic flourished in the cultural life of the 1920s. One important musical realization of *Neue Sachlichkeit* was the so-called *Zeitoper* (with its emphasis on *Alltäglichkeit*); but the term *Zeitoper* did not come into common usage until the late twenties, and even then there was disagreement about its specific meaning.[7] In the early years of the Weimar Republic, during the period of transition from *Hofoper* to *Staatsoper*, the present and future condition of opera was far from clear. A plethora of articles concerning the state of opera began appearing in various German music journals; "Die Opernkrise" was the catchword of the day.[8] Reduced budgets, worries about declining ticket sales, and fear of the increasing popularity of film made running an opera house an especially daunting task during the decade following the First World War.[9]

Intermezzo, Strauss's eighth opera, is seldom mentioned in surveys of twentieth-century opera, yet it is one of the first major German operas completed after World War I. Its novel musical-dramatic qualities and its ties to cultural life in the Weimar Republic have been ignored by most opera scholars, including those who have specialized in German opera in the 1920s. Clichéd perceptions of Strauss automatically caused him to be excluded out of hand from the discussions of the *avant garde*; these perceptions have only recently begun to be called into question. Indeed, if one probes beyond the autobiographical surface of *Intermezzo*, one finds a highly innovative work that was not only the prototype for Hindemith's *Neues vom Tage* (1929) and Schoenberg's *Von Heute auf Morgen* (1930)—as some scholars have already noted—but was, in its own way, a special kind of *Zeitoper* of the early 1920s. *Intermezzo* not only provides a fascinating angle on bourgeois culture in early Weimar Germany, but also offers an important picture of Strauss the composer at the threshold of his sixth decade—a composer who would continue to write for another quarter century.

Intermezzo is a problematic work; it encompasses a paradoxical conflation of the old and the new. Strauss's overriding aim was to create an entirely new genre of opera, and some of his innovations, especially as they relate to theme and dramaturgy, were quite bold indeed. Yet alongside these new ideas, Strauss relied upon methods and conventions that we have come to know quite well by this time in his musical career, ideas that served him successfully in the past. This study aims to untangle the network of new and old—of innovation and tradition—and to focus upon these dual elements within the context of artistic trends in Weimar Germany, as well as the composer's personal style.

Innovation

The originality of *Intermezzo* is apparent from the start: without any introduction the curtain swiftly rises, and we are thrust as voyeurs into the middle of domestic bickering. And beyond the *Alltäglichkeit* of a plot centering around the daily life of a composer and his wife, Strauss further highlights the action with numerous—often tongue-in-cheek—modernistic touches: Christine, the wife, goes over a detailed grocery list of food items to be packed for Robert's train trip, answers and makes telephone calls, reads the latest newspapers, and visits the family attorney in order to obtain a divorce.

This short scene with the lawyer represents *Alltäglichkeit* in a nutshell, for divorce serves as a sober negation of the prototypical operatic love plot, where love relationships are generally separated by death. A far cry from the scene with Ochs and the attorney in *Der Rosenkavalier*, Christine's frank, matter-of-fact scene in the lawyer's office was no doubt unprecedented in opera. Divorce would play an even larger role five years later in Hindemith's *Neues vom Tage*, where a divorce attorney is one of the leading characters.

Robert, who appears mostly in act 2, also contributes to the spirit of *Neue Sachlichkeit*, but in a different way, as evinced in act 2, scene 1 (the skat scene). Here the focus of the plot is, of course, Robert's discovery that his wife wants to dissolve their marriage due to her suspicion that he is having an affair. But just as important to Strauss is the down-to-earth, accurate depiction of leisure activity; he takes great pains to make the card game as realistic as possible. It is an integral part of the scene; the audience can, at times, truly follow the course of the game. Furthermore, by showing us a "behind-the-scenes" view of a composer, conductor, and singer (among other skat partners), Strauss strips the musical world of its exalted or romantic pretensions, something he had already begun to do in his prologue to *Ariadne auf Naxos* (where, however, the composer is still revered).

In the cozy atmosphere of a gentleman's game room (furnished with "modern paintings and sculpture"), we see a conductor off his podium, a composer away from his manuscript, and a singer far from the footlights. Robert Storch, the conductor and composer, enters the scene apologizing that "the rehearsal could not be cut short," to which the singer replies, "At the beginning of every [opera] season you always have a colossal eagerness for rehearsals, but by March it soon dies away." Ironic or even humorous references are made to such Romantic operas as *Otello*, *Der Freischütz*, and *Parsifal*, among others, by using lines from these works entirely out of context.

The Intermezzo *Preface*

Strauss firmly believed that he was embarking on an unprecedented project, a project so original that for the first time in his operas he felt compelled to write a preface to the score. In the final paragraph he concludes, semi-apologetically: "By turning its back upon the popular love-and-murder interest of the usual operatic libretto, and by taking its subject matter perhaps too exclusively from real life, this new work blazes a path for musical and dramatic composition which others after me may perhaps negotiate with more talent and better fortune."[10]

An earlier version than the one appended to the score was not published until 1949; it is decidedly more informal in tone.[11] Neither preface seeks to go beyond providing practical advice for the singer and conductor. At the end of the earlier version Strauss makes specific recommendations for performing the work: it should be produced in a small theater holding no more than a thousand people, the singer must eschew large and old-fashioned operatic gestures and should sing mostly *mezza voce* (consonants ff and vowels mf), only a full command of rhythm will enable the performer to give the impression of improvised dialogue with "absolute naturalism," and, finally, an adequate number of conscientious piano rehearsals is required ("Don't let one word or one eighth note escape you," Strauss warns the singer).

In short, the *Intermezzo* preface offers insights, no doubt based on Strauss's experiences as an opera conductor, about different types of vocal expression (such as spoken dialogue, secco recitative, accompanied recitative, and aria) from Mozart to Wagner. What Strauss wants above all is realism of expression, which comes from the intricate and often rapid interplay of these vocal styles. Strauss admits to wrestling with the problem of exploring manifold vocal styles in the *Ariadne* prologue and in parts of *Die Frau ohne Schatten*, but with only limited success. Strauss's concern for a natural mode of verbal expression and his expressed need for a new type of singer-actor recalls Peter Gay's description of *Neue Sachlichkeit* as a call "for realism in setting, accurate reportage, return to naturalistic speech, and, if there had to be idealism, sober idealism."[12]

More than any other character in the opera, Christine exemplifies the different types of vocal expression outlined in the preface. We hear her in a speaking voice when she talks on the telephone, gives orders to the servants, reads aloud from the newspaper, writes a letter, or quotes her husband. Dry recitative underscores such businesslike dealings as the scene with the lawyer's wife and landlord (act 1, scene 4: she inspects a room to be rented for the baron) or with the lawyer (act 2, scene 2: she tries to obtain a divorce).

Christine sings mostly accompanied recitative and arioso when she speaks with the young baron, or when she argues with her husband or servants. Only rarely does Christine sing in a lyrical style: as she sinks in reverie by the fireplace (at the end of act 1, scene 5), in the final scene of act 1 (the scene in her son's bedroom), and in the duet for Robert and Christine at the end of the opera.

The Strauss–Bahr Collaboration

Beyond the discussion of a "new" type of singing and acting, neither version of the Intermezzo preface offers much concerning Strauss's larger dramaturgical aims; these may be gleaned from his correspondence with Hermann Bahr. Hofmannsthal, who refused to cooperate with Strauss's new project, suggested Bahr as a possible collaborator, although Strauss would ultimately write the libretto himself. From the very beginning, Strauss had a clear vision of what this project should be. Bahr was at a decided disadvantage, for not only did he fail to understand fully Strauss's novel approach, but he had never before written an opera libretto.[13] Bahr's efforts failed to match Strauss's expectations, and the friendly clash of ideas, as evinced by their letters, illuminates Strauss's most fundamental views of the project.

Strauss had known Bahr personally since the time of the Elektra premiere in 1909. Bahr had written an important, laudatory review of the opera, and his future wife, Anna Mildenburg, had sung Klytämnestra for the later Viennese premiere of Elektra: she remained Strauss's favorite singer for that role.[14] That same year, Bahr wrote a three-act sex comedy, Das Konzert, which he dedicated to Strauss, and the composer was delighted with the work.[15] Bahr's play shares some superficial characteristics with Strauss's opera: both works begin with a musician preparing for a concert trip, and both involve symmetrical pairings of musician husband/paramour and paramour's husband/musician's wife.

Das Konzert is a remarkable work for 1909, a play exploring modern sexual relationships in various ways: the state of marriage in a modern world, the question of fidelity and the effect of sexual affairs on the marital relationship, sex roles in contemporary society (especially the role of women), and communication between the sexes. Das Konzert's search for the definition of the modern marital relationship surely anticipates not only Intermezzo but also Neues vom Tage and Von Heute auf Morgen. Indeed, for the final line of the latter work by Schoenberg, a child asks his parents (who have just reconciled their rocky marriage): "Mama, was sind das moderne Menschen?"

Strauss and Bahr discussed the plan for a modern Spieloper for the first time in Salzburg, probably on 24 September 1916.[16] It would be based on a real event in Strauss's marital life (dating from 1903) in which one Mitze Mücke (Mieze Maier in the opera) mistook Strauss's name for that of conductor Joseph Stransky, often called "Straussky" by his friends. On 5 October Bahr sent Strauss a scenario for act 1; the act 2 scenario followed a week later. But even as early as 5 October, Bahr wondered aloud to Strauss whether or not he was the right man for the job.[17] One can only imagine how Bahr must have felt writing a text based on such a personal event in the composer's domestic life.

Bahr's version differs significantly from the ultimate *Intermezzo*. He tones down the autobiographical aspect; Strauss is not portrayed as a musician, but as a professor of archaeology. His version of Christine is decidedly more sympathetic than Strauss's, where she abrasively scolds nearly everyone around her. In Bahr's treatment the Storch family has no children, and there is a strong maternalistic streak to Christine's relationship with Baron Lummer. Even Mieze Maier and the baron's father—who are only mentioned in Strauss's text—find their way in the cast of characters.

The substantive *Intermezzo* correspondence between Strauss and Bahr occurs between October 1916 and July 1917, and during that time they had some personal meetings as well. The two most important letters from that exchange are by Strauss dating from 21 October 1916 and 1 January 1917. In both letters he makes detailed criticisms of Bahr's work; those criticisms exemplify Strauss's creative aims better than any other source. The composer's remarks involve two major issues: characterization and dramaturgy.

Strauss believed that Bahr's characters were too stereotypical, especially Storch, who should not be the pedantic, learned type, but somehow more interesting and complex. More important, Bahr made Baron Lummer too appealing; his role was too large and multilayered. Lummer's impulsive, romantic personality is not unlike one of the leading characters (Franz Jura) in *Das Konzert*. Strauss wanted the young baron to be less central to the plot; he should develop in the action of conversation with Christine rather than having any monologues of his own. In essence, Strauss desired only two main characters: Robert and Christine (baritone and soprano, respectively), and it is thus hardly surprising that the composer portrayed Lummer as a tenor, the voice type that Strauss liked the least. The paucity of sympathetic tenor roles in Strauss's operas has been commented upon by numerous scholars.

But more important than matters of characterization were Strauss's criticisms of Bahr's handling of the drama; Strauss believed that many of the scenes were overwrought and self-contained. More than anything else, the composer wanted his librettist to allow more space for the music. The scenes and the characters needed to be more sketchlike. Strauss even enclosed a series of sketched-out scenes—labeled as being "fast nur Kinobilder" ("almost just cinematic pictures")—in which the music should say everything; the poet should provide only a few pace-setting "catchwords."[18] Bahr, who ultimately confessed that he simply could not visualize the characters in the same manner as Strauss, remained unable to satisfy the composer's demands, and he suggested that the composer write the text himself.[19]

The Symphonic Interludes and Cinematic Technique

Strauss's suggestions to Bahr point to the central role of the symphonic interlude in Intermezzo, a role important enough to be included in the opera's subtitle ("Eine bürgerliche Komödie mit sinfonischen Zwischenspielen"). Thus, the composer desired open-ended scenes that segué or even dissolve into orchestral interludes in a cinematic way. The influence of film, both as an artistic and business endeavor, can hardly be underestimated in Weimar Germany. By the late 1920s, Germany's film industry was the largest in Europe, surpassed only by the United States, and its potential to draw away opera audiences worried opera producers and composers alike.[20] Strauss's and Hofmannsthal's collaboration on the silent-film version of Der Rosenkavalier—only a year after the Intermezzo premiere—was partly in response to the increasing popularity of this burgeoning art form. Some of the later Zeitopern incorporated film as part of the actual staging.

There are a total of thirteen scenes in this two-act opera, and some are quite brief indeed. Act 1, scene 2, for example, lasts only three and a half minutes; scene 3 is just under three minutes. In the ninety seconds between those two scenes we go from a toboggan slope to a ballroom at the Grundlsee Inn. Other adjacent scenes take us from an attorney's office to a storm in the Prater, which, in turn, takes us back to the Storch villa. Space and time thus were intended to go beyond the staged scene, and only the symphonic interlude can make coherent the often rapid montage technique created by Strauss, a technique that shares important similarities with film.

The issue of diegetic vs. nondiegetic time has been a major focus in recent film criticism; the distinction is especially important to the study of film music.[21] If an opera or a film takes place over the course of a year, that would be its diegetic time span. Likewise, diegetic music would be music that takes place on stage or on film within the time frame of the narrative. Intermezzo's symphonic interludes thus serve as a nondiegetic musical mediator. With instrumental music that exists outside the narrative time frame, Strauss creates a kind of temporal continuity between spatially and temporally discontinuous scenes. The nonverbal status of the interlude allows it to "cross borders": between diegetic and nondiegetic worlds, between levels of narration, and between viewing time and psychological time.

Strauss's interludes exploit the audience's psychological capacity to make connections between images and gestures on the stage. In short, the nondiegetic symphonic interlude, because of its sovereign sonic and temporal continuity, masks both spatial and temporal contradictions. A good example of this mediating role, in which instrumental music suspends any real sense of time or space, is the letter that Baron Lummer "sends through the orchestra" to Christine. Toward the end of act 1, scene 6, the baron, who is too embarrassed to ask Christine for a loan in person, sits at his desk writing a letter requesting one thousand marks. The orchestral interlude commences as he begins writing the letter and shortly thereafter the curtain falls literally mid-sentence; the music continues. After the interlude the curtain rises with scene 7. Christine, letter in hand, exclaims: "He wants a thousand marks! He's surely mad!"

In this quasi-cinematic way, we find Strauss being his most successfully non-Wagnerian, for surely one major characteristic of Wagner opera is its capacity to expand time, where a mere glance in *Tristan* can be transformed into a lengthy orchestral passage, or where toward the end of *Parsifal*, act 1, "time becomes space," to use Gurnemanz's own words. Wagner's temporal expansion was, of course, a major point of criticism for Adorno, who suggested that his music "acts as if time had no end."[22] Generally speaking, film attempts the opposite—that is to say, temporal compression—where years can become minutes in front of our eyes.

Around a decade after *Intermezzo* Alban Berg turned to film in act 2 of *Lulu* as he compressed major events in her life over a year's time into a matter of minutes. However, the silent-film montage ("Arrest," "Detention," "Trial," "In Prison," etc.) would be largely incoherent without his nondiegetic film music (which, of course, obeys its own structural laws) that not only supplies the interconnecting thread but serves to alter our temporal perception. Strauss's reliance on dramaturgical techniques that border on the cinematic, thus anticipating an opera such as *Lulu*, is one of the most innovative aspects of *Intermezzo*. At least one critic made this observation following the premiere when he described the work as "Kinospiel mit verbindender Tonmalerei."[23]

Tradition

Strauss's stated goal in working on the *Intermezzo* project was to create "an entirely new artistic genre in style, form, and content," but *Intermezzo* is far from entirely new. It is an opera where elements of new and old sometimes operate side by side. Much of the opera is traditional Strauss, exploiting well-established aspects of his style that look back to *Die Frau ohne Schatten* and beyond. The quasi-cinematic relationship between short, open-ended scenes and nondiegetic orchestral music may have been a novel idea for Strauss, but there is nothing new about a symphonic impulse in his operatic scores. Strauss had already grappled with the problem of the symphonic interlude in opera with some of the complicated scene-change music in *Die Frau ohne Schatten*.

In a letter to Bahr, Strauss implies that he is still the old "Programmusiker" with respect to the role of the orchestra in filling in many of the details in *Intermezzo*.[24] And some reviewers of the premiere declared that they had not heard such orchestral vitality and freshness since the days of Strauss's tone poems. One critic described the work as a "lively dramatic symphony supplemented with scenery and voices,"[25] a description that recalls Strauss's declaration that *Salome* "is [a] symphony in the medium of drama."[26]

Die Frau ohne Schatten and *Intermezzo* share far more than technical similarities. The story of the Dyer, his wife, and their troubled marriage touched Strauss more deeply than any other part of the plot in the former opera. At the very beginning of their collaboration on the work, Hofmannsthal suggested that possibly the Dyer's Wife could be modeled "in all discretion" after Strauss's wife.[27] Few would doubt that Christine, patterned directly after Pauline, plays the central role in *Intermezzo*. Indeed, early on in the genesis of *Intermezzo*, Strauss envisioned a cycle of five domestic operas—to be composed over a decade—revolving around the central figure of his wife, but decided, soon enough, that one opera would suffice.[28] The role of Pauline de Ahna as an inspirational source for Strauss dates back to the 1880s. Beyond the Dyer's Wife and Christine, she likely inspired Don Juan, Freihild in *Guntram*, the "Heldens Gefährtin" of *Ein Heldenleben*, "Die Frau" in *Symphonia Domestica*, perhaps even Aminta in *Die schweigsame Frau*, and, of course, a host of lieder.

Given the numerous similarities between *Die Frau ohne Schatten* and *Intermezzo*, one is hardly surprised to find specific musical parallels as well. Similarities between the "Unborn-Children" motive and the very opening of *Intermezzo*, as well as the Empress's theme and Christine's *Träumerei* melody, have already been observed[29] (see example 1a and 1b). But the similarities go be-

Example 1a.   Example 1b.

Example 2.

yond that, for in Intermezzo Strauss manipulates that germinal opening motive in a way that parallels his manipulation of the "Unborn-Children" figure in the previous opera. Through augmentation, a "Reconciliation" motive is derived from Intermezzo's opening figure. Strauss creates a "Temptation" motive by augmenting the "Unborn-Children" theme in Die Frau (see example 2).

Sketchbooks at the Richard-Strauss-Archiv in Garmisch indicate that other melodic ideas in Intermezzo predate Die Frau ohne Schatten. The waltzes in Intermezzo not only recall the spirit of Der Rosenkavalier, but some actually date from that period of composition. The D- and G-major waltz themes used in the symphonic interlude between scenes 2 and 3 of act 1 (see example 3a–d) appear on folios 10 and 11, respectively, from a sketchbook (Tr.24: ?1900–1915), labeled a "collection of unused themes from old sketchbooks" ("Sammlung unverwendeter Themen aus den alten Skizzenbüchern"). They may very well be waltz themes that Strauss did not use for Der Rosenkavalier.

We know for certain that Strauss used part of a discarded version of Baron Ochs's waltz for the latter part of the G-major Intermezzo waltz. Folio 12 shows an early version of the familiar E-major waltz (see example 4a). Perhaps the most obvious difference is the eighth-note figure in the fifth bar; Strauss expands upon that idea in the fifth bar of the fourth system (see Strauss's

Example 3a. Tr. 24, fol. 10

Example 3c. Tr. 24, fol. 11

Example 3b. Intermezzo, act 1, reh. 140

Example 3d. *Intermezzo*, act 1, reh. 142

pencil annotation, "gut"). We see that idea from the fourth system, trans-posed to G, towards the end of the G-major waltz (see example 4b). Likewise, Tr. 13—a sketchbook mainly for *Salome*—contains fragments for a *Schuhplattler* that opens the third scene (see example 5a, especially the last two systems, and b). On the inside back cover of the sketchbook, Strauss writes: "Besides *Salome* contains: *Bardengesang* (Ha, stolzes Beil), *Der fromme Hirtenknabe* (Greif), *Schuhplattler*."

Strauss's characteristic melodic style, which remains unchanged in the *Intermezzo* interludes, allows him to borrow from the past without any threat to the overall coherence of the piece. But perhaps the most traditional as-pect of the *Intermezzo* score is Strauss's harmonic language and tonal layout—despite his declaration that he had rid himself of the "Wagnerian musical armor." *Intermezzo* is also no exception when it comes to Strauss's symbolic or representational use of keys, a technique to be found in most of his earlier works. Many of the keys Strauss chooses in his representational scheme cor-

Example 4a. Tr. 24, fol. 12

Example 4b. Intermezzo, act 1, 6 mm. after reh. 145

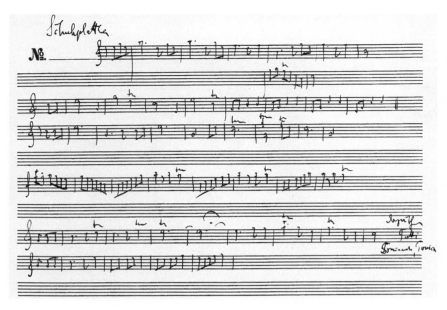

Example 5a. Tr. 13, fol. 52

respond to choices made in earlier works. Table 1 offers an overview of the tonal structure in *Intermezzo*.

A glance at table 1 shows that the opera begins in the no-sharps/no-flats everyday world of C major and ends in the elevated realm of F-sharp major. The second version of *Ariadne* seems a forerunner in this regard. Its C-major Prologue is likewise intended to represent the everyday in its behind-the-scenes view of the theater—with its mixture of spoken dialogue, recitative, and aria—but the opera ends in five flats rather than six sharps, and the symbolic difference between F-sharp major and D-flat major for Strauss is significant indeed. D-flat suggests the sublime in Strauss's music; it is the key of the final trio of *Der Rosenkavalier*, the duet ("Mir anvertraut") between Barak and his wife in act 3 of *Die Frau ohne Schatten*, and, of course, the end of *Capriccio*—his farewell to the stage.[30]

On the other hand, Strauss consistently uses F-sharp major to represent dreamlike or magical worlds. Don Quixote's dream of knightly adventures at the end of the third variation of that tone poem, the *Märchen*-like presentation of the rose in act 2 of *Der Rosenkavalier*, the Empress's act 1 entrance in *Die Frau ohne Schatten* ("Perhaps I shall dream myself back into the light body of a bird or a young, white gazelle!"), and Daphne's magical transformation into the laurel tree are all cast in F-sharp major. Moreover, Strauss's tonal sym-

Example 5b. Intermezzo, act 1, 5 mm. after reh. 148

Act I

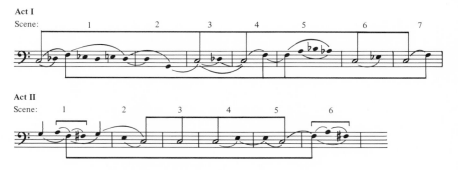

Table 1. Summary of tonal layout of *Intermezzo*

bolism also allows us to understand better the way in which reconciliation is depicted at the end of *Intermezzo*.

Strauss's stormy marital relationship with Pauline was no secret even before his *opera domestica*, and one wonders whether or not Richard (alias Robert) was fantasizing in act 2, scene 1 when he responds—to the skepticism of his colleagues—that he indeed has an ideal marriage. Strauss articulates Robert's defense of his marriage with a sudden shift to F-sharp major (see example 6). This shift is an important tonal anticipation of the ending (see table 1) where Robert and Christine ultimately find reconciliation. Some writers have criticized the final duet as being too sentimental, but I would gainsay that assessment. Strauss's use of F-sharp major suggests irony: that only the wave of a magic wand—in six sharps, no less—could create peaceful marital bliss between Strauss and his wife.

Strauss parallels the separation of the prosaic and lyrical by separating stable and less stable tonal areas, and some of the scenes are quite open-ended indeed. He often achieves this sense of suspended tonality through use of extended recitative. An excellent model for this technique is scene 1 of *Elektra*, where, although D is intoned in the opening and closing bars, the composer spends most of his time away from that key, and, instead, touches upon a number of other important referential harmonies to be fully realized later. Anthony Newcomb points out this progressive use of the old *recitativo secco* technique in Wagner's music.[31] Adorno, who takes a more critical stance, likens Strauss's use of recitative to a "centrifugal force" away from tonality despite the composer's strong tonal orientation.[32]

The opening scenes of *Intermezzo*'s acts 1 and 2 likewise touch upon tonal areas important to the rest of the opera. Although *Intermezzo* opens in C major, Strauss's creates a C/F duality from the start; this duality serves as a micro-

Example 6. Intermezzo, act 2, 5 mm. after reh. 22

cosm of Strauss's overall plan for act 1, which begins in C major and ends in F minor. But the opening scene of act 1 articulates some other significant key areas as well: D-flat major (which erupts in scene 3 as an enchanted Christine is swept off her feet by the young baron), E-flat (the *Heldenleben* key underscores the baron's cowardice as he writes, rather than asks face to face for money in scene 6), D major anticipates scene 2 (on the toboggan run), and E does not appear again until the end of act 2 as Storch returns with hopes of reconciliation. Act 2 is significantly shorter than act 1, and the layout of keys is less complex. Strauss frames act 2, scene 1 in G major, but within that frame he makes references to A, F, F♯, and C, which assume greater importance in the last two scenes of the opera (see table 1).

Thus, many of the scenes are not only dramaturgically but tonally open ended, and Strauss relies upon the symphonic interlude as a kind of tonal touchstone. It can sometimes dovetail into the next scene; other times it creates jarring juxtapositions. Within the first four scenes of act 1 we see both procedures (see table 1). The first interlude extends the end of the previous scene—in D major—and anticipates the next. The next interlude continues the circle of fifths through scene 3. There, C major modulates to D-flat (by way of A-flat), and the interlude continues that key, acting as a perpetuation of Christine's and the baron's rhapsodic moment. The sudden shift back to C major (articulated by dotted C^6 chords in the piano) in scene 4 is meant to shock us back into the world of the everyday, where we find Christine—now the baron's patroness—making a "white-glove" inspection of a potential apartment for him. The timbral change from lush orchestra to the percussive piano (which Strauss uses as a modern sound throughout the opera) contributes to that shock effect.

But localized shock effects, temporarily suspended tonalities, and surface dissonances aside, *Intermezzo* is a thoroughly tonal work. Even though the ratio of nondiatonic to diatonic material is significantly higher in *Salome* or *Elektra* than in *Intermezzo*, Strauss's fundamental approach is not all that different. In all three works the steadfast tonal underpinnings are articulated by the clarifying, affirming power of the cadential gesture. And without tonal clarity Strauss's network of associative harmonies would fall apart. Table 1 shows that as act 1 moves from bourgeois comedy to something more serious, the harmonies move to the flat side, finally to the relative minor of Christine's A-flat *Träumerei* ("Ein hübscher Mensch") at the end of scene 5.

The plot reaches its nadir in act 2, scene 3, as Robert wanders around the Prater in a raging storm, but that scene represents the turnaround of events as well; the case of mistaken identity is revealed, and the harmonies begin to move toward the sharp side. F-sharp major not only is a half step from the opening of act 2, but more importantly, it is a tritone from the opening of the opera.[33] The interval sets apart worlds of the everyday and fantasy (of C major and F-sharp major), perhaps even of Neue Sachlichkeit and Romanticism. Does the F-sharp major ending represent a return to Romanticism, a negation of his original intent, or do we interpret the ending as parody? Strauss leaves us with a question.

Reception

Reviews of the Intermezzo premiere in newspapers, magazines, and music journals were overwhelmingly positive. Many critics expressed a decided sigh of relief over the success of the new opera, given the mixed results of Josephslegende, Die Frau ohne Schatten, and Schlagobers over the previous decade. Eugen Thari of the Dresdener Anzeiger was surely not alone when he observed that Intermezzo ended a fallow period of around a dozen years following the premiere of Der Rosenkavalier.[34] One should keep in mind that worldwide popularity of Die Frau ohne Schatten was not achieved until after the Second World War.

But despite the fact that many believed that Intermezzo recalled Strauss's past glories, they also believed the opera to mark a significant departure, not only in the composer's output, but in the history of opera. In reviews one finds terms that would become regularly associated with the Zeitopern of the late 1920s, terms such as "Gusto der Welt," "Alltagsprosa," "Milieuechtheit," and "nüchterne Sachlichkeit." One critic suggested that the work should not be thought of as an "intermezzo," but rather as an "overture to a new era of German opera."[35] Even Paul Stefan, writing for the progressive Musikblätter des Anbruch,[36] and Arnold Schoenberg were favorably impressed, although Schoenberg did not see the opera until a couple of years later.

In a letter to Webern (3 May 1926), Schoenberg seems almost embarrassed to admit that he is favorably inclined toward the new opera: "I have recently heard Intermezzo by Strauss and must say, to my greatest surprise, that it was not at all unlikable."[37] But it was not so much Strauss's music as his text that appealed to the younger composer:

> I find it inconceivable that he can play comedy and make himself appear better than he is. For all that, he knows far too little as a poet. And since this presentation leaves me with the definite impression that one is dealing with a very genial, warm person—a consequence not of his art, but of his personality—it convincingly reveals a side of his personality that has actually captivated me.

Strauss's music was another matter indeed, according to Schoenberg, who found the score weak in invention and containing all too many sequences ("I can no longer endure these sequences any more: Strohfeuer! 'Trink ma noch a Glaserl!'"). But even then Schoenberg admitted that after repeated listenings he might like the music better, and perhaps he did, for two decades later he declared that Strauss "will remain one of the characteristic and outstanding figures in music history. Works like *Salome*, *Elektra*, *Intermezzo* and others will not perish."[38]

The *Intermezzo* text was not to everyone's liking. Some critics, even though they admired the work, admitted that the autobiographical text, taken out of context, was indiscreet, unpoetic, even downright banal; but within the framework of music and staging, all elements worked together to create a theatrically convincing whole. Opinions concerning the conversational vocal styles were mixed. Some marveled at the way Strauss set the potentially unmusical (scolding servants, playing cards, packing suitcases) to music with the rapid interplay of vocal styles. Others longed for more lyrical moments for the voice. Nearly all savored the numerous symphonic interludes, which, although they are used in novel ways, still have the sound of the "old Strauss." While many critics paid lip service to Strauss's new aesthetic aims as outlined in his preface, one wonders whether or not it was the return of a confident, older, neo-Romantic Strauss that so delighted its listeners. The interludes became so popular that, nine years after the premiere, Strauss published some of them (*Vier sinfonischen Zwischenspiele aus Intermezzo*) in a concert arrangement.

Given the favorable reception of the work, we must ask why *Intermezzo* faded from both the opera repertory (outside of Germany) and, more important, from history books concerned with this era. A technical explanation might be that the opera makes special demands on producers and singers alike. *Intermezzo* is not designed for the large opera house; it can only succeed in a smaller theater where the characters do not have to appear larger than life and, therefore, allegorical. And the work requires singers who can act with the sensitivity and nuance of stage actors.

But beyond that, *Intermezzo*, with its rejection of the universal, met a fate not unlike the other *Zeitopern* of the 1920s. Operas so tightly bound up with the here and now all shared the tendency toward obsolescence with the passage of time; they all seem to have a built-in temporal relevance. To criticize the *Zeitopern* on the sole basis of lasting influence is to overlook the central aesthetic aims of the genre.[39] It should be added, however, that *Intermezzo* has been far more successful over the past three decades than *Jonny spielt auf*, *Von Heute auf Morgen*, or *Neues vom Tage*.

Moreover, although the explicit autobiographical theme served as a vital catalyst that led Strauss to explore a new operatic genre, his choice of setting created some drawbacks as well. Not only did the element of self-portrayal potentially confine *Intermezzo* even beyond the intentionally limited scope of the *Zeitopern*, it also served to draw attention away from many of the more innovative aspects of the opera. Rudolf Hartmann, who himself first produced *Intermezzo* a year after the premiere, admitted that the nearly photographic reproductions of the rooms in the composer's Garmisch villa sparked a sensation but led to serious problems as well.[40] He remarked that since the end of the Second World War "it has been freed from the excessive autobiographical emphasis of its early productions and has given delight to a wide public."[41]

But the most obvious difference between *Intermezzo* and the *Zeitopern* of Krenek, Hindemith, or Schoenberg obviously lies in Strauss's musical language. Despite the spirit of *Neue Sachlichkeit* in the work's theme, staging, cinematic techniques, and vocal style, Strauss never rid himself of the Wagnerian musical armor that he so wished to shed. Strauss's post-Wagnerian style flourished during the Wilhelminian era, and it remained identified with that period. Many younger composers and critics found his tonal style incompatible with the art of a new age.

In 1927, conservative critic Ludwig Misch wrote an article exploring the meaning of the term *Neue Sachlichkeit* in music. Concluding that such art was detached and impersonal, he labeled it "Es-Musik" ("It-music"). "Ich-Musik" ("I-music"), on the other hand, embodied the subjective, expressive style of prewar Germany.[42] *Intermezzo* represents both worlds. Strauss's desire to create a modern, everyday setting along with a fresh, natural mode of vocal expression doubtless probes the realm of "Es-Musik." But *Intermezzo* is just as much part of the world of "Ich-Musik," both literally, with its autobiographical plot, and figuratively, with its backward glance at the style of a younger Strauss. It is his blurring of the borders between "sachlich" and "romantisch," between the everyday and the universal, that has made *Intermezzo* such a problematic, yet fascinating work, and an opera that has been unduly ignored.

Notes

1   "*Die Frau ohne Schatten*, das Schmerzenskind, wurde in Kummer und Sorgen während des Krieges vollendet. . . . Diese Kriegessorgen haben wohl auch der Partitur, besonders gegen die Mitte des 3. Aktes eine gewisse nervöse Überreizheit eingetragen, die sich schliesslich im Melodram 'entspannte!'" In *Richard Strauss: Betrachtungen und Erinnerungen*, ed. Willi Schuh, 3rd ed. (Zurich: Atlantis, 1981), pp. 244–45.

Bryan Gilliam

2 Letters of 16 August and 28 July 1916, respectively. In *Richard Strauss–Hugo von Hofmannsthal: Briefwechsel*, ed. Willi Schuh, 5th ed. (Zurich: Atlantis, 1978), pp. 359 and 354 (henceforth, *Briefwechsel*). My translation unless otherwise noted.

3 *Briefwechsel*, pp. 341–42.

4 See, for example, Theodor Adorno, "Richard Strauss. Zum 60. Geburtstag: 11. Juni 1924," *Zeitschrift für Musik* 91 (1924): pp. 289–95; Ernest Newman, "Strauss in England," *Neue Freie Presse* (8 June 1924); and Lazare Saminsky, "The Downfall of Strauss," *Modern Music* 1 (1924): 11–13 (the first two volumes of *Modern Music* were called *League of Composer's Review*).

5 Hanns Curjel, "Triumph der Alltäglichkeit, Parodie, und tiefere Bedeutung," *Blätter der Staatsoper* 9 (1929): 1–4.

6 From a letter by Hartlaub to Alfred H. Barr (8 July 1929), who quoted it in "Otto Dix," *The Arts* 17 (1931), p. 237. That quotation reappeared within the context of other statements by Hartlaub and others associated with *Neue Sachlichkeit* in Fritz Schmalenbach, "The Term *Neue Sachlichkeit*," *Art Bulletin* 22 (1940): 161–65.

7 See Susan Cook, *Opera for a New Republic: The Zeitopern of Krenek, Weill, and Hindemith* (Ann Arbor: UMI Research Press, 1988). Although this work essentially ignores *Intermezzo*, it represents the first major work on the *Zeitoper* in recent years and is a valuable source for anyone wishing to explore the German operas of this era.

8 Cook provides an extensive list of contemporary articles concerning the state of German opera in the 1920s on pp. 254–57.

9 In two short articles, Schoenberg expresses worry about the effect of film on the future of opera. See "Gibt es eine Krise der Oper?," *Musikblätter des Anbruch* 8 (1926), p. 209; and "The Future of Opera (1927)," *Style and Idea*, ed. Leonard Stein, trans. Leo Black (Berkeley: University of California Press, 1984), pp. 336–37.

10 The *Intermezzo* preface appears in English translation in Richard Strauss, *Recollections and Reflections*, ed. Willi Schuh, trans. L.J. Lawrence (London: Boosey and Hawkes, 1953), pp. 95–102; see also *Betrachtungen und Erinnerungen*, pp. 140–49.

11 This version appears only in *Betrachtungen und Erinnerungen*, pp. 135–39.

12 Peter Gay, *Weimar Culture: The Outsider as Insider* (New York: Harper and Row, 1968), p. 122.

13 In this sense we should not take for granted the relative ease in which Hofmannsthal made the transition from playwright to librettist as evinced by his work on *Der Rosenkavalier*.

14 So impressed was Strauss with her performance at the Vienna premiere that he gave her an *Elektra* sketchbook with the inscription: "Der genialen Darstellerin/der Klytämnestra in Wien/Frl. von Mildenburg/zu freundlicher Erinnerung/an ihren grössten Bewunderer./Der dankbare Componist der Elektra./Dr. Richard Strauss./Garmisch, 7. Mai 1909." The sketchbook is now in the Theatersammlung of the Oesterreichische Nationalbibliothek.

15 Hermann Bahr, *Das Konzert* (Berlin: Erich Reiss, 1909).

16 Letter of 14 September 1916 from Strauss to Bahr in Joseph Gregor, ed., *Meister und Meisterbriefe um Hermann Bahr* (Vienna: H. Bauer, 1947), p. 96.

17 Gregor, p. 97.

18 Letter of 1 January 1917 in Gregor, pp. 99–100.

19 Letter of 5 July 1917 in Gregor, pp. 101–2.

20 See n. 9.

21 One of the most important recent books on the subject is by Claudia Gorbman. See her *Unheard Melodies: Narrative Film Music* (Bloomington: Indiana University Press, 1987).

22 Theodor Adorno, In Search of Wagner, trans. Rodney Livingstone (Norfolk: Thetford Press, 1985), p. 42.

23 Richard Elb, "Aus Kunst und Leben. Strauss' Intermezzo" (? 9 November 1924). Unfortunately, the newspaper was not identified on my photocopy of the clipping. The suggested date is based on information from Dr. Franz Trenner of Munich.

24 Letter of 10 July 1917 in Gregor, p. 102.

25 Heinrich Platzenbecker, "Intermezzo von Richard Strauss," Neue Musik-Zeitung 5 (1924k): 116–17.

26 Ernst Krause, Richard Strauss: The Man and his Work, trans. John Coombs (Boston: Crescendo, 1969), p. 299.

27 Briefwechsel, pp. 112–13.

28 Letter of 12 July 1917 in Gregor, p. 104.

29 See Norman Del Mar's study on Intermezzo in vol. 2 of his Richard Strauss: A Critical Commentary of his Life and Works (London: Chilton, 1969), pp. 219–64; and Stephan Kohler's "Das eheliche Glück, ein Satyrspiel," in Hermann-Bahr-Symposion: "Der Herr aus Linz" (Linz: Linzer Veranstaltungsgesellschaft, 1987), pp. 191–98.

30 About the ending to Capriccio Strauss once asked collaborator Clemens Krauss: "Isn't this Db major the best conclusion to my theatrical life's work?" See Willi Schuh, Über Opern von Richard Strauss (Zurich: Atlantis, 1947), p. 101.

31 Anthony Newcomb, "The Birth of Music out of the Spirit of Drama," 19th-Century Music 4 (1981): 49–50.

32 Theodor Adorno, "Richard Strauss. Born June 11, 1864," trans. Samuel and Shierry Weber, Perspectives of New Music 1 (1965): 14.

33 We recall that Strauss separates himself from his wife by a tritone (F vs. B, respectively) in Symphonia Domestica; moreover, her theme is basically an inversion of his.

34 Eugen Thari, "Intermezzo von Richard Strauss," Dresdner Anzeiger, 5 November 1924.

35 Eugen Schmidt, "Intermezzo. Eine bürgerliche Komödie mit sinfonischen Zwischenspiele in zwei Aufzügen von Richard Strauss," Dresdner Nachrichten, 5 November 1924.

36 "Man darf getrost sagen, dass Strauss seit der Ariadne, seit dem Rosenkavalier so glückliche Stunden nicht mehr gehabt hat." Paul Stefan in Musikblätter des Anbruch 6 (1924): 412.

37 Ernst Hillmar, "Arnold Schönberg an Anton Webern: Eine Auswahl unbekannter Briefe," Arnold Schönberg Gedenkausstellung 1974, ed. Ernst Hillmar (Vienna: Universal, 1974), pp. 47–48.

38 Arnold Schoenberg, "On Strauss and Furtwängler (1946)," in H.H. Stuckenschmidt, Schoenberg: His Life and Work, trans. Humphrey Searle (New York: Schirmer Books, 1978), p. 544. The memoir appears in the original English in this translation of Stuckenschmidt's work.

39 Cook goes even further, suggesting that the issue of lasting influence "ignores the social and political realities of the age." See Cook, p. 6.

40 The visual connection with Strauss was made even stronger in early productions by the fact that the Storch character often wore a mask bearing a strong resemblance to Strauss.

41 Rudolf Hartmann, Richard Strauss: The Staging of his Operas and Ballets, trans. Graham Davies (New York: Oxford, 1981), p. 163.

42 "Man kennt im täglichen Sprachgebrauch den Gegensatz von 'sachlich' und 'persönlich.' Sollte die musikalische 'Sachlichkeit' nach dieser Analogie 'Unpersönlichkeit' bedeuten?— Allerdings das ist der Sinn. Schon vor mehreren Jahren wurde die Antithese 'Ich-Musik'— 'Es-Musik' geprägt, wobei der 'Es-Musik' die Sympathien der Jüngsten zufielen." Ludwig Misch, "Neue Sachlichkeit," Allgemeine Musikzeitung 54 (1927): 614.

Index

Bryan Gilliam is Associate Professor of Music and Director of Graduate Studies at Duke University. He has published articles on Anton Bruckner, Erich Wolfgang Korngold, and Kurt Weill, and is the author of *Richard Strauss's Elektra* (1991). Gilliam has also edited *Richard Strauss and His World* (1992) and *Music and Performance During the Weimar Republic* (1994). He is currently writing a biography of Richard Strauss.

Kofi Agawu is Professor of Music at Yale University. Günter Brosche is Director of the music collection at the Austrian National Library. Stephen E. Hefling is Professor of Music at Case Western Reserve University. James Hepokoski is Professor of Music at the University of Minnesota. Timothy L. Jackson is Assistant Professor of Music at Connecticut College. Michael Kennedy is Chief Music Critic, *Sunday Telegraph*. Lewis Lockwood is Professor of Music at Harvard University. Barbara A. Petersen is Vice President of Concert Music at Broadcast Music Incorporated (BMI). Pamela M. Potter is Assistant Professor of Music at the University of Illinois. Reinhold Schlötterer is Professor of Music at the University of Munich. R. Larry Todd is Professor of Music at Duke University.

Library of Congress Cataloging-in-Publication Data
Richard Strauss : new perspectives on the composer and his work /
Bryan Gilliam, editor.
Includes index.
ISBN 0-8223-1207-7 (cloth: alk. paper)
ISBN 0-8223-2114-9 (paper: alk. paper)
1. Strauss, Richard, 1864–1949 — Criticism and interpretation.
I. Gilliam, Bryan Randolph. II. Series: Sources of music and their interpretation.
ML410.S93R515 1992
780'.92 — dc20   92-7675 CIP   MN